Advance Praise for

Mindfulness for Teachers

"Essential information on a subtle topic, presented with clarity and simplicity, and beautifully written, Patricia Jennings 'gets it' about being a teacher. She has been there, and now she is back with a great story about about the enormous value of mindfulness and she has the evidence to back it up. Teachers, take one of your most valuable possessions—*your time*—to read this thoughtful and thorough book!"
                                        —Robert L. Selman, Roy E. Larsen Professor of
                                    Human Development and Education; Professor of
                                        Psychology in Psychiatry, Harvard University

"Jennings blends years of personal practice with classroom experience and research to create a pertinent resource for any teacher wishing to begin or enrich a cultivation of mindfulness. An understanding of the human brain, and its' reactions to stress, are provided as a pathway to guide teachers to build a self-care practice that acts as a model for students and a foundation for classroom wellness. Through refined attention to and mindfulness of daily habits and actions, Jennings illustrates how repeated forms of inquiry can operate as pedagogical techniques for learning."   —Jennifer Dauphinais, Magnet Resource Teacher,
                                    Quinnipiac STEM Magnet School, New Haven, CT

"*Mindfulness for Teachers* draws on research, theory, and Patricia A. Jennings' extensive experience in education to present a very readable set of guidelines for creating a mindful and caring classroom. This impressive book should be required reading for teachers during their training. The ideas here will help *any* teacher develop a greater awareness and find greater joy and personal fulfillment in teaching."   —Mark T. Greenberg, PhD, Bennett Chair of
                                    Prevention Research, Pennsylvania State University

"This book is a wonderful resource for teachers. Patricia A. Jennings has a real understanding of the challenges teachers face. Utilizing her strong foundation in mindfulness practices, she provides effective exercises and a wealth of information to support educators both inside and outside the classroom."
                                        —Sharon Salzberg, Co-Founder of the Insight
                                    Meditation Society and Author of Real Happiness

Mindfulness for Teachers

The Norton Series on the Social Neuroscience of Education

Louis J. Cozolino, Mary Helen Immordino-Yang, Series Editors

The field of education is searching for new paradigms that incorporate our latest discoveries about the biological underpinnings of processes related to teaching and learning. Yet what is left out of these discussions is a focus on the social nature of human neurobiology, the interactive context of learning, and the quality of student-teacher relationships. The "interpersonal neurobiology of education" is a fresh perspective that will help teachers and administrators better understand how the relationships among educators, students, and the social environments they create within classrooms and schools promote brain development, support psychological health, and enhance emotional intelligence.

The Norton Series on the Social Neuroscience of Education publishes cutting-edge books that provide interdisciplinary explorations into the complex connections between brain and mind, social relationships and attachment, and meaningful learning.. Drawing on evidence from research in education, affective and social neuroscience, complex systems, anthropology, and psychology, these books offer educators and administrators an accessible synthesis and application of scientific findings previously unavailable to those in the field. A seamless integration of up-to-date science with the art of teaching, the books in the series present theory and practical classroom application based in solid science, human compassion, cultural awareness, and respect for each student and teacher.

Norton Books in Education

Mindfulness for Teachers

*Simple Skills for Peace and
Productivity in the Classroom*

Patricia A. Jennings

Foreword by Daniel J. Siegel, MD

W. W. Norton & Company
New York • London

Note to Readers: Models and/or techniques described in this volume are illustrative or are included for general informational purposes only; neither the publisher nor the author(s) can guarantee the efficacy or appropriateness of any particular recommendation in every circumstance.

For information about permission to reproduce selections from this book, write to Permissions, W. W. Norton & Company, Inc., 500 Fifth Avenue, New York, NY 10110

For information about special discounts for bulk purchases, please contact W. W. Norton Special Sales at specialsales@wwnorton.com or 800-233-4830

Manufacturing by LSC Communications Harrisonburg
Book design by Paradigm Graphic Design
Production manager: Leeann Graham

ISBN: 978-0-393-70807-3 (pbk.)

W. W. Norton & Company, Inc.
500 Fifth Avenue, New York, N.Y. 10110
www.wwnorton.com

W. W. Norton & Company Ltd.
15 Carlisle Street, London W1D 3BS

11 12 13 14 15

To my husband André who has provided the love, support, and encouragement I needed to write this book.

Contents

Foreword

by Daniel J. Siegel, MD

Why should you take the time to read a book on "mindfulness for teachers"? What's the bottom-line about all this contemporary talk about mindful awareness and its importance for well-being and efficacy in our personal and professional lives? This beautiful book by Patricia ("Tish") Jennings answers these important fundamental questions with comprehensive and clear cutting edge science, compelling stories, and practical applications for classroom life that can profoundly enhance your experience as an educator.

But what does "mindfulness" really mean?

Mindfulness is a way of being aware of what is happening within us and around us with a clear focus of attention on moment-to-moment experience that enables us to be fully present for life. In many ways, cultivating mindfulness means we develop the ability to *sense* life deeply and also to *observe* our experience as well. This linkage of these two differentiated streams of awareness—sensing and observing—reveals how mindfulness can be considered an "integrative practice," one that links differentiated elements to each other. This book is a part of the new Norton education series that builds on our mental health series based on the interdisciplinary approach of interpersonal neurobiology. From that broad scientific perspective, integration is the heart of health. Studies of mindfulness training and the structure and function on the brain reveal, for example, that mindfulness promotes the growth of important integrative fibers that help us with the regulation of emotion, attention, thought, and behavior. These executive functions in ourselves, and in our students, can be cultivated with mindfulness training.

Mindfulness cultivates integration within us, creating an inner sense of calm and clarity. And mindfulness cultivates an interpersonal way of being integrated with others as we become more empathic, compassionate, and connected to those around us.

But how is being "mindfully aware" any different than simple everyday "awareness"?

With mindful awareness we can both sense and observe our *internal* states. When we sense our emotions, for example, we can feel the passion and vitality of life fully. But as we also are observing our emotional states, we can sense them without becoming reactive or impulsively acting on them. In this way, we achieve a state of equanimity, being open to what is happening as it is happening, being fully emotional, but not becoming locked into pre-programmed ways of behaving because of our emotions. Mindfulness is a form of freedom from being taken over by our own neural processes.

In a similar way, being mindfully aware allows us to sense and observe what is going on around us with clarity and openness, enabling us to be receptive to *external* signals from other people and our larger environment. As we sense this connection with other people and the world, we can feel this vibrant sense of being alive and involved in the world. As mindfulness enables us to also observe these signals from our external environment, we are not on automatic pilot and instead have a "space of mind" that gives us the ability to pause before simply reacting mindlessly. This openness within us is a form of receptivity that contrasts to the automaticity of being reactive. Being simply aware can sometimes mean we sense things, but react without observation. Being open and receptive gives us strength. It allows us to pause before acting on an impulse. This receptive state of both sensing and observing also means that we will be more perceptive of life as it unfolds as we do not limit our view of the world, or ourselves, by becoming locked up into prior judgments or expectations that filter and constrain how we see and hear and understand life as it unfolds.

Simply put, being mindful means we can choose to be receptive rather than reactive.

From an interpersonal neurobiology perspective, mindfulness works to create well-being because it is an integrative practice. What is being integrated? We differentiate sensing from observing and then link them within mindful awareness. We focus an observing-self in a respectful and accepting way toward the experience of a sensing-self and embrace the distinction and the importance of each. Sensing and observing are distinct, but both can be linked. That's what the integration of being mindful means. In this book you'll read about the "Wheel of Awareness" which was created to integrate consciousness. As an integrative practice itself, it also promotes mindful awareness.

As integration creates health, compassion, and creativity, we can understand how cultivating the integrative state of mindful awareness would be associated with many positive outcomes in our inner and interpersonal lives. So you might not be surprised, then, to discover that researchers exploring the impact of mindfulness training on children, adolescents, and adults have revealed a wide range of positive outcomes including: improvements in executive functions such as the regulation of attention, emotion, behavior, and relatedness; physiological enhancements in our immune function; elevations in the enzyme (telomerase) that maintains and repairs the ends of our chromosomes; and even preliminary findings suggesting the optimization of the control molecules on our genes (epigenetic regulatory histones and methyl groups) that help prevent certain forms of disease. No kidding! Studies also show that for professionals, such as teachers and physicians, mindfulness training enhances empathy and reduces burnout.

Not bad for a practice that essentially costs nothing but gives you everything from health enhancement to more satisfaction and meaning in your work.

But "where is the catch?", you may be wondering. If this were a medication, you'd ask about side effects and costs. And if this were a pill, there'd be a lot of advertisements promoting its sale, for sure! But the only "catch" is that it often takes your intention, your motivation, and your action to cultivate mindful awareness in your life. Some of us come to mindfulness as a trait without the need for training for its initial growth, but each of us can benefit from learning to strengthen or develop anew this important way of being present. The *intention* can come from waking up and realizing that it's never too late to add a health-promoting, meaning-enhancing life habit to your daily routine. The *motivation* can be a bit more challenging—you're busy, tired, overwhelmed, and you just don't have the time, so forget it. And the *action* needed, well this is where the rubber hits the road. It actually doesn't take much behavioral change in terms of time to make a significant change in your life—both personally and professionally.

If you are anything like me, you may feel more comfortable getting the intention, motivation, and action in place if you have the scientific reasoning and research that reveals how this simple but powerful way of being aware may actually work. And while there's always a lot more to know than whatever we scientifically believe at the moment, we do have a pretty good general notion of how and why mindful awareness is so important to cultivate in our individual and collective lives.

Tish Jennings has created a masterful book to give you not only this scientific background, but also the real life examples from the classroom setting to reveal how mindfulness helps. She then goes on to offer empirically proven practices for you as a teacher to create in your own life that can help promote more mindfulness in your life. Dr. Jennings is herself is a former teacher who knows classroom challenges and opportunities from the inside out. And as she transitioned from teacher to researcher, she has not forgotten these important practical lessons. Demonstrating the power of mindfulness training for teachers to enhance their own lives and improve the experience of their students through the Cultivating Awareness and Resilience in Education (CARE) program she was chiefly responsible for designing and implementing, our expert guide has learned empirically what it takes to bring mindfulness to real life practice.

This is a magnificent book to help you develop your intention, motivation, and action. You are in wonderful hands with this guide to cultivate a way of being aware that will enhance your own life and the experience of your students. Welcome and enjoy!

Daniel J. Siegel, MD, is the founding editor
of the Norton Series on Interpersonal Neurobiology

Preface

*My Journey from Preschool Teacher to Scientist
and Why I Wrote This Book*

This book has emerged from my over 40 years of experience as a mindfulness practitioner, an educator, and a scientist. I wrote this book for everyone who cares about transforming our schools into environments that promote human development—in the fullest sense of the word—and where our children and young adults can reach their full potential. This has been my lifelong goal, and I am incredibly grateful to have the opportunity to share my experience and ideas in the form of this book with the hope that it contributes to this goal.

My intention in writing this preface is to explain why I wrote this book and to give the book context by telling the story of my journey from a preschool teacher infusing my lessons with mindful awareness to a social scientist developing and studying mindfulness-based interventions for teachers and students. This book will share with you what I have learned from these experiences so that you can apply them in your personal and professional life.

My story begins during my childhood, when I discovered the power of mindful awareness to heal. As a result of a series of traumatic events, I found myself orphaned at the age of 15. Trauma can tear you off your moorings. It can shatter your sense of self and your place in the world. It was the late '60s, and the effects of trauma were not well understood. Because I appeared to be functioning well, no one considered that I might need counseling or other psychological support, so I had to figure out how to heal myself.

In high school, I had a teacher who helped me a great deal and who inspired me to become a teacher myself. Ms. Curtis taught creative writing for advanced English students. During this troubling time, she provided the encouragement and support that I desperately needed. Besides our regular writing assignments, we were required to turn in journals to her every week. In these journals we could write whatever we wanted about our lives. She carefully read each entry and responded in writing with insight, kindness, and thoughtfulness.

With Ms. Curtis's encouragement, I began to express grief in the form of very dark poetry. She provided a safe way for me to express my sadness and despair by seeing me for who I was, honoring what I had been through, and helping me transform a horrible experience into art. Through her encouragement, I entered and won a poetry competition. Without a safe way to express and transform my overwhelming grief and feelings of hopelessness, it would have been difficult to overcome them and to go on to have a successful life. I graduated from high school a semester early and was out on my own at age 17.

While I managed well academically, I had lost any sense of security and suffered from existential anxiety. Feeling that my religion had failed me I began to search for ideas and philosophies that might help me make sense of my situation. I was fortunate to find a Zen meditation teacher. Ever since then, for over 40 years, I have practiced some form of mindful awareness. As I drifted around searching for approaches and teachers, I found myself in Boulder, Colorado, in 1974, then a mecca for contemplative seekers. I went to teachings and studied with many teachers from various contemplative traditions. As I experimented with a wide variety of ideas and practices, I would always return to a simple mindfulness practice.

I found that the simple practice of sitting quietly and cultivating present-moment awareness resulted in a heightened clarity and calmness and an objective perspective of my experience. I discovered that I am not my anxious thoughts and feelings, that these are fleeting symptoms of the mind's tendency to grasp, reject, and worry about the past and the future. I learned that by simply sitting with the present moment, I could achieve peace.

The next chapter in my story is about how I became a teacher. After several years in Boulder, I relocated to the San Francisco Bay area, where I studied education and earned a master's degree, a teaching credential, and a Montessori certificate. For over 22 years I taught in a variety of educational settings both public and private, including an inner city Oakland elementary school, a locked mental health facility in San Francisco, and several Montessori preschool and elementary programs.

I founded a Montessori school where I began to integrate mindfulness into my teaching. I was attracted to the Montessori approach because of the contemplative nature of Montessori instructional methods. Lessons are presented to students silently, in the form of practical demonstrations. I found giving these lessons to be wonderful opportunities to apply mindful awareness to my teaching. Before I presented a lesson, I took a brief moment to center myself, to be fully present. To my surprise, I found that by bringing my full mindful awareness to each teaching moment, I was providing a scaffold that gave my students an opportunity to share this experience of mindfulness with me.

I wasn't giving instructions in mindfulness; I was teaching mindfulness through my example by teaching mindfully. My lessons became lessons in both academic content and mindful awareness. After the lessons, the students would often access the same mindful awareness as they engaged in the learning activity I had shown them. I had discovered how valuable the teacher's own mindful awareness is to her students' learning. I had also discovered that children could learn to be mindful by observing mindful behavior among adults. While I regularly included direct mindfulness instruction in my daily teaching routine, I found that the mindfulness they learned from the lessons was much more powerful because it enhanced the understanding of the content.

Next my story shifts to how I became a teacher educator. While I was teaching, I began working as an adjunct professor in a university teacher education program. I taught a variety of education courses, including classroom management. At the same time I supervised student teachers, regularly visiting their classrooms to observe their progress and provide mentoring and leading regular seminars.

Observing classrooms was an excellent opportunity to apply mindful awareness to another aspect of my work experience. New insights arose that shifted my work in another direction. During these 15 years of teaching classroom management strategies while mindfully observing student teachers who had taken my class, I discovered that the teacher's own social and emotional skills are a strong predictor of effectiveness.

I observed firsthand how emotional reactivity interferes with teaching and learning. I especially noted how teachers' emotional reactivity was derailing their efforts to manage student behavior. I knew that my mindful awareness practice helped me manage my emotions and classroom, but this was the early '80s and it wasn't the right time to integrate a mindfulness-based approach into teacher education. However, it became very obvious to me that teachers' emotions can interfere with teaching and that mindfulness might hold the key to helping them.

The last chapter in my story tells how I grew from an educator to a scientist. In 2000, my son graduated from high school and I decided to return to graduate school. I was accepted into the doctoral program in human development at the University of California, Davis, and studied adult development with a focus on stress and coping, looking for ways to address and support teachers' social and emotional competence and resilience.

In 2004, I learned about an exciting new research project just getting under way at the University of California, San Francisco (UCSF). In 2000, a group of scientists met with His Holiness the Dalai Lama to explore the question of how to apply mindful awareness to reducing the harm caused by destructive negative emotions. At this meeting, emotion expert Paul Ekman, meditation teacher B. Alan Wallace, and a team of psychologists, including Mark Greenberg, met to develop an intervention that combined mindfulness and emotion skills instruction. They called it Cultivating Emotional Balance (CEB). The intention was to present this program to groups of individuals working in professions where negative emotions could be detrimental to others. For the first study, they settled on teachers. When I discovered this, I immediately contacted the study's principal investigator, Margaret Kemeny, to find out how I could become involved.

I joined the study team and spent two years working on the project, eventually becoming the project director. During this time I attended the CEB trainings and postdoctoral training seminars in health psychology at UCSF. For the study, we collected a wide range of data to assess the physical signs of stress among the teachers in our sample.

As I learned more about the stress response, I came to realize that the classroom environment can be a setup for serious stress-related health problems. In a sense, both teachers and their students are "captives"—they can't leave during class without suffering adverse consequences. Furthermore, the social and emotional dynamics of a room full of children or adolescents can be intense and sometimes chaotic.

Under pressure, some students become disruptive, distracted, and even defiant, and teachers may become anxious, frustrated, embarrassed, and hopeless. From this perspective, it's easy to see why teachers are burning out and students aren't learning. The stress response is derailing our teaching and our students' learning.

The idea of applying a mindfulness-based approach to supporting teachers' well-being made perfect sense. Furthermore, if we could give teachers the skills to better manage these social and emotional demands, the classroom climate would improve and so would student behavior and learning.

During my time at UCSF, I became one of the first to receive a Francisco J. Varela Research Award for Contemplative Science from the Mind and Life Institute to conduct a small pilot study of the CEB teachers, exploring whether their participation in the study had a positive effect on their classroom climate. The results were promising and led to a long-term program of research that has grown to include projects supported by several federal grants, including a large randomized controlled trial of teachers, classrooms, and students in New York City.

But I have moved ahead of myself in this story. In 2006, I was offered a position at the Garrison Institute as director of the Initiative on Contemplative Teaching and Learning. One of the projects I initiated there was the CARE (Cultivating Awareness and Resilience in Education) for Teachers program. An extension of the CEB program, CARE is more specifically tailored to address the stressors of teaching. A longer description of this program can be found at the end of Chapter 7.

While I was still at the Garrison Institute, I joined the faculty at the Prevention Research Center (PRC) at the Pennsylvania State University to work with Mark Greenberg on the first federally funded study of CARE. I found the PRC to be a very supportive environment for this work. I had the opportunity to collaborate with like-minded scientists and doctoral students on several mindfulness-based studies besides CARE.

In 2013, I was offered an opportunity to return to teacher education as an associate professor at the Curry School of Education at the University of Virginia, an internationally recognized leader in teacher education. This was a dream come true. I was hired specifically to integrate the work I had been doing in teacher professional development on CARE into teacher education. Furthermore, I became the Curry School representative to the Contemplative Sciences Center, a university-wide, interdisciplinary center developed to promote the contemplative sciences and educational approaches across the university. My journey had brought me back to working with students who would become teachers, and now I had an opportunity to bring mindfulness into this work.

This book is a culmination of these over 40 years of experience. I hope that it will make a valuable contribution to the transformation in education that has been catalyzed by mindfulness by providing valuable ideas and helping to build important skills among the thousands of teachers, educators, parents, and leaders who are committed to this transformative process.

Acknowledgments

I am incredibly grateful for the opportunity to share these ideas with you and I appreciate your attention and interest. I have many people to thank who have contributed to my thinking that led to this book. These include in alphabetical order: Paul Ekman, Barbara Fredrickson, Joan Halifax, Jon Kabat-Zinn, Sharon Salzberg, Dan Siegel, and Tsoknyi Rinpoche.

I owe a debt of gratitude to my editors at W. W. Norton, A. Deborah Malmud and Ben Yarling. Ben provided excellent feedback that really helped me craft this book.

I would like to thanks Mark Greenberg, who has been my mentor and devoted supporter over the past decade. Special thanks to my dear friends and colleagues Richard Brown and Christa Turksma. Working with them to develop CARE for Teachers has been one of the most rewarding experiences of my life.

I wish to acknowledge and thank all those who have worked on the CARE research projects. A special thanks to Joshua Brown, the Co-PI on our NYC research. Without him and his outstanding team, we would never have been able to successfully accomplish this important study. Thanks to the Penn State research team: Sebrina Doyle, Jennifer Frank, and Deborah Schussler. Thanks to our previous PSU research team members, Karin Snowberg and Michael Coccia. Thanks to the Fordham University research team: Regin Tanler, Damira Rasheed, and Anna DeWeese.

I also wish to acknowledge my friends and colleagues at the Garrison Institute who provided the opportunity for us to create the CARE for Teachers program and to help provide leadership in this new field. Special thanks to Adi Flesher, who took over as director of the Initiative on Contemplative Teaching and Learning after I left. Also special thanks to Jonathan and Diana Rose, executive director Robyn Brentano, and the Institute's board of directors, along with all the wonderful staff.

I am grateful to my friends and colleagues on the Garrison Institute Education Leadership Council for their years of contribution to the field: Trish Broderick, Richard Brown, Marian David, Adele Diamond, Mark Greenberg, Tobin Hart, Linda Lantieri, Peggy McCardle, Jerry Murphy, Laura Rendon, Liz Robertson, Kimberley Schonert-Reichl, Pamela Seigel, Mark Wilding, Rona Wilensky, and Arthur Zajonc.

An added thanks to Jennifer Frank for reviewing this manuscript. Her comments and suggestions were much appreciated. Also special thanks to Rachel Abenavoli, who spent hours helping me keep track of references for this project.

I thank my family: my sisters Penny Jennings and Pam Jennings Calabrese, my niece Katie Calabrese, and my son and daughter-in-law, Isaac and Lacey Goldstein. Finally, I wish to thank my husband, André La Velle. Without his love and support, I would not have been able to successfully transition from teacher to scientist. Nor would I have been able to write this book. Thank you so much!

Introduction

Mindfulness for Teachers is the result of my over 40 years of personal and professional experience as a teacher, teacher educator, and scientist. It is informed by my deep appreciation for, and commitment to, the teaching profession.

While our educational systems are facing huge problems, I remain optimistic. Challenging situations offer great opportunities for change. We may be poised to be part of a dramatic transformation in education. While there has been a growing recognition that our society needs greater mindfulness and heartfulness, science is showing us how the simple practice of attending to the present moment can change lives. This book applies this new knowledge to the art of teaching. As you read this book, you will learn ways to apply mindful awareness in your daily life to reduce stress and improve your teaching and your students' learning.

Teachers Make a Difference

When you ask people to name someone who has made an important difference in their lives, there is a high probability that they will tell you about a teacher. These stories often have a common thread—the student felt that their teacher saw and respected them for who they were, and in this way provided a means for personal transformation. Over the course of my career, I have found that teachers are some of the most altruistic people I meet, devoted to making a positive difference in the lives of the children they teach.

However, the fact remains that many of us today are not well prepared for the social and emotional demands of the classroom. Students are coming to school less prepared, while at the same time new levels of accountability demand that we demonstrate academic improvement under difficult conditions, often without the necessary support systems. Under these stressful conditions, we become more likely to burn out and leave the profession at a time when, more than ever, we a need workforce of calm, supportive, and understanding teachers.

In 2012, the MetLife Survey of the American Teacher reported,

> Teachers are less satisfied with their careers; in the past two years there has been a significant decline in teachers' satisfaction with their profession. In one of the most dramatic findings of the report, teacher satisfaction has decreased by 15 points since the MetLife Survey of the American Teacher measured job satisfaction two years ago, now reaching the lowest level of job satisfaction seen in the survey series in more than two decades. This decline in teacher satisfaction is coupled with large increases in the number of teachers who indicate that they are likely to leave teaching for another occupation and in the number who do not feel their jobs are secure. (p. 3)

These data are alarming. At a time when our educational system is in crisis, having large numbers of teachers leave the profession would add stress to an already deteriorating situation.

It's really no wonder that we teachers are stressed out by our jobs. Whether in kindergarten or in high school, teaching is a highly demanding activity. Not only do we need to know our content material well, but we need to deploy our attention so we are aware of the entire class while also being able to focus on one or two students at a time. We need to attune ourselves to the group to assess the level of engagement and understanding as well as the social and emotional dynamics of the classroom. And we need to do this without becoming anxious or irritated, without over-controlling or under-controlling.

However, teacher education focuses primarily on content and pedagogy, often overlooking the social, emotional, and cognitive demands of teaching. New teachers can easily become overwhelmed by these demands and the demands of daily lesson planning, organization, assessment, and classroom management.

Added to these demands is the increasing number of children who come to school with unmet needs. Children at risk of psychological and behavioral problems often pose challenges for unprepared teachers. These students have more difficulty attending to learning activities, sitting still, and getting along with their peers. They can disrupt lessons by creating chaos in the classroom, something many of us dread and try to avoid at all costs. When frustration builds, we become emotionally exhausted, an early sign of burnout.

Skills for the 21st Century

Today there is a great deal of talk about 21st century skills. What are these skills and how can schools promote learning them? While this question has been debated widely, two factors rarely mentioned are adaptation and resilience. The fact is, we don't know much about the world for which we are preparing our children. However, the current pace of change in our society does not seem to be abating. It's a good bet that our children will need to be adaptive to succeed in their constantly changing economic, social, and cultural environment.

Children's brains are incredibly adaptive and resilient, but our current education system does not cultivate these faculties. Rather, our schools too often drum out these gifts through an emphasis on rote learning and rigid, fact-based testing. Furthermore, in most cases, our classrooms do not mirror how adults typically work in our modern economy. Most high-level work today in every sector of our economy involves the collaboration of individuals within interdisciplinary teams who have a variety of skills and abilities and coordinate their efforts to analyze and solve problems and to create innovations. This type of work requires a high degree of social and emotional competence, creativity, and higher-order thinking. Because of the constantly changing social, cultural, and economic landscape, it also requires flexibility and adaptation.

The Aim of This Book

Mindfulness for Teachers was written to help teachers cultivate the skills they need to promote a calm, relaxed, but enlivened learning environment that can prepare children for the future by fostering creativity, innovation, collaboration, and cooperation. This sort of classroom requires a teacher who is fully aware and present as she or he teaches and interacts with students, parents, and colleagues, and you now have the tools to be that teacher.

This book will help you develop the skills you need to orchestrate healthy and supportive classroom dynamics, boost your enjoyment of teaching, and cultivate your students' love of learning. Each chapter introduces a special topic in the application of mindful awareness to teaching and learning and a series of activities you can do to practice and apply what you've learned to your teaching.

In Chapter 1, "What Is Mindfulness?," I open with an overview of the concept of mindful awareness, both as a state of mind and as a personal trait that can be cultivated and enhanced through practice. I introduce the concept of interpersonal mindfulness and how it relates to teaching. I introduce Dan Siegel's (2007) wheel of awareness, a model of how we can apply mindful awareness to our inner and outer experience in order to improve our psychological functioning. I review research on the specific effects of mindfulness-based interventions, focusing on how these interventions reduce stress and improve self-awareness, self-regulation, and reflective capacities, which are necessary for effective teaching. The chapter concludes with a series of mindful awareness activities you can practice on your own.

Chapter 2, "The Emotional Art of Teaching," explains how practicing mindful awareness can help you explore and better understand your emotional life. Teaching is an "emotional practice" (Hargreaves, 1998), and teacher and student emotions affect classroom dynamics. This chapter contains information about the functions of emotions and how emotional reactivity affects teaching and learning. I describe how to apply the wheel of awareness to exploring your emotional experience. This chapter also introduces the field of social and emotional learning and the added value of mindfulness-based approaches. The chapter's skill-building exercises are designed to help you explore and understand your emotional experience.

Chapter 3, "Understanding Your Negative Emotions," addresses negative or unpleasant emotions like anger, fear, and sadness. These emotions arise when you feel threatened, and they help you protect yourself by triggering the fight, flight, or freeze reaction, but they trigger these reactions whether the threat is real or imagined. This type of emotional reactivity develops into patterns of behaviors that can be easily triggered without your conscious awareness, and can derail your most well-intentioned efforts. I cover this information in depth, explaining what we know about the brain's role in emotional experience. Practicing mindful awareness can help you notice uncomfortable emotions so that you can understand and regulate them with more consciousness rather than automatically reacting when your emotions are triggered. The skill-building section of this chapter includes activities designed to help you practice mindfully working with uncomfortable emotions.

Chapter 4, "The Power of Positivity," explores the power of positive emotions like happiness and gratitude and demonstrates how important these positive emotional states are to effective teaching and learning. Positive emotions broaden your perceptions and build your resilience and connections with others. They also support creativity, critical thinking, and promote exploration—three foundational skills for learning. This chapter introduces mindful awareness activities that will help you generate and savor positive emotions alone and in the context of your classroom to build a warm and supportive community of learners.

Chapter 5, "The Heart of Teaching," begins with information and strategies to promote self-care, because caring for others requires that you first care for yourself. The chapter introduces simple strategies for teaching care and reinforcing caring behavior among your students. You will also learn how to improve your listening skills and how to generate compassion for students and families who are experiencing deep pain and suffering. We end the chapter with two practices and two activities designed to help you develop and employ these skills.

In Chapter 6, "Orchestrating Classroom Dynamics," I apply the principles learned in previous chapters to supporting optimal classroom dynamics. I highlight how mindfulness can help you cultivate a composed teaching presence that fosters respect and care among your students. You are a powerful role model, showing children how to be emotionally honest, firm, and responsive. In this chapter, I have applied a mindfulness-based perspective to community building, relationship management, establishment and reinforcement of rules and procedures, conflict management, instructional processes, and responses to challenging student behavior. The skill-building section of the chapter provides several activities to help you apply this learning to improve the dynamics of your classroom.

In Chapter 7, "Mindfulness and School Transformation," I explain how mindfulness may help us build the collective will to transform our schools into learning environments that promote creativity and innovation to meet the needs of an unknown future. While educators and policy makers have struggled over school reform for decades, mindfulness may help catalyze the transformation education urgently needs. This chapter introduces the organizations and individuals who form the vanguard of the mindfulness-in-education movement. These are pioneers who are transforming our classrooms, schools, and whole districts. I survey the evidence-based programs and the research that is demonstrating that mindfulness reduces stress and improves well-being for students and teachers. The chapter ends with an inspirational message of hope for the future of education.

The end of the book contains a wealth of resources that will enable you to learn more and help you join this growing movement. These include bibliographies, links to websites of programs for students and teachers, links to free audio files of teachers leading mindfulness practices, and links to mindfulness apps.

Finally, a few words about the anecdotes contained in this book. Many are based on true stories from my work as a teacher, teacher educator, and program developer. In some cases, the stories are fictional accounts to demonstrate an idea, or they are an amalgamation drawn from mine and others' experiences. In most cases, names have been changed. In several cases, I mention individuals by name and I have their permission to do so.

Mindfulness for Teachers

Chapter 1

What Is Mindfulness?

In this chapter you will learn about mindful awareness, how it can be cultivated with practice and how it can be applied to improve your teaching, the quality of your classroom environment, and the relationships you build with your students. I will survey the research on the effects of mindfulness, focusing on improvements in well-being, self-awareness, self-regulation, and reflective capacities.

You will learn a fundamental mindful awareness practice involving focusing attention on the breath. You will also learn the practice of setting intention, an exercise designed to help you reconnect with your motivation to teach and to renew and maintain your commitment to the teaching profession. Finally, you will learn a very brief mindful breath awareness practice you can use to calm down when you need to. Practiced regularly, these simple activities can help you build the resilience to handle the everyday ups and downs of teaching so you can create and maintain a learning environment where your students can thrive, socially, emotionally, and academically.

Mindfulness Is Present-Moment, Nonjudgmental Awareness

Mindfulness is a particular state of consciousness that involves awareness and acceptance of whatever is happening in the present moment. You can think of it as "fullness of mind," because you bring your full, undivided attention to the present moment. The term *mindfulness* has been used in various contemplative traditions to refer to very specific types of meditative states and practices. For the purposes of this book, I use the term generically. This approach is purely secular, based upon the most current science.

Practicing mindfulness means monitoring, in real time, your experience, and doing so in a nonjudgmental way (Kabat-Zinn, 1994). When you are experiencing mindful awareness, you are fully present to what is happening in the here and now, rather than dwelling on the past with thoughts such as "I hope things went okay in class yesterday with the substitute" or concerns about the future like "What am I going to do about this student?"

Mindfulness involves three fundamental processes: forming intention, paying attention, and adjusting your attitude (Shapiro, Carlson, Astin, & Freedman, 2006). The act of practicing mindfulness is intentional—a purposeful act. We focus our attention on the present moment and attend to it with acceptance, care, and discernment. Mindfulness is also "heartfulness" in that it promotes both an open-minded and open-hearted apperception of the world reminding us of its intrinsic goodness and beauty.

The term *mindfulness* can be used to indicate both a state of mind and a more enduring personal trait or disposition. While research suggests that some people may be naturally more mindful than others (Brown & Ryan, 2003), it has also demonstrated that over time, and with practice, the state of mindfulness becomes consistently more accessible and more traitlike.

There is also evidence that practicing mindful awareness is associated with beneficial changes in the brain that may support self-regulation (Hölzel et al., 2011). Through practice we can strengthen our capacity to incorporate mindfulness into our daily lives until it becomes a habit of mind (Roeser & Zelazo, 2012).

Mindful awareness can be practiced in various formal and informal ways. Formal mindful awareness practices (MAPs) include forms of sitting meditation and contemplative movement activities like yoga and tai chi, a Chinese martial art involving a series of slow, mindful movements.

The two basic forms of formal sitting meditation practices are called *focused attention* and *open monitoring*. Focused attention involves bringing mindful awareness to a particular target, such as the breath, and working toward maintaining focused attention on the target. Open monitoring involves openly and nonjudgmentally monitoring the content of your experience from one moment to the next.

At the end of each chapter I will introduce various formal and informal mindful awareness practices for you to learn and apply to your work as a teacher. At the end of this chapter, I introduce several introductory formal practices, including focused attention. I introduce open monitoring at the end of Chapter 2.

Mindful awareness can also be practiced informally, in the midst of your daily activities. At any given moment you can bring mindful awareness to the richness of your present-moment experience in all its dimensions: external sounds, objects, other people or animals, and internal thoughts, sensations, and feelings.

Informal mindful awareness practice involves the flexible application of attention, awareness, and acceptance. It is a kind of "meta-awareness" in which you notice everything in your consciousness, like an observer watching a movie, and adopt an attitude of acceptance of everything that is happening.

For a demonstrative example, imagine you are sitting peacefully on the bank of a beautiful river focusing your attention on the waves of the water. You notice boats going by, but you don't focus your attention on them. Then this big, beautiful party boat floats by.

There's music, and people are dancing on the deck. It looks like a lot of fun. Pretty soon your mind has left the shore and is on the boat, wondering where it's going and where it's come from. Then, like waking from a dream, you suddenly realize you've become distracted by the boat and you bring yourself back to the riverbank to focus on the waves again.

Practicing mindful awareness is like this. When your mind has wandered into disruptive thoughts about the future or the past and you're no longer present to the here and now, you recognize it and consciously bring your attention back to the present moment. This sequence of intentionally engaging in present-moment awareness, becoming distracted, noticing your distraction, and then bringing your attention back to the present is the practice of mindful awareness itself.

Just as physical exercise builds strength, flexibility, and endurance in your body, mindful awareness practice builds cognitive and emotional skills that cultivate inner strength, resilience, a sense of purpose, and the capacity for continuous learning and flexible adaptation in the face of change and life's challenges.

Observing Judgments

The attitude of acceptance is often referred to as "nonjudgmental" awareness. However, as you begin formal practice, you may notice yourself engaging in judgmental thoughts, especially if you are new to the practice. As you sit quietly attending to your breath, you may begin to think about the way you are practicing (e.g., "I am doing this wrong") or about how your mind darts around aimlessly (e.g., "My thoughts are driving me crazy").

This is a common experience and is perfectly normal. Here's the point: As I practice mindful awareness, I can simply notice these thoughts. I don't try to stop them or judge them, but just notice them and then let them go, recognizing that I am not my thoughts. The thoughts are there, but I don't get wrapped up in them or let them carry me away. I don't need to judge my judgments, just observe them.

As I apply informal mindful awareness practice to my everyday experience in the classroom, I notice how often my judgments take me out of the present moment. Judgments take the form of impulses to reject or to grasp something in our experience. If we judge something as bad or distasteful, our impulse is to reject it. If we judge something as enjoyable or beneficial to us and we have a strong desire to obtain it, our impulse is to grasp on to it and try to acquire it.

When I mindfully observe my thoughts, I begin to notice these tendencies. For example, I might find myself thinking, "Sam is really disrupting the class. I want the principal to transfer him out," or, "Mr. Garcia always gets assigned student teachers, and I could really use one." Both of these impulses grab my attention and take me away from mindful acceptance of the present moment.

Nonjudgmental awareness does not imply lack of discernment. Judging involves imposing our beliefs and expectations on our present-moment experience rather than being fully aware of what is actually happening.

For example, Marcus is rummaging around in his backpack rather than paying attention to me as I explain a math problem. It's a test prep week, so I'm already feeling pressured to make sure my students attend so they'll do well. Marcus's activity is starting to distract the other students, and I find myself becoming annoyed with him. From past experience, I know he can easily get distracted and disrupt the class.

Automatically I start to judge him: "He's always getting into trouble. What's he going to do this time?" My judgment frames my mindset, prompting me to prepare for the worst and to be ready to jump on him at the slightest provocation.

By regularly practicing mindful awareness, I develop the capacity to recognize these thoughts and feelings rather than getting caught up in them. As soon as I notice my frustration and annoyance and their associated physical sensations and thoughts, I can stop, take a breath, and let go of them, and then I can recognize that I'm making snap judgments and assumptions about Marcus.

That doesn't mean I ignore Marcus and let him do whatever he wants. It means that I can focus my attention on what he is really doing and respond to this, rather than assuming that he's preparing to cause trouble, and overreacting. I can also notice my tendency to assume that he is intentionally trying to make my job more difficult when in actuality his behavior is probably motivated by numerous factors that have nothing to do with me, such as lack of parental support and developmental immaturity.

When I notice my judgment, I can intentionally broaden my awareness of Marcus. I realize that his pencil is broken and he's trying to find another so he can take notes. Rather than hastily jumping on him for not paying attention, I can offer him a new pencil so he can stay on track.

In this way, I accomplish three important things: (1) I calm myself down (why get into a tizzy about something if I don't have to?), (2) I avoid a confrontation with Marcus that would damage my relationship with him and create tension in the learning environment that might derail other students' learning, and (3) I strengthen my relationship with Marcus by responding to his need.

My intention in writing this book is to help you apply mindful awareness to your daily life as a teacher. As you do so, teaching will become easier and more enjoyable. You will build a set of internal resources that will build strength and resilience, preventing overwhelm and burnout. You will deepen your relationships with your students by being more fully present to them as they are, rather than as you would like them to be.

Finally, you will become more responsive and proactive and less reactive. You will find that you are calmer and more focused even in the midst of the chaos that is typical when large groups of young people congregate. Your composure will act as a catalyst, allowing you to shape the social and emotional environment by modeling exemplary behaviors and through firm but gentle direction.

This calm, broadened awareness will help you recognize and respond to teachable moments and develop creative ways to present content to your students, enlivening your teaching and stimulating your students' learning.

Interpersonal Mindfulness

What I have described above is intrapersonal mindfulness: the present-moment, nonjudgmental awareness of internal processes, including thoughts, feelings, and bodily sensations. Mindfulness can also be applied to how we relate to others. We call this interpersonal mindfulness.

My colleagues and I developed a definition of interpersonal mindfulness that we apply to our work with both teachers and parents (Duncan, Coatsworth, & Greenberg, 2009). This definition involves the development and practice of the following behaviors:

- Listening with full attention to others
- Present-centered awareness of emotions experienced by oneself and others during interactions

- Openness to, acceptance of, and receptivity to others' thoughts and feelings
- Self-regulation: low emotional and behavioral reactivity and low automaticity in reaction to the everyday behaviors of others
- Compassion for oneself and others

A central tenant of the wisdom traditions from which a secular approach to mindfulness has been adapted is that mindful awareness involves a sense of connectedness—the recognition that as human beings we are essentially the same and we need to care for one another to survive and flourish. This recognition promotes a deep sense of respect and compassion for others and the wish to alleviate their suffering.

In the field of education today, we emphasize the exploration of which professional dispositions are required to teach well (Dottin, 2009; National Council for Accreditation of Teacher Education, 2008), also referred to as "habits of mind." Habits of mind are defined as "those dispositions toward behaving intelligently when confronted with problems, the answers to which are not immediately known" (Costa & Kallick, n.d., para. 2). Practicing mindful awareness can help us cultivate such habits as resilience in response to challenges, nonjudgmental awareness of and reflection on our experience, flexible problem-solving, emotion regulation, and caring, empathetic, and compassionate responding to others (Roeser, Skinner, Beers, & Jennings, 2012).

When I find myself caught up in painful thoughts and feelings and behave badly, my mindful awareness practice helps me recognize what I'm doing, stop, and forgive myself. Then I can take the necessary actions to repair any harm I may have caused others.

The application of interpersonal mindfulness helps me recognize and understand when students, parents, and colleagues have similar challenging moments. From a place of empathy, I can generate compassion for others, even in the midst of a difficult interpersonal situation, and provide the social support they need rather than getting caught up in defensiveness or hostility.

The process of engaging in interpersonal mindfulness often begins with listening. Years ago when I was teaching kindergarten, I had a parent come to me in a rage. A classmate had hit his four-year-old daughter and he was furious.

Young children have not developed mature abilities to self-regulate and sometimes resort to aggressive behavior when they are very angry. When children hit in school settings, it often happens so quickly that it's very difficult for a teacher to prevent. While hitting is not uncommon in kindergarten settings, parents are often horrified by this behavior.

It was late in the afternoon when this father called me. He was yelling so loudly I had to hold the receiver away from my ear. I let him talk and then suggested that we meet to discuss the issue in person. We scheduled a meeting for the next day.

That evening I noticed my anxiety growing in anticipation of the meeting. Dread formed in the pit of my stomach. My mouth was dry and my mind was spinning with thoughts about what to say to him. These thoughts ranged from extreme defensiveness ("He hit her so quickly that I couldn't stop it") to self-righteous indignation ("I will not be treated like this. He is so disrespectful!").

Then I began to empathize with the parent, recognizing how hard it must be for him to see his daughter hurt. I focused on my goals for the meeting: my intention to be fully present for this parent and to facilitate a conversation that would resolve his concerns. Slowly I felt the anger and defensiveness fall away.

The next day, I met with the father. By now he was somewhat subdued, but his rage erupted again as he described how he felt when he learned that another child had hit his daughter. He began to blame me, accusing me of not providing adequate supervision and endangering his child. Rather than trying to defend myself, I listened quietly. I noticed my body tense up and the knot in my stomach return, but I kept breathing and allowed these feelings to subside.

As I did this, I began to notice his pain and suffering. I could empathize with him. The urge to protect his child from harm was primal and brought out an intense rage against the perceived threat which, in that moment, I represented.

I noticed the power of his rage, the intensity of the glare in his eyes, his clenched fists and the harsh tone of his voice. After a few minutes of mindfully observing and listening to his tirade, his ferocity began to wane. My mindful presence took the wind out of his sails; without a defensive or angry response from me, his rage ran out of fuel.

Suddenly he stopped in midsentence, looked around sheepishly, and said, "Wow, I'm really going on about this, aren't I?" I gently smiled and said, "It's really tough when your child gets hurt and you want to protect her. I understand how you feel." From that point on, our conversation changed.

I told him that, unfortunately, hitting happens in kindergarten and it's really difficult to catch. I told him about the proactive steps we were taking to help the children prevent aggression by teaching them the assertiveness they needed to stop another child from hurting them. In role plays, children practiced telling another child, "Don't hit me!" I gave him suggestions for teaching his daughter these techniques at home. He left the meeting relieved and ready to help us prevent hitting in the future. Furthermore, he came to realize that he couldn't protect his young daughter from every painful situation and that the best way he could help her was to provide her with skills rather than attacking and blaming her teacher.

In this example, I began to apply interpersonal mindfulness by listening to the father with my full attention while maintaining a present-centered awareness of my emotions. As I calmed myself, I was able to recognize, understand, and accept his thoughts and feelings. Even though his anger was directed at me, I understood that his emotions were motivated by his urge to protect his daughter, not to hurt me.

This recognition helped me continue to self-regulate. I maintained focus on my breath so I could stay calm and generate empathy and compassion for the father. I think my calm demeanor, the expression of concern on my face, and my silence allowed the father to hear himself and to recognize his overreaction.

Interpersonal mindfulness helps us recognize how our behavior affects our students. Our students learn social values primarily by observing and responding to our behavior. Being mindful of our values involves recollecting and reflecting on our actions with honest evaluation, and mature discernment—rather than being unconsciously reactive. Practicing mindful awareness helps us to see things as they really are—with clear comprehension—and to interact with others and our environment with intentionality, clarity, kindness, and compassion. It also helps us be kind to ourselves when we find ourselves acting in ways we regret.

One day when I was teaching kindergarten, I noticed a boy named Javier staring intently at the fishbowl in our classroom. At first I thought he was wasting time and needed to be redirected to his work. But I took a moment to notice my judgment, stopped myself from interrupting, and spent a few minutes observing him. We were in the middle of a unit on fish, so I realized that in observing the fishbowl, he might, in fact, be applying the knowledge I had presented about basic fish physiology.

As I helped other children, I occasionally glanced at him. He stayed at the fishbowl for a good 10 minutes, just staring at the fish. When he was finished, he came over to me with a huge smile on his face. He looked as if he had just made the most important scientific discovery in his life. He said, "Ms. Jennings, fish can't snap their fingers!" I smiled back, recognizing that he had integrated the study of fish with his own interest in finger snapping, which he had just mastered.

In this example, simply taking the time to notice my judgment of Javier's behavior allowed me to self-regulate so I could be open, accepting, and receptive to his thoughts and feelings, and fully present to him and his discovery. Rather than judging him for wasting time, I became aware of his interest in the fish and was able to share his thrill of discovery.

When I teach, it often feels like a constant flurry of activity, demands, and distractions. One student needs my help with problem-solving. Another needs me to help her stay on track. I have to monitor another's behavior while remembering the content I am teaching. This barrage of demands can create the illusion that there is no time to mindfully attend to what's going on and to listen to my students fully. When I bring mindful awareness to my teaching, time slows down. When my mind isn't distracted by a flood of thoughts about the past and future and I am present to what is happening now, I find I have more time than I realized, and I begin to notice the needs of my students. When I find myself becoming anxious because I think my class is chaotic, I can stop, calm down, and mindfully observe what is happening. In these moments, I often realize that the chaos is in my mind and that the class is actually just fine.

Mindfulness, both interpersonal and intrapersonal, can play an important role in effective teaching. Mindful awareness and mindful behavior help us maintain composure, compassion, and sensitivity to our students' needs and interests while helping us build the resilience required to maintain our well-being in a highly demanding work environment.

Practicing mindful awareness while teaching allows us to manage the classroom proactively. We notice when children are about to go off task or become disruptive, and we can position ourselves to prevent problems. To be aware of what is happening in the whole classroom at any given moment and at the same time respond to individual children's needs, we must be able to shift our attention from the whole classroom to an individual child, and back again, with comfort and regularity. This requires a high degree of attentional flexibility, which we can build by regularly engaging in mindful awareness practices.

Concurrently, we must process a barrage of emotion-laden information. On a regular basis, we monitor and manage conflict situations that arise between children. Some students present challenging behavior that we find emotionally provocative. Parents and administrators can be critical and demanding. Furthermore, we face the pressure of high-stakes testing and the challenges of unprepared students, many of whom have social and behavioral problems that receive inadequate support.

Because we spend a great deal of time focusing our attention on these demands and subject matter, we may not be aware of our own emotions or those of our students. Furthermore, despite working in a highly emotionally challenging environment, we are expected to maintain an even keel and meet the needs of students, parents, and administrators calmly and professionally.

When we take time to notice our own emotional experience, it can help us understand the roots of our emotional reactivity and to find ways to better manage it. Let's explore this idea with an example from a teacher who applied mindful awareness to her emotional state, allowing her to engage with her students in a new way.

Karen is an English teacher in a private prep high school. The school has very high expectations for its students. As a new teacher, she was assigned to the teachers' least favorite class: freshman English. At a mindfulness workshop, she expressed anxiety about teaching. Her demeanor was timid and insecure. However, Karen was very responsive to the mindful awareness practices and the instructions on how to apply them to teaching.

On a subsequent training day, I noticed a dramatic change in her demeanor. She stood with more presence and looked more confident. We began the workshop by asking participants to share their experiences of applying mindful awareness to their teaching. Karen was the first to raise her hand, and she shared an amazing story.

One day, she had come to class prepared to teach a grammar lesson. It was a few weeks before the holiday break, and she faced a class of fidgety freshmen. The last thing they wanted to do was learn grammar. She said to her class, "Today we will be learning about subjunctive clauses." The whole class moaned and complained, "I hate grammar! Why do we need to learn this stupid stuff?"

Facing this onslaught of negativity, she wanted to run away and hide. But she didn't. She remembered what she had learned in the workshop and began to pay attention to her body. She felt the surge of stress hormones flood her body and her knees begin to tremble. She was able to bring mindful awareness to the bodily sensation that she interpreted as fear.

Then she began to take some deep belly breaths to calm herself. The tirade continued, but she made a conscious effort to stop taking it so personally. Once she was calmer, she began to notice her students' emotions. They were powerfully bitter and sarcastic. She wondered if she could direct this energy to learning something useful.

She said, "Okay, I hear that you really hate grammar. Tell me more about this. Why do you hate it so much?" As her students began to explain their feelings about grammar, she had an idea.

"Okay, here's what we're going to do. I want you to write a poem about why you hate grammar. But there are two rules you have to follow. You cannot use the word *hate* because that's just too easy. Come up with a more articulate way to express your feelings. The second rule is that you have to include a subjunctive clause in your poem."

Excited by the challenge, her students settled down and started to work on the assignment. By the end of class, they had turned in a slew of outstanding poems. They were incredibly bitter and sarcastic, but they all avoided the word *hate* and included a subjunctive clause.

As Karen told this story, her face lit up as if she had finally discovered the secret of managing a rowdy bunch of teenagers. She had successfully engaged them in a productive learning activity rather than hopelessly trying to control them.

Months later, I returned to this school for a visit and ran into Karen. I asked her how things were going, and she said, "To tell you the truth, earlier this year, I was thinking that I wasn't cut out to be a teacher and was on the verge of quitting, but the workshop changed all that. I'm really enjoying teaching now." The confident smile on her face supported her words.

Practicing mindful awareness can help us manage stress and improve our teaching and our students' learning. This simple practice can help us take behavior and tough situations less personally. Then we can step back, reflect, and figure out how to manage the situation in a new way—a way that engages and channels the students' energy rather than fighting against it.

The Wheel of Awareness and the Eight Senses

Let's take a moment to think about the question, "What is mind?" While we've been learning about mindfulness and mindful awareness, we haven't yet explored the nature of mind itself. Daniel Siegel, the founder of the field of interpersonal neurobiology, has defined mind as "an embodied and relational process that regulates the flow of energy and information" (Siegel, 2012, p. 2).

In this book, we will explore how to promote the mind's regulatory balance of energy and information flow. We experience mind as an emergent, transactional, and interpersonal process. Energy and information flow within us and between us, and the mind regulates this process.

We have the power to shape this process when we intentionally direct our attention. We can mindfully attend to inner and outer experience through eight senses. Siegel describes what he calls the "wheel of awareness" as a metaphor for this process (Siegel, 2007).

Imagine a wheel. The hub is our awareness. The rim contains all the possible objects of awareness, anything we can perceive through our eight senses. The spokes represents our attention.

Figure 1.1

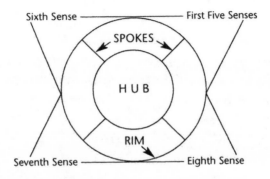

From *The Mindful Brain: Reflection and Attunement in the Cultivation of Well-Being* by Daniel J. Siegel. Copyright © 2007 by Mind Your Brain, Inc. Used by permission of W. W. Norton & Company, Inc.

Let's take a trip around the wheel of awareness as it is depicted in Figure 1.1, and explore the possibilities. We'll start with the first five senses of sight, smell, hearing, touch, and taste, located on the upper right side of the figure. These senses give us information about the outer, physical world. We can focus our mindful awareness on input from these senses.

For example, we can focus our attention on a glorious rose. We see the subtle range of pinks across the petals, we smell the delicious sweetness, and we feel the contrast between the soft petals and the sting of the thorns. We can notice the blending overtones of wind chimes ringing, and taste the tangy sweetness of an orange. When we bring mindfulness into our sensory experience of the outer world, we notice its richness and beauty. We realize how often we go about our lives numb to our incredible world.

Next we move counterclockwise around the wheel to the sixth sense, located on the upper left side of the wheel. Our sixth sense involves our inner bodily perceptions. Bringing mindful awareness to our inner experience, we can feel inside our body. Siegel calls this the "embodied mind." We notice the stiffness in our neck and shoulders after a hard day at work. We notice bodily sensations that we associate with emotions. We can feel our jaws clenching and the tension and heat rising to our heads when we become angry. We can feel the dread growing in the pit of our stomach when we are afraid.

Our language contains many expressions that communicate these experiences: "hot headed," "burning with rage," "sick to his stomach with terror." These physical sensations result from the automatic bodily functions designed to help us survive. They are triggered by the fight, flight, or freeze response that begins in the limbic system of the brain. As we develop the ability to apply mindful awareness to these bodily sensations, we can notice ourselves reacting emotionally before our emotions get the best of us.

Continuing counterclockwise around the wheel, to the lower left side of Figure 1.1, we have the seventh sense. We can direct mindful awareness to the content of our conceptual mind—thoughts, images, beliefs, attitudes, assumptions, biases, and intentions (Siegel, 2010).

As we practice mindful awareness, we begin to notice that our mind has a mind of its own, so to speak. We notice how our mind distracts us, drawing our attention away from the focus of our practice to an endless number of issues related to grasping and rejecting the future and the past. "What should I eat for lunch today?" "I was so stupid yesterday. I wonder if she's still angry with me?" "How will I solve this problem?" As we notice that our attention has wandered off, we gently bring it back to the present moment.

Siegel calls this awareness of the cognitive mind's process "mindsight" because it gives us insight into the way the mind works (Siegel, 2010). We realize that others have the same experience, and this gives us insight into how others may be thinking as well.

Traveling around the wheel counterclockwise to the next stop, we find the eighth sense, located on the lower right side of the figure. The eighth sense is relational. It is our ability to attune ourselves with another person. When I walk into a room where there has just been a heated exchange, I can feel the tension without anyone having to tell me. When I share a happy moment with a student, we are attuned to each other for that moment. When we apply mindful awareness to the eighth sense, we are practicing interpersonal mindfulness.

When I look into my son's eyes, I can feel the deep love we share. When I'm teaching and the whole class is engaged, there is a sense of joint attention, the excitement of discovery, and the joy of learning together. As you will discover in Chapter 6, mindful attention to the relational senses of your students can help you orchestrate the dynamics of the classroom to promote student engagement and prosocial behavior.

The Positive Effects of Practicing Mindful Awareness

Increasingly, psychologists are using mindfulness-based interventions (MBIs) to successfully relieve a variety of mental and physical ailments. For over 25 years, researchers have studied the effects of these interventions, and interest has grown dramatically over the past decade as the promising results of this research have become better known.

The most widely studied mindfulness-based intervention is Mindfulness-Based Stress Reduction (or MBSR), developed by Jon Kabat-Zinn, founder of the Center for Mindfulness (Kabat-Zinn, 2009). Kabat-Zinn began his work decades ago by applying mindfulness meditation training to helping people cope with medical conditions that traditional medicine was unable to cure, like chronic pain. Numerous rigorous studies have found that MBSR reduces stress, promotes well-being, makes psychological functioning more adaptive, and enhances cognitive functions, including attentional skills (Chiesa, Calati, & Serretti, 2011; Ivanovski & Malhi, 2007; Keng, Smoski, & Robins, 2011).

Furthermore, MBIs enhance regulatory psychological processes that serve as a buffer against psychological distress, promote resilience (Jimenez, Niles, & Park, 2010), and enhance awareness of bodily sensations, improving emotion regulation (Desbordes et al., 2012). Other benefits include increases in positive mood, empathy, and immune system functioning; reductions in stress and anxiety; a reduced incidence of relapse after treatment for depression; and decreases in substance abuse (Chiesa & Serreti, 2009; Davidson et al., 2003; Ma & Teasdale, 2004; Ostafin & Marlatt, 2008; Shapiro, Brown, & Beigel, 2007). MBIs also promote cognitive flexibility (Kashdan & Rottenberg, 2010) and self-reflection (Farb et al., 2007). In this way, they may help teachers overcome the tendency toward emotional reactivity in response to student behavior that contributes to emotional exhaustion and burnout (Chang, 2013; Jennings & Greenberg, 2009).

Focused attention and open awareness may have different effects upon the cognitive functions associated with creativity. One study found that open awareness promotes divergent thinking (Colzato, Ozturk, & Hommel, 2012). This type of thinking facilitates the generation and consideration of multiple ideas and solutions critical to situations that require a high degree of creativity.

Recent research has demonstrated that MBSR promotes significant changes in brain structure associated with improvements in learning and memory processes, emotion regulation, self-referential processing, and perspective-taking, all of which are skills critical to effective teaching and learning (Hölzel et al., 2011).

We are still not entirely sure exactly why mindfulness-based programs and therapies are so helpful. One suggestion is that by practicing awareness in this way, we strengthen the connections between the prefrontal cortex and the limbic system of the brain and, as a result, are better able to use our executive functions to override emotional reactivity. This may promote a decentering process whereby we are able to psychologically step back and observe our thoughts and feelings, not allowing them to take over (Feldman, Greeson, & Senville, 2010). Having greater distance from disturbing thoughts and feelings may make it easier for us to see them as just thoughts and feelings, rather than critical realities that demand our full attention.

When we experience distress or become "stressed out," we tend to be easily triggered and react automatically in ways we may not realize. The tone of our voice becomes harsh. We overreact. As we learn to apply mindfulness to our life experiences, we become more aware of our reactivity and perceive the triggers that throw us out of our decentered (in a good way), mindful, more accepting states of mind. In other words, by practicing mindful awareness, we can take things less personally, disrupt our cycles of negative reactivity, strengthen our attention, and engage in more effective problem-solving (Safran & Segal, 1990).

Over the past decade, researchers have turned their attention to exploring whether MBIs might provide the skills teachers need to effectively manage stress and create and sustain socially and emotionally supportive learning environments. This exploration began with the idea that MAPs could be generally beneficial for people working in the helping professions. Today there are several programs showing evidence that they may help teachers reduce stress and promote resilience and efficacy. These programs are described in detail in Chapter 7 under "Evidence-Based Programs for Teachers."

Skill-Building Practices

Now that you know what mindful awareness is, how it can be applied to teaching, and how it can support your ability to be composed and fully present in your classroom, let's address how to practice it. I'll start by describing two basic mindful awareness practices and then give you instructions.

A daily mindfulness practice can help you strengthen your "awareness muscles" so you can more comfortably apply them to your teaching. There are numerous approaches to mindful awareness practice. Maybe you already have a practice, and if you do, I encourage you to continue with whatever routine you have established. If you are new to this work, I encourage you to find a regular time for formal, sitting practice that you can maintain on a daily basis. I find that it works best for me to take this time first thing in the morning.

If you feel you need more support, find an MBSR program in your area and enroll in the eight-week program (see the resources section at the end of this book for more information on this and other recommended programs, as well as books and guided practice recordings). It's also very helpful to find a teacher who can provide instructions in person to support your understanding of the practice. As an alternative, try daily exercise with the practices described below. You may wish to record yourself reading the instructions; in this way, you can create a customized audio recording for your guided mindful awareness practice.

Focused Attention

The first and most basic form of mindful awareness practice is often called *focused attention*, and it involves intentionally directing and maintaining attention on a target. This practice helps the mind settle. This form of practice involves intentionally but gently resting your attention on your breath, noticing the sensations of each inhalation and exhalation. If you are new to MAPs, this is where I suggest you begin your practice. This practice will help you build awareness of interior experience and has a calming effect on your body. It involves three primary aspects: posture, focus, and distractions. It is ideal if you can create a space where you can practice every day without distractions.

Practice sitting in a chair or on a cushion on the floor. If you sit on a chair, it helps to rest your feet flat on the floor. If the chair is too tall, you can use a cushion to rest your feet on. Sit forward on your chair so that your lower back is not leaning on the back of the chair. If you practice sitting on a cushion, place a firm, supportive cushion under your hips and cross your legs in front of you. An alternative is to use a meditation bench that allows you to sit with your legs tucked under the bench.

Sit erect but not too stiff. Visualize that your spine is suspended from a thread coming from the top of your head and attached to the ceiling. This will help keep your posture upright without straining. Gently place your hands in your lap in a way that feels comfortable. Your arms should hang from your shoulders without tension. Your hands can lie on your thighs or be folded in your lap.

Next, notice your face. It should be relaxed. You may notice that your jaw is tight. See if you can relax the jaw and all the muscles of the face. Your eyes can be open or closed, whichever feels most comfortable. If you close your eyes, do so gently; don't squint or force them closed. If you'd rather keep your eyes open, relax your gaze and look slightly downward. Some meditation instructors will encourage you to practice with your eyes open to help you make a bridge between mindful awareness and your everyday waking life. However, some teachers find this distracting, and others consider either option just fine. You can experiment with this aspect of the practice to see what works best for you.

In this exercise, the primary focus is on the experience of breathing. Pay attention to the simple, ordinary experience of breathing. Sometimes this can be difficult, because when attention is focused on the breath, there's a tendency to try to alter it by taking deeper or longer breaths. However, in this practice, you want to breathe as normally as possible.

When attention is placed on the breath, the richness of the simple act of breathing comes alive: the sensation of the cool air entering the nostrils; the air filling the airways and the lungs; the feeling of the diaphragm moving the abdomen up and down with each breath; the moist, warm air leaving the nostrils. During this practice, it's best to focus your attention on one of these sensations. You can choose the focal point that naturally tends to draw your attention.

Once you've settled into the practice, distractions will probably arise. Your mind will wander away from the breath. The practice is to simply recognize that your mind has wandered and to gently bring your attention back to the breath.

How you approach this process of noticing that your mind has wandered and bringing it back to the breath is very important. Attention should be directed with gentleness, nonjudgmentally. Harsh criticism won't help you practice any better. It's important to recognize that this wandering is a natural part of the mind's activity, and that bringing the attention back to the breath is the practice itself.

It's also important to deal gently with distractions. You might become distracted by a particular thought, feeling, or physical sensation. You might lose track of your breathing because of a pain in your neck or shoulders. You might think about a student who has you concerned. You might remember something you were supposed to do and be worried you'll forget if you continue practicing. When you notice yourself getting distracted, you could immediately go back to attending to the breath. However, it's best to take a moment to notice the distraction (e.g., "My sore neck is distracting"). By doing this, you learn about the patterns and content of your inner experience.

When your mind wanders off, you can notice that it's been wandering and name the nature of that wandering—for example, "thoughts," "sore knee," or "bird sounds"—and then bring your attention back to the breath. Over time, the ability to keep your focus while at the same time being aware of your surroundings will develop. With practice, mindful awareness can be applied to everyday living so that you experience the richness of the present moment more fully and more consistently.

Mindful awareness is characterized by curiosity and openness to both the nature of experience and the quality of the awareness itself without judgments or preconceptions. This may include noticing and exploring any preconceptions that arise. For example, as I focus my attention on my breath, my mind begins to wander. "I wonder what we're having for lunch." My first impulse may be to think, "Oh no! I'm distracted; I'm thinking about lunch. I can't do this." Rather than being swept away with these judgments, I can simply notice that I was distracted and that I judged myself for being distracted. Without belaboring the issue, I can gently redirect my attention back to the breath.

A common misconception is that we're supposed to stop thinking during practice. If you hold this misconception, you may feel that practicing mindful awareness is not for you because you can't stop thinking. It's very important to recognize that even the most advanced practitioners have distracting thoughts. Thoughts and feelings arise during practice. This is natural. The point is to notice the distracting thoughts and feelings and gently bring the attention back to the practice. Over time, your mind will begin to settle.

Here's a metaphor that many find helpful. Imagine a glass of clear water. Now imagine that you pour a spoonful of dirt into the glass and stir. The water becomes muddy and opaque. If you stop stirring and let the water and the dirt settle, soon the water is clear again and the dirt has formed a layer of sediment at the bottom of the glass. Your mind is like the glass full of dirt. If you allow your mind to settle, it will become clear. You can settle into the present moment with clarity of mind.

Over time, with practice, you will become more aware of your thoughts and feelings. You will notice which thoughts and feelings tend to capture your attention and which are easier to release. While this sounds simple, at first it may be quite difficult. Sometimes you may barely be able to keep your mind focused on one breath before it wanders off in thought. But the practice of noticing this drift and consciously bringing your focus back to the breath is exactly what makes the exercise useful.

You will also begin to recognize that you are not your thoughts. You will notice that your mind has a mind of its own, so to speak, and that thinking is somewhat automatic. With time, the thoughts will become less salient and your mind will settle into a quiet calm where the thoughts are more like background noise and don't capture your attention as often. This increases the flexibility and focus of your attention. It helps you learn that you can shift your attention, and notice when your attention is not on target. Just as physical exercise builds muscle, mindful awareness practice builds attentional focus and flexibility.

Once you have attained a stability of attention, you will begin to recognize the impermanence of your inner experience. Thoughts and feelings come and go. As you learn to approach your experience with acceptance, spaciousness, and generosity, you will realize that what you experience in any given moment is simply the "as is" of that moment. You will begin to see how often your thoughts result in a misapprehension of the present. You may notice that you are projecting experiences from the past or expectations for the future onto the present moment.

Setting Intention

The practice of setting intention—realizing your sense of purpose—can provide powerful support for personal transformation: becoming the teacher you wish to be. This simple exercise can help you to be more present and aware throughout the day.

Take a moment to reflect on why you became a teacher. Think about the values that motivated you. Our values provide us with motivation, vision, and direction for our intentional behavior. We can reflect upon our actions to determine whether or not they are in alignment with our intention. Throughout the day, we can take a moment to check in to see if we are on track.

For example, I envision a world where teachers and other adults support children with compassion and calm but firm limit-setting. In my daily work life, I might set an intention to notice when I'm feeling annoyed and calm myself down before overreacting. Taking time to reflect on how I want to behave and setting my intention acts as a reminder. I find I am more likely to be aware of my feelings and to remember to calm down when I need to. If I forget, I can just notice and remember next time. It's like a navigation system that reminds me when I'm off course and helps me get back on track. I set my intention at the beginning of my mindful awareness practice time. When I take a moment to recall my intention for maintaining a regular practice, it helps me keep motivated to do it every day.

Setting an intention is not the same as setting a goal. If I don't reach a goal, I may feel disappointed, as if I failed. Setting intention doesn't assume that I will reach an end point, but that I will stay on course. Setting intention is gentle and forgiving. Throughout the day, I can check my intention to see if I'm still on track. I can always adjust it if necessary, or re-set it and go on with my day.

I invite you to start with a very simple practice. Consider your intention for the remainder of this day. Spend a few moments contemplating this question. For example, you may decide, "My intention is to spend the rest of this day being calm and centered." Once you have settled on your intention, focus your attention on it for a short period of time. This is how we "set" our intention.

I recommend that you practice setting your intention every morning and check it during the day. It only takes a minute to reflect on the day, consider what you want to happen today, and decide how you want to behave. For example, I might think, "My intention is to enjoy my class today" or "Today I intend to find something positive to enjoy" or "My intention is to remain calm during transition times."

Many teachers I have worked with find it helpful to set their intention right before they get out of their cars to go into the school. They often check their intention during lunch or breaks between classes. Some set their smartphones to remind them. You can keep an intention journal to help yourself remember your intentions.

Three Breaths

Sometimes we need to take a pause in our day and punctuate it with a moment of mindful awareness. *That transition was hectic and the classroom is a mess. The principal made an announcement over the intercom just as I was getting to the meat of my lesson.* Frustrations happen and we begin to get triggered. When this happens to you, you can rely on a brief and very simple exercise to calm your nervous system. Simply take three long, slow, mindful breaths.

To practice this exercise for the first time, it helps to put your hands on your abdomen. You want to breathe with your diaphragm so your body fills with air. You should feel your abdomen rise on the inhalation and fall on the exhalation. Feel the flow of the air as it fills your body from your nose to the bottom of your lungs. Then feel the air flow out of your body. Repeat this a total of three times.

Be careful not to hyperventilate. Your breaths should be relatively slow and deep but not uncomfortable. Don't hold your breath or try to inhale or exhale too quickly. After the third breath, allow your breathing to return to normal and notice any changes in your body.

Now that you have two basic exercises to practice as well as an exercise to use during hectic moments, you are on your way to developing mindful awareness. I encourage you to spend some time developing a routine for daily practice. Find times in your day when you can naturally fit the basic practices into your schedule. You don't need to spend a lot of time on them; if you can start with just five minutes a day of focused attention and one minute to set your intention, that's fine. It's the regularity of the practice that is most important. Over time, as the practice becomes more natural, you can begin to extend the time to 10 minutes or longer.

In the next chapter, you will learn how applying mindful awareness can refine the emotional art of teaching.

Chapter 2

The Emotional Art of Teaching

At its core, teaching is an "emotional practice" (Hargreaves, 1998). Positive emotions such as interest, curiosity, and joy form the basis for the motivation to learn, and for the development of a sense of security and connectedness critical to building an effective learning community. On the other hand, negative emotions such as sadness, fear, and anger can inhibit the learning process.

The classroom contains a rich soup of intrapersonal emotional experiences (those that take place within the teacher and each student) and interpersonal emotional experiences (those that take place between peers, between the teacher and each student, and as a social experience of group emotion). Just as I experience my own emotions and simultaneously have an emotional relationship with each of my students, each student has both internal and external emotional experiences.

Added to this complexity are the social subgroups that form within classrooms, such as close friendships, "partners in crime," rivalries, and cliques. To top it off, emotional contagion can draw the entire group into synchronized emotional experience, for better or for worse. When you consider the vast array of social interactions and emotional experiences that take place in a classroom each day, it's truly astonishing.

In this chapter, we explore the nature of emotions and the critical role they play in teaching and learning, both consciously and unconsciously. You will learn how to apply mindful awareness to your emotional experiences to help you recognize, understand, and effectively regulate those experiences internally and externally. You will learn how the social and emotional climate affects student learning and behavior, and how to apply mindful awareness to recognizing, understanding, and regulating students' emotions, behavior, and learning.

When we master our emotions, we can harness their power to artfully orchestrate learning environments that promote prosocial behavior, engagement, and academic success. As a result, teaching becomes enjoyable and rewarding, reinforcing our commitment to the profession and building the resilience we need when challenges arise (Fredrickson & Cohn, 2008).

What Are Emotions?

There is a growing consensus among emotion researchers that emotions can be defined as "multicomponent response tendencies—incorporating muscle tension, hormone release, cardiovascular changes, facial expression, attention, and cognition, among other changes—that unfold over a relatively short time span" (Fredrickson & Cohn, 2008, p. 778). Typically, the experience of emotion begins with a rapid conscious or unconscious appraisal of a particular situation that triggers the reaction (Lazarus, 1991).

Charles Darwin (1872/1998) proposed that emotions are innate, universal functions that evolved to ensure survival. Early in his career, psychologist Paul Ekman wanted to test Darwin's theory. This was back in the early 1960s when behaviorism was the dominant approach to psychology. It was a risky move, early in his career, to embark on this research, because many behaviorists argued that emotional reactions were simply socially conditioned responses (McGill & Welch, 1946).

Traveling to the highlands of New Guinea, Ekman studied the local tribal people who had never before been exposed to Westerners and therefore were not subject to our social conditioning (Ekman, Sorenson, & Friesen, 1969). Ekman reasoned that if these people associated the same facial expressions with events and situations that are commonly associated with an emotional response among Westerners, this would demonstrate the universality of emotional expression. He found that they not only interpreted the expressions in the same way as Westerners, but when asked to pose expressions in response to hypothetical situations, these expressions were easily understandable to people in the West (Ekman, 2007a). For example, he might ask a tribesman to show him what expression he would make if someone close to him died. The expression on the tribesman's face was the same sad expression that we would recognize: the downturned mouth and eyes.

Ekman found universal expressions for happiness, sadness, anger, fear, disgust, and surprise. These basic emotions can be found in every culture, and they have clear adaptive functions that are evident in their associated physiological, cognitive, and behavioral responses. For example, if I am physically threatened, I will likely begin to feel anger, and a flood of hormones and neurotransmitters will prepare me to defend myself. My heart rate and breathing will accelerate, energizing my extremities in preparation for a fight. My face will contort into a fearsome expression, my voice will become loud and harsh, and my eyes will glare—reactions all intended to frighten my attacker.

The more we understand our emotions and our emotional patterns, the better we can manage them. When situations provoke strong emotions, we can apply mindful awareness to the experience itself. This gives us more response options, because awareness provides some space between the experience and the reaction, allowing for a conscious response rather than an unconscious emotional reaction. Viktor Frankl, an Austrian psychiatrist and Holocaust survivor, described this experience in this well-known quote: "Between stimulus and response there is a space. In that space is our power to choose our response. In our response lies our growth and our freedom".

There is dimensionality to emotional experience that creates a sort of landscape with hills and valleys and constantly changing weather. Scientists have developed a number of theoretical models to explain these various dimensions. In this book, it is not my intention to cover all of these theories. Rather, I want to introduce some basic dimensions of emotional experience to familiarize you with the territory and provide a map and some navigational tools for you to use as you explore your emotional life as a teacher. The three basic dimensions that I will cover are valence, intensity, and arousal.

Valence

The most salient dimension of emotion is what's called the pleasant–unpleasant valence (also referred to as the positive–negative valence). Every emotional experience is associated with pleasant or unpleasant sensations. Fear can create an unpleasant feeling of nausea in the pit of your stomach. Love is often associated with a pleasant, warm sensation around the heart.

Many researchers and educators working in the area of social and emotional learning like to avoid using the words *positive* and *negative* to describe emotions and prefer to use *comfortable* or *pleasant* and *uncomfortable* or *unpleasant* because the words positive and negative give the impression that positive emotions are good and negative emotions are bad.

I want to clarify that this is certainly not the case. Both play critical roles in our survival and well-being. For the sake of convenience, I use the words *positive* and *negative* here, with the understanding that the emotions they describe are neither good nor bad.

Intensity

Every emotional reaction can be experienced across the continuum of intensity, from very subtle to extremely intense. On the low end, anger can be experienced as mild frustration, annoyance, irritation, or bother. On the high end, anger can be experienced as blinding rage.

When I am teaching, subtle emotional experiences are often hard to notice because my attention is so focused on the outside (i.e., delivering my lesson and keeping my students' attention). When the emotional intensity slowly rises, I may find myself suddenly feeling and expressing anger. It's as if the anger crept up on me unexpectedly.

However, if I occasionally take a brief pause to notice that I'm starting to become frustrated or annoyed, I can take a breath (or three breaths if necessary), calm down, and continue, making whatever adjustments are necessary to respond in a thoughtful rather than reactive way to the situation that triggered my frustration.

Arousal

Emotions can also arouse or subdue us. Typically, anger is an arousing emotion because it prepares us to fight. In contrast, sadness tends to subdue us to help us save our resources so we can better manage loss. The artful orchestration of the social and emotional dynamics of the classroom involves managing our students' emotions.

You will notice that students learn best when there is a moderate level of positive emotion and arousal. When a task is both interesting and challenging, but not too challenging, students tend to feel engaged. We can promote our students' interest by approaching the content with our own interest and excitement.

We can help students maintain engagement by differentiating instruction to match students' learning styles and ability levels (Tomlinson, 1999). If the material is too difficult for some students, they may lose interest and give up. If it's too easy, some will become bored and easily distracted.

Emotional Reactivity

Teaching is an especially emotionally demanding profession (Hargreaves, 1998; Jennings & Greenberg, 2009). When I consciously respond to emotionally charged situations, rather than unconsciously and automatically reacting to them, I enhance my effectiveness, resilience, and enjoyment of teaching. Over time, when I don't manage my emotions well, teaching can exhaust me. This is why it's useful to explore how emotional exhaustion can lead to teacher burnout, and learn ways to prevent it. Later in this chapter, I'll show you two reflection activities designed to help you recognize and understand your emotional triggers and patterns and a simple activity you can use to help you pause, notice how you are feeling, and calm down.

When it comes to managing strong emotions, the classroom context poses unique challenges. Few other work contexts demand the capacity to maintain a composed professional demeanor while managing a group of 20 to 30 youngsters who may or may not be prepared to sit still, listen, learn, and get along with others. We are held accountable for our students' achievement, even when multiple factors beyond our control influence their motivation and capacity to achieve.

Furthermore, when things get tough, we must manage our emotions while they are occurring, in the face of the challenge. Unlike other professionals who can excuse themselves and take a break when they're experiencing strong emotions, we are literally trapped in the classroom and must manage both the situation and our emotional response to the situation in the moment.

This is a setup for physiological catastrophe. When we experience strong emotions that we feel we can't control or express, it's like driving with our foot on the accelerator and the break at the same time, and we're bound to do some damage. Under these conditions, stress hormones flood the body. These hormones are designed to help us deal with short-term challenges. However, when they remain elevated for long periods of time, they can have toxic effects on the body (McEwen, 1998).

How Emotional Reactivity Affects Teaching

Once I was teaching a lesson to my fifth-grade class about the digestive system, and several students found the subject of bodily functions both funny and embarrassing, as is typical for 10-year-olds. They made wisecrack remarks in response to important points I was trying to make or in response to my attempts to stimulate discussion as the other students giggled. Everyone but me thought it was all quite amusing.

As my annoyance and frustration grew, I found it difficult to stay focused on the lesson. I felt as if I was going to explode, but I knew that would only make things worse. So I held in my anger. Fuming, I finished the lesson, but I was disappointed in myself. I was so angry I couldn't think straight. I forgot important points in the lesson and I felt at a loss about how to respond to their behavior. I also felt exhausted and embarrassed. My students had gotten the best of me.

Later on, when I began to supervise student teachers, I noticed how common this experience is among student teachers and their mentors. I began to understand the importance of emotional experience to teaching and learning, and I wondered if these common daily experiences of frustration contributed to teacher inefficacy and burnout. I realized that when we're in the midst of teaching, it's often difficult to notice how we're feeling because our attention is directed outward, to the task at hand. If I don't notice an emotional reaction as it begins to build, it becomes difficult to regulate and I may end up doing something I regret. This becomes especially important when it comes to managing student behavior.

For example, I was once observing a student teacher who was enrolled in the classroom management course I was teaching as part of a teacher preparation program. In the course, I was teaching an Adlerian approach to behavior management (Dreikurs & Soltz, 1964) (see more about this approach in Chapter 6). The approach involves two steps: assessing the motive for the behavior and then applying the strategy that most appropriately matches the motive.

In the case I'm referring to, a student was involved in a power struggle and was refusing to clean up an activity to prepare for recess. After reminding the student several times, the student teacher, clearly frustrated, said in a harsh tone, "If you don't clean this up, you'll have to stay in and miss recess." The student said, "Okay, I'll stay inside," and the teacher lost the battle.

She had set up a situation that was bound to fail because it wasn't possible for her to stay inside with the student; he really had to go outside with the rest of the class. She gave him an option that wasn't really an option, and she delivered it as a threat with a harsh tone of voice. Trapped by her own mistake, she barked, "You have to clean this up now!" and quickly cleaned up the activity for him, then ushered him outside.

After class, I spoke to her about the incident. She said, "I tried what you told us to do in class. I gave him a consequence. But it didn't work. I think he likes to make things hard for me." I explained that the tone and delivery made the comment a threat of punishment rather than a consequence, and that she had threatened a punishment that wouldn't work because she couldn't stay inside with the child and the child couldn't stay inside alone. From the surprise she expressed in response to my comments, it was clear that she was unaware of the harshness of her vocal tone and facial expressions. Her impression of herself was that she had been calm and objective, rather than angry and frustrated.

She was so annoyed by the situation that she was unable to recognize that she had set herself up for failure by making an empty threat. Nor did she recognize how she had reinforced his defiance by cleaning up the mess for him. She had been so focused on getting him outside that she didn't see how her behavior was contributing to the power struggle.

Convinced that the whole situation was the student's fault, the teacher took his behavior personally, assuming that he was trying to make things difficult for her. She didn't perceive the role that she had played in his reaction to her attempts to manage his behavior. Next I'll describe how applying mindful awareness of our emotional experience can help us notice how we're feeling in the moment so we can respond, rather than automatically and unconsciously reacting, to challenging experiences.

Applying the Wheel of Awareness to Emotional Experiences

In Chapter 1, we learned about the wheel of awareness and how we can direct our mindful awareness to each of the eight senses. When I mindfully explore my emotional experience, I can engage my senses to help myself recognize and regulate my emotions. I can notice the physical sensations that come with emotion, such as the tension I feel in my shoulders when I'm angry, and the thoughts and thinking patterns that reinforce the emotion.

I also notice various sensory experiences, such as changes in the tone of my voice. I may notice changes in others' facial expressions in response to my emotion and perceive the emotional energy that is exchanged between individuals. Practicing mindfulness helps me become more aware of all these dimensions.

Emotional experience is often like a musical crescendo. It can begin with very subtle signals that grow more pronounced as the intensity builds. If I am aware of the subtle signals at the beginning of the crescendo, I have a better chance of regulating the emotion before it gets the best of me.

For example, when I become frustrated, I first notice tension in my jaw because I'm clenching it. I also notice my hands clenching into fists. As the frustration grows, my shoulders become tense and creep upward, and my face becomes hot and contorts into an angry expression. My eyebrows gather at the midline of my face, my eyes glare, my mouth frowns. My voice might become very harsh. To other people, I must look pretty scary!

In fact, when I get like this, I have noticed that my students usually respond in one of two ways. Some automatically become defiant, even though I haven't said anything. They interpret my expression as a threat and can easily become defensive. Others become frightened and withdraw. They look away from me and avoid eye contact. Neither of these responses is conducive to learning. In fact, either response can derail learning altogether and damage the relationships I am trying to build with my students.

At times like these, I notice that my thoughts reinforce my anger and that it becomes very difficult to think about the situation objectively. I tend to ruminate about how bad a behavior is and imagine that the student is doing it on purpose to make my life difficult. The strong emotions inhibit my ability to analyze the situation and apply my knowledge to discovering possible strategies for responding effectively, so I tend to react automatically in ways that often make the situation worse.

It's important to clarify that I am not advocating that we should never express emotions like anger. If we are feeling angry, it is impossible to completely inhibit its expression, and there are times when the expression of anger is important and useful. However, as we develop a more mindful approach to our emotional experience, we learn to synchronize with the experience and modulate emotional expression in a way that is more conscious, respectful, and effective.

We can even model the process of regulating our emotions so our students can learn to regulate their own. For example, when I am very angry, I can say to my class, "I'm feeling very frustrated right now, and it's hard to teach when I'm frustrated. I'm going to stop and take some deep breaths right now so I can calm down." I have found that when

I do this, my students tend to calm down, too. Most students don't want their teacher to lose her temper, and when given a chance they will encourage their peers to stop the behaviors that the teacher finds frustrating. Also, by regulating our own emotions, we are teaching by example. Often we accidentally model behaviors that are exactly the opposite of what we're trying to teach.

In the next two chapters, I will describe how to apply mindful awareness to both "positive" and "negative" emotions. As you become more knowledgeable about emotions and how to recognize and regulate them, you will find you have more options than you thought to skillfully respond to situations. You will also find that you emotional life is more enriching both personally and professionally.

Emotions Are Survival Mechanisms

Emotional functions allowed human beings to survive against impossible odds. As a result of new discoveries in human genetics applied to anthropology, we now know that every human being alive today is a descendant of a small group of perhaps less than 10,000 living on the east coast of Africa approximately 74,000 years ago ("Humans Change the World," n.d.). At that time, there were dramatic climactic changes that threatened with extinction the large variety of proto human populations in Africa. To escape drought, what remained of our ancestors migrated east to the Rift Valleys near the coast of Africa.

Despite near extinction, in less than 2,500 generations, a blink in evolutionary history, we migrated from Africa along the coast to Australia; into the Middle East, central Asia, and Europe; across the frozen strait to North America; and all the way to the southern tip of South America. Throughout these migrations, our ancestors found innovative ways to adapt to extreme heat and extreme cold, severe drought, and the need to travel across water; to harness fire and domesticate animals and plants; and to create culture and civilization.

To say the least, we are the most adaptable, intelligent animal on the planet. Why is this so? The key to this exceptional adaptive capacity was the development of our modern brain. The prefrontal cortex is one of the most recently evolved parts of our brain. This large brain area is what separated us from our earlier proto-human ancestors. It allowed us to remember the past and apply this learning to the future by imagining and planning. Education became the very transmission of culture that allowed humans to adapt to a wide variety of environments.

Another key to our survival was our strong social and emotional bonds. We needed our social group to survive. We evolved the ability to communicate through speech and writing, and our strong bonds created cohesiveness that promoted cooperation, innovation, and joint problem-solving.

Much of our learning comes from social and emotional conditioning that creates shortcuts for learning important things quickly. As children, we learned what was right and wrong from the responses of others around us. These lessons are firmly imprinted in our emotional makeup. For example, my family valued punctuality. If we were late arriving somewhere, even by just a few minutes, and even if we had a good excuse, we were in big trouble. Our parents would express extreme dissatisfaction and we might even be grounded.

As a result, when I'm running late, I feel very anxious and guilty. This is an emotional program, or script. When I'm wrapped up in this script, I have trouble noticing it. I take it very seriously. But when I can step back and observe the experience objectively, I can see that my strong emotions are really reacting to my thoughts of the past (parental judgment) and future (fear of judgment from others), not my actual experience in the present moment.

It has been argued that the same adaptive function that helped us to survive threatens to impair our survival in this fast-paced modern world (Baumann & Taft, 2011). Our brain developed under very different conditions than those we face today. The pace of change increases as each year passes. "Shortcut learning" by conditioning—like learning not to be late, as described above—evolved to help us function in an environment that was relatively static. When human beings lived in a world that did not change much, we could count on the shortcut to be adaptive most of the time.

Today, however, learned shortcuts can actually impair our adaptation because they interfere with our ability to respond flexibly to various situations. For example, since I learned to fear being late, it's difficult for me not to feel anxious when I'm running late, even when being on time isn't that important.

We no longer live in a relatively static environment. Rapid change has become the constant, making shortcut learning less useful. As children, we grow up learning things that will be obsolete in less than a decade. As our culture becomes more globally integrated, constants give way to ongoing change. Learning needs to evolve. Mindfulness allows us to notice and overcome our automatic shortcut learning so we can approach each situation with freshness. We then have available a myriad of possible responses rather than one or two shortcut reactions.

Social and Emotional Learning

Today parents, educators, and policy makers recognize the need for a broad educational agenda that includes the development of social and emotional competencies. We want young people to learn to succeed academically, but we also want them to learn to manage relationships in skilled and respectful ways; practice positive, safe, and healthy behaviors; make ethical and responsible contributions to their peer group, family, school, and community; and demonstrate basic competencies, work habits, and values as a foundation for a meaningful life and engaged citizenship (Elias et al., 1997; Jackson & Davis, 2000; Learning First Alliance, 2001; Osher, Dwyer, & Jackson, 2002).

The Collaborative for Academic Social and Emotional Learning (CASEL) defines social and emotional learning as instruction that promotes social and emotional interpersonal and intrapersonal competencies. Intrapersonal competencies include self-awareness and self-management. Interpersonal competencies include social awareness, responsible decision-making, and relationship skills (Zins, Weissberg, Wang, & Walberg, 2004). Years of research have demonstrated that social and emotional learning not only improves school culture and student behavior but also improves academic achievement (Durlak, Weissberg, Dymnicki, Taylor, & Schellinger, 2011).

While there are many excellent commercially produced social and emotional learning programs available, children primarily learn these skills by example (Fox & Lentini, 2006). Teachers and parents have the opportunity to demonstrate these competencies in the ways they interact with children and other adults. As teachers, we set the tone of the classroom by developing supportive and encouraging relationships with our students; designing lessons that build on student strengths and abilities; establishing and implementing behavioral guidelines in ways that promote intrinsic motivation; coaching students through conflict situations; encouraging cooperation among students; and acting as role models of respectful and appropriate communication and behavior.

To teach in this way, we must have a high degree of self-awareness. We must be aware of our emotions and emotional patterns and tendencies and know how to cultivate and use emotions such as joy and enthusiasm to motivate learning. We need to have an accurate understanding of our capabilities and recognize our emotional strengths and weaknesses while being kind and compassionate toward ourselves.

To be a good role model, we also need to have a high degree of social awareness so we can understand how our behavior and expressions of emotion affect our interactions with students. Our goal is to recognize and understand our students' emotions, build supportive relationships through mutual understanding and cooperation, and effectively negotiate solutions to conflict. It's important to be culturally sensitive so that as we develop relationships with students, parents, and colleagues, we take into account that people have different perspectives that we respect.

In the field of social and emotional learning, we often refer to "prosocial" behavior or values. By *prosocial*, we mean promoting positive social and emotional experiences within ourselves and among others. Prosocial values includes empathy, compassion, perspective-taking, cooperation, and gratitude. Prosocial behaviors include helping, caring for, using good manners, including, welcoming, and speaking up against cruelty and injustice. To help our students learn these ways of being, we must demonstrate prosocial values in our own behavior and make responsible decisions based on an assessment of factors, including how our decisions may affect ourselves and others, and take responsibility for these decisions and actions.

We must know how to manage our emotions and behavior, and also how to manage relationships with others even when faced with emotionally provocative situations. We must regulate our emotions in healthy ways that facilitate positive classroom outcomes without compromising our health. We must effectively set limits, firmly but respectfully, yet be comfortable with the level of ambiguity and uncertainty that comes from letting students figure things out for themselves.

While these characteristics are considered ideal, most of us received little if any explicit pre-service or in-service training aimed at our own personal development. There has been an expectation that anyone who wants to be a teacher should come to the position with these competencies already developed. However, the level of social and emotional competence required to perform in this way is not possessed by the average adult. Furthermore, we now know that these skills and dispositions can be learned.

When we lack the social and emotional competence to handle classroom challenges, we experience emotional distress that can have an adverse effect on our job performance and eventually lead to burnout, which threatens teacher–student relationships, classroom management, and classroom climate (Jennings & Greenberg, 2009).

Understanding Burnout

Today we hear a lot about teacher burnout. In fact, approximately 50% of new teachers leave the profession after only five years. This figure is higher in schools that serve large number of children at risk. The National Commission on Teaching and America's Future (NCTAF) estimated that the cost of teacher turnover among public school teachers in the US is more than $7.3 billion a year (NCTAF, 2007). Given that the individual and societal costs of teacher burnout are so high, it's an important issue to address.

Why do teachers burn out? The teaching profession has become more demanding over the past three decades. Increasing numbers of children are coming to school unprepared, many with serious behavior problems as early as preschool (Gilliam, 2005). Research indicates that teachers often face situations that provoke emotions that are difficult to manage. When this happens, their classroom management efforts lack effectiveness, the classroom climate is less than optimal, and they may experience emotional exhaustion, provoking a "burnout cascade" (Jennings & Greenberg, 2009).

Burnout results from a breakdown in teachers' ability to cope over time, and is viewed as having three dimensions: emotional exhaustion, depersonalization, and feelings of lack of personal accomplishment (Maslach, Jackson, & Leiter, 1997). Emotional exhaustion is the chronic state of physical and emotional depletion that results from the inability to cope with stress and emotional demands. When teachers become emotionally exhausted, they feel overextended and exhausted by their work and no longer find it enjoyable or rewarding.

When teachers feel this way, there is a tendency to resort to depersonalization as a coping strategy. To cope with the challenges of a disruptive classroom, teachers may develop a callous, cynical attitude toward students, parents, and colleagues. For example, when an emotionally exhausted teacher is having a particularly difficult time with a student, he may perceive that student as being innately bad. He may convince himself that there's nothing anyone can do about her, so why try. He may even speak about her in ways that express his depersonalized perception of her—for example, "She's just a little monster" or "She's a holy terror."

The last stage of the burnout process involves a feeling of failure or lack of personal accomplishment. At this point, many teachers decide they just can't hack it and leave the profession. However, there are many teachers who feel trapped in their jobs because they have already invested so many years toward their pension and keep working despite their burnout.

This is a bad situation for everyone involved. Research has found that burned-out teachers are less likely to demonstrate sympathy and a caring attitude toward their students, have less tolerance for disruptive behavior, and are less dedicated to their work (Farber & Miller, 1981). Working in a state of burnout day after day can cause serious physical and mental health problems, and students exposed to a burned-out teacher may be harmed. They may lose their interest and enthusiasm for learning and may develop negative impressions of school and teachers in general (Zhang & Sapp, 2008).

Considering that teachers rarely receive training on how to manage the social and emotional challenges of the classroom, it is not surprising that among teachers, attrition is on the rise (Auguste, Kihn, & Miller, 2010). Unlike practitioners in many other professions, we teachers are constantly exposed to emotionally provocative situations in a classroom setting where we have limited options for self-regulation.

When kids push our buttons, we have to manage our emotions so we can keep teaching. We must keep our cool and act professional under conditions that most people would find extremely difficult. If we don't have the skills to manage our emotions effectively, we may try to suppress them putting a strain on our stress response system.

Teachers' emotional exhaustion and classroom climate are closely related. As teachers become emotionally exhausted, the social and emotional climate of their classroom deteriorates, creating a vicious cycle of negativity.

Enhancing our social and emotional skills may prevent emotional distress and, in turn, the burnout associated with teaching. In particular, the intrapersonal dimensions of self-awareness and self-management build resilience and support our ability to cope with the emotional demands of teaching. This is where mindfulness plays an important role.

Practicing mindful awareness can help us build these competencies. As we apply mindful awareness of our emotional experiences, we build greater self-awareness. We develop the ability to recognize our emotions and understand the role they play in our teaching. Mindfulness also helps us develop self-regulation. We learn to understand and anticipate our emotional patterns of reactivity. Research has demonstrated that practicing mindfulness builds connections in the brain that support our ability to regulate emotions (Hölzel et al., 2011).

Emotions and Classroom Management

Over the past several decades, classroom management has experienced a paradigm shift toward a more democratic, proactive, and authoritative approach. This approach promotes student cooperation and prosocial behavior by establishing supportive learning communities and interpersonal relationships, assertive limit-setting, and the use of guidance and preventive strategies rather than autocratic and coercive measures such as punishment (Angell, 1991; Bredekamp & Copple, 1997; Brophy, 2006; DeVries & Zan, 1994; Ginott, 1993; Glasser, 1988, 1998; Kohn, 1996; Levin & Nolan, 2014; Noddings, 2005; Watson, 2003). Research has shown that these approaches promote students' commitment to school, prosocial behavior, and academic engagement and achievement at all levels (Durlak et al., 2011; Marzano, Marzano, & Pickering, 2003; Osher et al., 2007; Watson & Battistich, 2006).

The proactive approach necessitates self-regulation among both teachers and students for the development of a learning environment where students behave out of a sense of shared responsibility, rather than to avoid punishment or earn rewards (Weinstein, 1999; Woolfolk Hoy & Weinstein, 2006). To manage a classroom in this way—to assimilate and apply this new orientation toward classroom management in order to achieve a healthy classroom climate and positive student outcomes—social and emotional competence is essential.

Back in the 1970s, the US government funded the first large-scale research studies investigating which teacher behaviors were most related to positive student outcomes. The results of this research produced a shift in approach from one that emphasized the enforcement of rules to one that also attended to students' need for supportive relationships and opportunities to learn self-regulation (Weinstein, 1999).

This paradigm shift emphasized teacher social and emotional competencies that had not previously been required. For example, classroom management shifted from the simplistic, punish/reward "bag of tricks" approach to a more nuanced and individualized approach requiring thoughtful decision-making and reflection (i.e., through self-awareness and awareness of others). The shift involved a change from managerial practices intended to control student behavior to practices promoting students' capacity for self-regulation and their motivation to engage in prosocial behavior. To make this shift, teachers need high degrees of self-awareness, sensitivity, and thoughtfulness in their decision-making so that they can observe, understand, and respond respectfully and effectively to student behaviors.

For example, under the old paradigm, when a child misbehaved, the teacher typically responded with punishment. In contrast, under the new paradigm, a teacher spends more time at the beginning of the school year getting to know each child and building a learning community, at the same time assessing each student's ability to self-regulate and therefore comply with behavioral expectations. When inappropriate behavior occurs, the teacher responds by providing assistance and support to help the child behave appropriately rather than punishing him or her.

To do this requires high degrees of self-regulation, both attentional and emotional. As we teach, we need to be able to attend to many things that are happening simultaneously without feeling overwhelmed. We need to maintain our own composure as we supervise our class so we can respond thoughtfully rather than reacting unconsciously and automatically to any given situation. Practicing mindful awareness promotes these self-regulatory skills so we can better manage these demands.

Withitness

The paradigm shift in classroom management was presaged by the work of Jacob Kounin. Wanting to know why some teachers could keep their students on task better than others, Kounin studied 80 first- and second-grade classes, each of which contained at least one child identified as having emotion regulation problems. He found that the most effective teachers noticed subtle changes in their students' emotions and behavior and responded proactively, letting the students know they were aware of them and responding matter-of-factly by reminding them of the task at hand (Kounin, 1970). He called these teachers "with it" because they were particularly aware of what was going on in their classrooms.

Withitness requires self-awareness, social awareness, self-management, and relationship management (sound familiar?), giving teachers the capacity to attentively monitor and act responsively in the classroom, prevent disruptive behavior, and support on-task behavior. Marzano and his colleagues (2003) found that what they called the "mental set" of the teacher has the largest effect in reducing disruptive behavior. *Mental set* refers to "a heightened sense of situational awareness and a conscious control over one's thoughts and behavior relative to that situation" (p. 65).

Mental set also refers to a teacher's degree of emotional objectivity (related to the social and emotional learning dimension of self-management). Teachers who remain cool under pressure, addressing disciplinary issues matter-of-factly without taking behaviors personally, are the most effective classroom managers.

Let's see how a teacher's proactive mindset plays out in an example from a teacher I'll call Ms. Ferrera. Ms. Ferrera has noticed that one of her students, Yolanda, is having a hard time focusing on her work. Rather than immediately redirecting her, Ms. Ferrera spends a few minutes observing Yolanda's distracted behavior. Yolanda has a tendency to disrupt the class by bothering other students during seat work, but Ms. Ferrera knows she's not trying to make her job difficult. Yolanda just has a hard time focusing her attention and managing her emotions.

As she observes, Ms. Ferrera notices that the child's hair is disheveled and she is chewing on her pencil. Quietly she approaches Yolanda and asks her if she is okay. Yolanda says she has a headache. Knowing that Yolanda's home situation is less than ideal, Ms. Ferrera asks, "Are you hungry?" Yolanda nods her head yes. Ms. Ferrera decides to end the seat work early and have snack time so Yolanda can have something to eat. Ms. Ferrera suspects that Yolanda came to school without eating breakfast. The gnawing hunger is making it hard for her to concentrate on her work.

Community Building

When students feel a sense of community in their classrooms, they are more cooperative and helpful, demonstrate more concern for others, and are less prone to disruptive behaviors (Battistich, Solomon,

Watson, & Schaps, 1997). To build such a community, we can provide opportunities for students to collaborate with others and reflect upon the experiences and needs of their peers. This helps them learn prosocial values such as kindness, empathy, compassion, and perspective-taking; reflect upon their behavior as it relates to the needs of others; develop and practice social competencies such as good manners and conflict resolution; and learn to participate in joint decision-making with regard to classroom rules and guidelines.

When a student's need to belong in and make valuable contributions to a community is satisfied, he or she is more inclined to behave in accordance with the classroom's and school's community values, reducing the need for the external control of adults. In other words, building a community of learners helps avoid the need for coercive discipline altogether.

Practicing mindful awareness can add value to social and emotional learning programs designed to build a community of learners. With practice, we can strengthen brain functions that are responsible for emotion and attention regulation, resilience, empathy, and compassion in support of social and emotional learning (Jennings, Lantieri, & Roeser, 2012).

Motivation

Human beings are born with an innate curiosity and motivation to learn and discover. From the time we are born, we want to learn to walk and talk. We spend hours practicing rolling, crawling, and finally walking. We focus intently on our family members as they talk to us and respond with gurgles and smiles.

Amid the struggle to learn, we find joy and fulfillment in each new discovery and in each skill we master, no matter how difficult the process. The joy motivates our learning. This type of motivation is called intrinsic because the motivation is rooted in the experience of mastery itself, rather than in any extrinsic reward.

Emotions play a critical role in motivation. Effective teachers encourage engaged student learning by generating enthusiasm and passion for the curriculum (Fried, 1995). Setting the conditions for promoting intrinsic motivation requires greater social and emotional competence than does the use of extrinsic methods such as rewards and punishment. Rather than simply creating rules and responding to offenses with punishment, we must establish a strong, cohesive community that allows student autonomy and cooperative learning and promotes the joy of discovery and learning for its own sake.

My teaching career began with early childhood education. I found that the joy of learning was alive and well among my preschoolers. Later, as I faced my class of fifth-graders, I often wondered what had happened to the intrinsic motivation these children had had as infants, toddlers, and preschoolers. When did the joy of learning dissolve into tedium? How could I spark this joy and enthusiasm for learning? This is when I discovered how much my own emotional state affected my ability to motivate my students. The more interested and excited I was about the subject matter at hand, the more my students were as well.

However, there were so many times when this enthusiasm was hard to maintain. John would be bothering the boy next to him. Two girls in the back would be talking. Someone would drop a book and that would send me off track. After starting out thinking I was going to excite my students with a captivating history lesson, these small interruptions would completely throw me off. Frustration would build and get the best of me. Deflated, I would start trying to put out the fires with admonitions and treats. "John, keep your hands to yourself," I would snap. "Girls, pay attention, this will be on the test." "Let's pay attention, everyone." By the end of the day, I would be exhausted, wondering what had happened to my good intention to deliver an exciting, engaging lesson.

Over the course of each day, my emotional state would change dramatically. Like a day that starts out sunny, I would meet my students in the morning with joy and enthusiasm for the lesson of the day. But when students didn't immediately respond and even became disruptive, I would become annoyed. Like a dark cloud, my frustration would obscure the sunny enthusiasm and grow into a thunderstorm of anger.

As I mentioned earlier, when I lost my temper, my students responded in one of two ways. Some became fearful and quiet. The others gave me looks of defiance, but settled down nonetheless. My thunderstorm had created a palpable shift in the emotional climate. My students were quiet, but they were not ready to learn. My anger had triggered the fight, flight, and freeze reactions in their developing physiology. Had someone walked into my classroom at that moment, they would have felt the tension in the room.

If you've experienced something similar, you're not alone. In the coming chapters, you will learn how practicing mindful awareness will help you recognize and manage the strong emotions that derail your teaching and your students' motivation to learn.

Skill-Building Practices

In Chapter 1, you learned a type of mindful awareness practice that involved focusing your attention on the sensation of breathing. The purpose of this practice is to develop stability of attention. In this chapter, you will learn another form of practice called open monitoring. This involves openly and nonjudgmentally monitoring the content of your experience from one moment to the next.

The next two skill-building practices are reflection activities that involve recalling and focusing your attention on the emotional experience associated with two memories: (1) being helped by a teacher and (2) helping a student. These activities are intended to help you tune in to how you and your students feel when you respond to their needs. Memory is a powerful tool for mindfully exploring your emotional experience and for learning to recognize and understand your emotional patterns.

Open Monitoring

Remember when you learned how to maintain mindful awareness of your breath during focused attention practice? This is a great way to ease into the next practice, called open monitoring. However, once you are comfortable with focused attention practice, it's important to open yourself to the next stage as soon as your mind has stabilized. In open monitoring you broaden your awareness to the whole panorama of present-moment experience.

To begin, start focusing your attention on the inhalation and exhalation of the breath. This will help your mind settle. Do this for about 5 to 10 minutes. Once you feel that your mind has settled somewhat, loosen your attention on the breath and allow your awareness to broaden and settle into the full experience of the present moment.

In the state of open awareness, you are aware of everything, but not focused on anything in particular. It's like sitting in the center of the wheel of awareness and taking in everything within the present moment at one time without grasping or rejecting anything. You're not grasping on to the thoughts or feelings you experience, just noticing them like clouds passing by.

You may find that your mind becomes "captured" by a thought, an emotion, or a sensation. Your attention becomes drawn away from open awareness and focused on the thought, emotion, or sensation. When this happens, simply notice that your attention has been captured, name what grabbed your attention, and then loosen your mind back to open awareness. For example, you may notice yourself thinking, "What should we have for dinner?" In this case, you note the distraction and name it "thinking." If you notice the ache in your knee, you note it and name it "sensation." Then return to open awareness.

Over time, you will find your mind resting in what has been called "choiceness awareness"—meeting each sensory experience directly, without mediating thoughts. In this state, you meet each moment with freshness and your mind is not clinging to anything.

During this practice, if you find it becoming difficult, you can always return to focused attention on your breath. Sometimes practitioners go back and forth between the two types of practice, focusing their awareness on the breath when their mind needs to settle and broadening their awareness when their mind has stabilized again.

Classroom Reflection #1

Think about a teacher who made a difference in your life. If you can't recall a teacher, see if you can recall an adult who provided support to you and expressed that he or she cared about you. It could be a parent or another relative. Once you settle on one person, sit in a comfortable, mindful posture in which your back is erect but not rigid, your head is held high, your shoulders are relaxed, and your hands rest lightly in your lap. If you are sitting on a chair, your feet should be flat on the floor or on a cushion.

Now focus your attention on your breathing for a few minutes. As you inhale, feel the cool air entering your nostrils and filling your lungs. Feel the warm air exit as you exhale. Take some time to simply be present to the breath—the air going in and out of your body. If your mind wanders, simply notice what has drawn your attention away, and then gently bring your attention back to the breath.

Now I invite you to shift your attention to the memory of the person you have chosen for this exercise. See if you can bring a picture of this person to mind. At first, this may be an intellectual exercise, but as you practice, you will become more able to recollect details about the past. As you focus your attention on the memory of this person, try to remember as many details as you can about the way he or she looked and dressed. What color was his or her hair? Did he or she wear glasses? Try to bring the memory to life.

Next, I invite you to recall a specific point in time, a situation where this teacher (or other adult) expressed his or her care for you and did something to help you or support you in some way. Try to recall details about the situation. Where were you? Who were you with? What was everyone doing? Try to recreate the scene in your mind. Next imagine yourself stepping back into the scene, like stepping into a movie.

Now you are back in that situation again with this teacher (or other adult), and this person is expressing his or her care and helping you in some way. Notice how you feel as you experience this care, help, and support. Notice any sensations in your body. There might be a sense of temperature or color. You may feel sensations in particular parts of your body. Explore in as much detail as you can how it feels to be cared for and supported. Savor this experience.

Now spend a few minutes writing down what happened and how you felt.

Classroom Reflection #2

Think about a student you are trying to help. Perhaps she is struggling with school in some way, or maybe he has problems getting along with his peers. Most likely there are many children you are trying to help in some way. For the purposes of this exercise, choose just one. See if you can bring a picture of this child to mind. Try to recall as many details as you can about the way he or she looks and dresses. Once you have recalled this student, sit in a comfortable, mindful posture and focus your attention on your breathing.

Feel the gentle breath filling your lungs with air. Feel the warm air exit as you exhale. Next, see if you can recall a specific point in time, a situation when you did something to help this child. Try to recall details about the situation. Next imagine that you are back in that situation again with this student, helping him or her. Notice how you feel as you help this student. Notice any bodily sensations. You may notice a sense of temperature or color. You may also feel different sensations in various parts of your body.

Now spend a few minutes writing down what happened and how you felt.

Emotion Journal

One way to develop a better understanding of your emotional experience is to journal it. When you spend time reflecting on an emotional experience, you learn more about your emotional landscape and how to best navigate its ups and downs. One way to do this is to use the table below to record your experience.

In the first column, describe what happened in a situation in which emotion, positive or negative, pleasant or unpleasant, had an effect on your teaching. Write down just the facts, exactly as the situation happened, as if you were watching it on camera. In the second column, describe the physical sensations you felt during the situation. In the third column, write down the thoughts you had during the experience. When you're finished, notice how you feel. Can you identify the emotion that you associated with this situation? Can you see what triggered this emotion? Over time and with practice, you will begin to notice patterns of emotional reactivity. The more you recognize these patterns, the more you will be able to anticipate emotionally charged situations and deal with them proactively.

The Facts	Physical Sensations	Thoughts

Chapter 3

Understanding Your Negative Emotions

Try this. Think about a student you find challenging, then recall the last time she or he did something that made teaching difficult. Perhaps he interrupted your lesson, or maybe she bothered a classmate. Whatever it was, just think about it for a few minutes. What emotions does this memory elicit? Do you feel annoyed? Frustrated? How does your body feel? Maybe you notice tension in your shoulders or jaw.

Just a brief memory can trigger uncomfortable negative emotions. In this chapter we'll explore these negative emotions: what triggers them; what effects they have on our bodies, our thinking, and our behavior; and how we can apply mindful awareness to help us recognize and manage negative emotions before they get the best of us.

Emotional Mastery

Understanding and mastering negative, unpleasant emotions gives you an edge when you're teaching. As you will see, the emotional mastery you can develop through mindful awareness will make classroom management easier and more effective. Moreover, when you are no longer constantly exhausted by negative emotional reactivity, teaching will become more enjoyable and rewarding. And when your classroom climate is socially and emotionally supportive, your students will learn better.

So what are emotions for, anyway? As you learned in Chapter 2, Charles Darwin (1872/1998) hypothesized that emotions are biologically determined functions that support survival. He believed that these functions are universal—that every human being experiences and expresses the same emotions in similar ways under similar conditions. Paul Ekman's research supported Darwin's hypothesis (Ekman & Friesen, 1971).

Ekman and Friesen (1971) also demonstrated that cultures have different rules about how certain emotions should be expressed, and under what conditions. In this way, cultural mores may conceal the universality of emotion expression. However, Ekman and Friesen also discovered that, despite these cultural emotion display rules, emotions leak out in the form of microexpressions, fleeting facial expressions that are impossible to hide.

So, for example, even though it may not be socially acceptable to show anger in Thai culture, people of that culture who appear to be smiling may still show evidence of anger in the form of momentary changes in expression. Their eyes will briefly glare, their brows will furrow, and their mouth may turn down quickly in the midst of an attempt to maintain a smiling expression. Furthermore, if you look closely, you will see that the smile is not genuine, but forced. A genuine smile involves crinkling of the muscles on the outsides of the eyes, something difficult to fake. People may turn up their mouth in a smile, but if their eyes are not smiling, it's not authentic (Ekman, Davidson, & Friesen, 1990).

Ekman and his colleagues expanded their list of basic emotions to include a range of positive and negative emotions that are not all encoded in expressions formed by facial muscles. These include amusement, contempt, contentment, embarrassment, excitement, guilt, pride, relief, satisfaction, sensory pleasure, and shame.

Emotions have common triggers that all relate to a single theme: survival. According to Ekman (1994), emotions have the following characteristics:

1. Occurrence as a result of automatic appraisal of a situation
2. Commonalities in antecedent events or triggers
3. Presence in other primates besides human beings
4. Quick onset

5. Brief duration
6. Unbidden occurrence (i.e., they are not under conscious control)
7. Distinctive physiology to enhance survival
8. A distinctive (universal) signal (i.e., expression)

These characteristics differentiate our emotions from other experiences. They provide us with the ability to respond to life quickly, without planning, in ways that have been adaptive in our evolutionary past.

It's important to differentiate emotions from moods, because although both play an important role in teaching and learning, they do so in different ways. A mood resembles an emotion, and mood feeling states are similar to emotional feeling states. The primary difference is that moods last longer than emotions and may not be directed at an object. For example, we can be in an irritable mood for no particular reason, but if we are angry or frustrated, that anger or frustration is typically directed at a person, object, or situation.

Moods predispose us to certain emotions. If I come to work irritable, I'm more likely to become angry easily and snap at a student whose behavior I find annoying. Things that normally don't bother me may seem intolerable.

Each primary emotion is associated with a mood. As I've just highlighted, irritability predisposes us to anger. If we're feeling blue, we are predisposed to sadness. If we're anxious, we're predisposed to fear. The same is true for our students. If Peter comes to school feeling anxious, he may tend to react to my anger with fear. If he's feeling irritable, he may tend to react to my anger with defensiveness and hostility.

While negative emotions evolved to help us survive under conditions of threat, today we experience high levels of emotional stress, primarily because of psychological threats rather than physical threats. We may fear being judged or criticized, losing our job, or not being respected. We may feel anger when a student interrupts our lesson, a parent complains about her child's grade, or an administrator doesn't provide the support we need. Negative emotional reactivity in response to psychological threat causes emotional stress. While it may be only my self-esteem that is really threatened, my body reacts as if my life is threatened. However, this reaction may not be adaptive under these conditions. In fact, over time it can be very harmful to my health (Sapolsky, 2004).

Stress and the Body

When our life or the life of a loved one is threatened, our bodies automatically react in ways that give us an incredible survival edge. We've all heard the stories about ordinary people doing extraordinary things in life-threatening circumstances. For example, a mother has been reported to lift a car off her child after a car accident. While science has not been able to verify these rare incidents, it's clear that the experience of threat has a significant impact on our physiology that gives us an advantage by activating the stress response.

The field of mind-body medicine has contributed a great deal to our understanding of the stress response. This complex process begins in the brain. Our nervous system has two parts: One is conscious (e.g., I am consciously moving my fingers as I type this sentence), and the other is automatic, or autonomic. The autonomic nervous system manages our heart rate, respiration, and everything else that our body does without our conscious effort. If we had to consciously pay attention to whether or not we were breathing, we probably wouldn't live long!

Our autonomic nervous system, in turn, is composed of two subsystems: the sympathetic and the parasympathetic. You can imagine that the sympathetic system is like the accelerator of a car: It gets things moving. The parasympathetic system is like the break: It slows things down. When the two subsystems are synchronized, our autonomic nervous system helps our body regulate and adapt in response to challenging situations, supporting our survival.

The sympathetic system triggers the release of the organic chemicals adrenaline and noradrenaline. Adrenaline or epinephrine, as we call it in the US, is excreted by the adrenal gland in response to activation of the sympathetic system. Norepinephrine is released by sympathetic nerve endings throughout the rest of the body. These are the chemical messengers that trigger the stress response.

During the fight or flight response, the sympathetic system is activated into a state of hyperarousal. The hypothalamic-pituitary-adrenal axis (HPA axis) is a complex series of interactions among the hypothalamus, the pituitary gland, and the adrenal glands. The hypothalamus and the pituitary gland are located in the brain, and the adrenal glands are located above the kidneys. These interactions constitute the neuroendocrine system's response to stress that controls bodily functions such as digestion, immune response, emotion, sexual functions, and energy management to promote survival.

In a stressful situation, a whole cascade of rapid changes occur in the body. Let's imagine that I'm experiencing a real physical threat: A bear is chasing me. The adrenal gland shoots epinephrine into my bloodstream. This powerful chemical travels throughout my body, triggering changes in my organs and tissues to maximize my survival so I can run away. The airways of my lungs relax to maximize my breathing capacity and metabolism. My heart pounds, sending blood flowing to my leg muscles to help me run as fast as possible.

To access extra energy, the epinephrine activates the adenosine triphosphate–creatine phosphate (ATP-CP) system, the "first responder" of the various metabolism systems. While all metabolism systems run on ATP, a small amount of ATP is stored in muscles in case of an emergency like this one.

Functions such as digestion, immune response, and reproduction shut down. When life is threatened, these are low-priority functions. Dopamine, a natural painkiller, is produced in the brain, permitting me to keep running, even when my legs would otherwise give out due to pain. My vision narrows to help keep me focused on the bear and prevent distractions. There's only one thing that's important: survival.

When the sympathetic system delivers epinephrine to my heart muscle and makes it beat faster, it's playing the role of a neurotransmitter. If any cell, including a neuron, secretes a messenger that travels through the bloodstream to activate distant parts of the body, it's called a hormone. The hypothalamus, about the size of an almond and located just above the brain stem, is the master hormone regulator of the body.

The hypothalamus uses a variety of hormones to regulate the body. Some stimulate and some suppress certain functions. An important class of hormones involved in the stress response system is the gluco-corticoids. These are secreted by the adrenal gland and function similarly to epinephrine. However, their actions are not as immediate. The epinephrine works instantaneously, while the glucocorticoids can continue working over longer periods of time.

Any time we perceive a threat, the various hormonal reactions involved in the stress response happen very quickly and automatically. They occur whether the threat is physical or psychological. And here's the rub: While they were designed to help us survive physical threats, they react the same way when we feel psychologically threatened (as we may often feel in the classroom setting), despite the fact that these reactions may not be adaptive or helpful for dealing with psychological threat. In fact, if sustained for any length of time, the stress reactions, intended to help us survive, become toxic themselves.

Here's why: For one thing, the stress response can have a very detrimental effect on the cardiovascular system. If I am being chased by a bear, I need my heart to pump oxygen to my muscles so I can run as fast as possible. However, if I am fuming about that parent who is giving me a hard time about the failing grade I gave his daughter, well, my heartbeat is increasing too, but for no adaptive reason.

Hypertension—elevated blood pressure—is bad for the heart. When blood pressure is elevated, the blood returns to the heart with a "bam," wearing it out. The left ventricle is the part getting slammed by the returning blood flow. Over time, the muscle wall becomes thicker to protect against the increased blood flow. Now the heart is lopsided. One side is heavier than the other, increasing the risk of an irregular heartbeat.

When the stress response is sustained over time, bad things happen at the periphery of the circulatory system too. The places where blood vessels branch off from one another are vulnerable to the increased blood pressure, and eventually become damaged. The body tries to repair the damage by engaging the inflammatory system. However, adrenalin makes the blood thicker by signaling the platelets to clump together. These clumping platelets begin to get stuck in these damaged areas, creating blockages or atherosclerotic (artery-hardening) plaques.

A substance called C-reactive protein (CRP) is produced in the liver in response to injury. It travels to the damaged blood vessels to help reduce the inflammation. It helps trap bad cholesterol in the inflamed tissue. By measuring CRP, researchers have discovered that emotional stress can cause hypertension and atherosclerosis. High blood pressure can also dislodge the plaque that forms on blood vessels, resulting in a moving piece of plaque that travels downstream and can clog a smaller artery. If it lodges in a coronary artery, you've got a heart attack. If it lodges in the brain, you have a stroke.

Once the cardiovascular system is damaged, it becomes highly susceptible to further stress; it just can't handle it. And when the stress response is extended over a long period of time, the system begins to have difficulty shutting itself off. In chronically overstressed people, the parasympathetic system becomes impaired, and it becomes more difficult to slow down or decrease stress-induced reactions.

Stress affects the metabolism in a bad way too. As we have already seen, the body mobilizes all its resources to prepare to handle threat. This preparation includes pumping a bunch of glucose and cholesterol into the bloodstream. While this might help the individual run away from the bear, it increases the risk of metabolic difficulties, including insulin resistance, which causes big problems if the person has Type 1 diabetes.

The stress response is typically associated with a situation appraised as dangerous or threatening in some way, either physically or psychologically. If we feel we have some power in the threatening situation, such as when a student's behavior interrupts our lesson, we may immediately feel anger and respond with the fight response. If we feel powerless, such as when the principal is judging us unfairly, a threatening situation may evoke fear and the flight or freeze response.

In either of these situations, whether sooner or later, our fear may turn to anger. As Chapter 2 brought out, the classroom setting is a perfect setup for the stress response, because when we're teaching and something happens that we interpret as threatening, we can't escape. We have to deal with the emotionally provocative situation while we are teaching. The sense of being trapped and powerless accentuates the feeling of threat.

Our stress response evolved to help us learn about the dangers in our environment and to adapt to them quickly and automatically. Stressful emotional experiences "program" us to respond in a particular way without thinking. For example, my friend and colleague Christa was bitten by a vicious dog when she was very young. This experience was extremely traumatic, resulting in an extreme fear of dogs. Any time she would hear or see a dog, she would become paralyzed with fear.

In this way, Christa became conditioned to fear all dogs, even if they were not dangerous. However, she didn't want to be disabled by her fear of dogs, so she worked hard to desensitize herself. She intentionally spent time with dogs that she knew were good-natured and friendly so she could become used to being around dogs without the overwhelming feeling of fear. Over time, Christa was able to overcome her fear of dogs, and now she has a dog herself.

The stress response evolved to help us adapt to an environment that was relatively stable. For most of human history, we lived in the same geographic location in small tribal groups. If you lived in a land where there were dangerous wolves, it would be adaptive to have a strong fear of wolves. However, today we live under conditions that change rapidly and rarely expose us to physical threat. This function, designed to help us adapt, may now have limited adaptive capacity, and it may in fact be maladaptive under many circumstances.

On a regular basis, especially in our teaching life, we are getting ourselves into major emotional fusses over psychological threats, which are not something that the stress response can help us with. Yet our stress response kicks in nonetheless, wreaking havoc on our bodies. Mindfulness helps us recognize the stress response and the emotions, physical sensations, and cognitive processes associated with it. When we are aware, we can manage our reactions and reduce our stress, improving our health and well-being.

Negative Emotions in the Classroom

In the last chapter, we learned how positive emotions can help us create a warm and supportive learning environment. However, given the stresses of the classroom, it's not always easy to cultivate positive emotions, especially when challenging student behaviors interfere with our ability to perform our primary instructional role. It's no wonder that teachers so often report that they find it difficult to regulate negative emotions when they are teaching (Carson & Templin, 2007; Sutton, 2004).

While as teachers we regularly face situations that provoke our anger, contempt, disgust, sadness, and frustration, we must be professional. We must learn appropriate ways to regulate these feelings in the classroom setting (Hargreaves, 2000). Research on teachers' emotions has found that while we recognize the importance of regulating our emotions, we are less successful at hiding our emotions from our students than we think (Carson & Templin, 2007; Sutton, 2004; Sutton & Wheatley, 2003). Children are very sensitive to adults' emotions, and they can sense how we feel.

We can see why children have this sensitivity to the emotional states of the adults around them. In our evolutionary past, it would have been critical for children to be tuned in to the emotions of the adults around them in order to learn about the dangers in their environment and how best to respond to them. Also, when kids come from unstable, chaotic home environments, they can become hypervigilant to adult emotions that might be threatening. They are on high alert so they can protect themselves in case someone becomes violent. This hypervigilance can result in emotional dysregulation. The emotional challenges that we face in the classroom often involve dealing with students who have problems with self-regulation. These are the kids who are at the highest risk of developing behavior disorders and are in most need of our support (U.S. Department of Health and Human Services, 1999).

Not surprisingly, teachers' reports of stress and emotional negativity are strongly correlated with student misbehavior (Yoon, 2002). As disruptive student behavior increases, teachers' negative emotions increase. Indeed, research has found that teachers routinely experience negative emotions such as anger, disgust, and contempt in response to student behaviors (Carson & Templin, 2007; Hamre & Pianta, 2001; Pianta, Hamre, & Stuhlman, 2003; Sutton & Wheatley, 2003).

As many of us have experienced, this stress is magnified when we have more than one or two disruptive students in our class. Even those of us who would normally cope quite effectively under less stressful conditions can become coercive and harsh under these circumstances (Conduct Problems Prevention Research Group, 1992).

When we become overwhelmed by negative emotions, we lose our enthusiasm for cultivating and maintaining positive relationships with our students. Research has demonstrated that under the influence of negative emotions, teachers become less involved with, less tolerant of, and less caring toward their students (Blase, 1986).

Our negative emotions may have long-term effects on our students, too. Bridget Hamre and Robert Pianta (2001) conducted a study to explore these long-term effects. They asked kindergarten teachers to report on their feelings about their students. As you would expect, teachers expressed strong negative reactions in response to some of their students. Hamre and Pianta then followed these students through the fourth grade and found that they did more poorly than their peers in terms of their social and emotional development.

Kids that enter school with self-regulation problems tend to provoke negative emotions in their teachers. Often the teachers' reactions reinforce the kids' self-regulation problems, rather than helping them learn to self-regulate.

What Is a Script?

We all have a database of stored emotional memories that influence the way we think, feel, and behave. Experiences associated with strong negative emotions create patterns of neural networks in the brain that are stored in the memory. Ekman (2007a) calls these influential emotional memories "scripts," or conditioned responses.

Each negative emotion has an evolutionary function—a theme that is prewired into our system to protect us against danger. For example, if a car comes at us, we instinctively react with fear and jump out of the way without thinking. However, throughout our life, we develop our own individualized emotional patterns based on our experience. Scripts are shortcuts; they enable us to react to a situation quickly and without thought. They were most likely very functional for humans when we lived as hunter-gatherers and the kinds of threats we might encounter in our environment were more predictable than they are today.

Today our scripts can create problems for us. They can cause us to automatically react to situations in ways that may not be appropriate. This is because scripts interfere with our perceptions of reality. Something happens that we automatically interpret as a threat based upon a script. Even if the current event is not the same as the past event that programmed the script, we interpret it as similar.

For example, my colleague Christa's script about dogs caused her to falsely perceive even friendly dogs as a threat. By practicing mindful awareness, we can learn to recognize and weaken the effects of our scripts so we can respond to situations with greater awareness rather than automatically and unconsciously reacting.

Emotionally conditioned scripts develop when we are exposed to a situation that elicits a strong, negative emotion. Ekman (2007a) has described several factors that determine the likelihood that an emotional experience will result in a script. One factor is the closeness of the event to the evolutionary theme of the emotion. For example, one survival theme related to anger is the perception that our goals are being thwarted. Thus, when a student interferes with my ability to accomplish my mandated instructional goals (upon which my continued employment depends), I may feel anger, and I may easily develop the script, "She's trying to make my job difficult." However, this may be a misinterpretation. It is unlikely that the student's behavior is really intentional and premeditated.

Another factor is the similarity of the event to the original emotional trigger. So, for Christa, a similar dog would still be more likely to elicit fear than one that looks different. The third factor is how early in life the trigger was learned. The earlier it was learned, the more difficult it is to recognize and unlearn the script. A fourth is the intensity of the initial trigger. The stronger the emotional reaction, the greater the likelihood of developing a strong script and the greater the difficulty in recognizing and weakening it. A fifth factor is density—how often the emotion is triggered in a similar situation, again and again. One final factor is individual affective style; people who emotionally react faster and with greater intensity will have more difficulty overcoming the power of the script.

Scripts in the Classroom

We can't help but bring a lifetime's worth of scripts to the classroom with us. Many of these scripts are rooted in the way we were raised. As children, we learned that some behaviors are very bad and deserve punishment. When we see our students acting in these ways, these scripts come to the fore. When this happens, our perceptions are distorted and we have the tendency to overreact.

We may assume that a student's behavior is conscious and intentional when it's more likely the result of poor regulation, trauma, or something going on outside of school. Our scripts may exaggerate our perceptions and blow things out of proportion. We may think a student misbehaves more frequently than he actually does. Finally, our scripts may lead to a tendency to act on unconscious biases without realizing it.

Kids develop scripts about teachers and school. When students have poor relationships with their teachers, they begin to dislike and fear school. Eventually this may lead to feelings of alienation and disengagement from school. When students feel alienated, they are at much greater risk of developing antisocial behaviors, delinquency, and academic failure (Dwyer, Osher, & Warger, 1998).

This is not surprising. A kid comes to kindergarten unprepared for the demands and expectations of the school and classroom environment. He doesn't know how to sit still and focus his attention on a task. He isn't used to being around so many children his age. He has difficulty keeping his hands to himself and is generally disruptive. His teacher has three or four other kids in the class with similar problems, compounding the challenges. Dealing with all the disruptions is emotionally exhausting, and she loses patience with him.

Frustrated and overwhelmed, she makes him sit in the corner for time-out or sends him to the office. He doesn't understand why she's angry and decides she's just mean and doesn't like him. The other kids model the teacher's behavior. Since it appears that the teacher doesn't like the student, they decide they shouldn't like him either. Soon the other kids are rejecting him during recess. It's no wonder he hates school and doesn't want to attend.

It's also no wonder that he becomes easy prey to older kids looking to recruit gang members. Everyone needs to feel they belong to a social group. If students feel rejected by their teachers and their peers at school, they will look elsewhere for a sense of belonging. Learning to manage our emotional reactions can help us help these kids. If we can notice our tendency to react and regulate this reaction, we can become positive role models for our students and help them adjust to the demands of the classroom environment rather than pushing them away.

Mindfulness Can Help

So you may be asking, "How does mindfulness fit in?" Attending mindfully to what is happening can help you recognize your emotional patterns and respond to them consciously rather than blindly reacting to emotionally provocative situations. Practicing mindful awareness builds your capacity to recognize your scripts and disengage from your scripted emotional tendencies.

In education, we speak a great deal about reflective practice—the capacity to reflect on our actions so we can continually learn from our experience (Schön, 1983). However, in practice, this is typically superficial, focused on what we did or didn't do and how our students responded. Mindfulness helps us to be deeply reflective. We can apply mindful awareness to deepening our reflection on our emotional patterns and the scripts associated with them. Thus, when we reflect on a challenging situation, we can bring awareness not only to what happened, but how we felt about it, what we were thinking about it, and how these thoughts and feelings affected our behavior.

We can mindfully apply the eight senses of the wheel of awareness to our emotional experiences. When we practice regularly, we become more aware of our internal emotional landscape. We notice the subtle ups and downs of our feeling state and the physical sensations that clue us in to the early stages of our emotional reactivity.

When we develop "mindsight," we can observe our thought processes and recognize the role they play in reinforcing both the reactivity and the associated scripts distorting our perception of what is actually occurring in the moment. At the same time, we can observe our students' feelings and behaviors more objectively. This allows us to become attuned to our class. With a deep understanding of the social and emotional dynamics of the classroom, we can orchestrate an effective learning environment. When we begin to practice mindfulness regularly, the physical sensations and thoughts associated with important feelings become very obvious, because these are usually what take us away from the awareness of the present moment by "capturing" our attention.

For example, suppose that during my morning focused attention mindfulness practice, my mind wanders and I begin to think about the day. I wonder, "What shall I have for lunch?" This innocent thought elicits a memory of yesterday, when I had to miss lunch because James was disrupting the class again and I kept him in my classroom during lunch for a time-out. I start ruminating about James and his frustrating behavior.

By the time I realize that I've become distracted by these thoughts, I'm already experiencing the early stages of an anger reaction. I notice the subtle changes in the tension in my body as my shoulders creep up and my jaw and hands begin to clench. This gives me a clue that I need to be especially mindful in my interactions with James because I might tend to project a script onto his behavior.

When, during practice, we notice that we've become distracted, it helps to pay attention to the distraction and its effect—objectively, as an observer. In the example above, I can recognize that I've become distracted by these thoughts and notice the frustration and the associated physical sensations. Once I recognize what has happened, I can let go of the thoughts and feelings and bring my attention back to my breath.

After practice, record the experience in a journal, if you feel that would be useful. Notice what distracted you and how you feel, and think about this distraction. If you do this regularly, you will learn a great deal about your scripts and emotional patterns. And once you understand why you have negative emotions, how they evolved to help you survive, and how they make you think and feel, you can become more aware of your emotional reactivity before it gets the best of you. Then, throughout the day, when you notice the subtle sensations in your body and the thought patterns that go with them, you can stop, take a breath, and calm down before you do something you may regret. This practice also helps prevent the stress-related health problems you learned about earlier in this chapter.

The Effects of Negative Emotions: Contract and Defend

As we have learned, negative emotions support our survival by initiating reactions that involve physical and psychological contraction as a means of defense. Just as our large muscles contract to prepare us to fight or flee, our perceptions also contract. Research has demonstrated that when we are feeling intense negative emotions, our attentional focus narrows (Easterbrook, 1959). This helps us focus our full attention on the threat, but it also limits our ability to see the bigger picture and take in the context of the situation.

Although I describe emotions as discrete, they often blend together. I can feel happy and sad at the same time— for example, happy that my son is getting married, but sad to realize he's all grown up and I won't see as much of him anymore.

Next you will learn more about each of the particular "negative" emotions, the physical sensations and thought patterns associated with them, their evolutionary functions, and the roles they often play in the classroom. Finally, you will learn practical skills to promote emotional mastery.

Anger

As we have seen, anger is a constellation of feelings that range from mild irritation to rage. According to Ekman (2007a), the most common situation that triggers in us anger of any degree is one in which our goals are being thwarted. We also feel anger (and fear) when we think someone is trying to hurt us physically or psychologically. Another driver cuts us off on the road; someone takes the parking place we've been waiting for; a lazy clerk closes the drugstore five minutes early when we really need a prescription; a student interrupts us for the umpteenth time when we're trying to get through a lesson that will help prepare the class for a high-stakes, standardized test. These are all common situations that trigger anger.

Anger arises even when we know that the behavior was an accident. However, it is usually stronger when we think the person is intentionally trying to hurt us or thwart our goals. As Ekman notes, "Anger controls, anger punishes, and anger retaliates" (Ekman, 2007a, p. 111).

Anger is the most dangerous emotion because it is highly volatile and provokes an urge to cause harm to the perceived cause. Once we become angry, our biological wiring predisposes us to stay angry. It is also highly contagious. It's difficult not to become angry in the presence of an angry person, especially if we feel that her or his anger is unjustified or is directed at us.

When it comes to anger, there are a lot of individual differences. Some people have "short fuses" and are quick to anger. They are easily provoked and their anger can be intense. Others are "slow burners" who do not become angry easily, and their anger may not be so intense. Some people stay angry longer than others.

Part of becoming mindful about our emotions is to become familiar with our emotional patterns. Do I become angry easily? What usually provokes my anger? Is my anger more or less intense than the anger of others? Does my anger last longer than most people's? These are the dimensions of our emotional experience that form a landscape to explore.

While anger is a powerful emotion, most of us can control our tendency to lash out and hurt others when we feel angry because the executive functions of the prefrontal cortex of the brain help us inhibit this tendency. Our executive functions, often called the CEO of our brain, handle the regulation and control of cognitive processes such as working memory, reasoning, planning, and problem-solving.

There are some people who, due to an illness or brain injury, cannot control their automatic tendency to lash out. However, this is rare.

The emotion regulation process commonly involves two cognitive processes: reappraisal and suppression (Gross, 2002). Reappraisal involves changing the way we perceive a situation in order to reduce the effect of the emotion. Suppression involves inhibiting the expression of the emotion. While both involve cognitive control, reappraisal actually decreases the intensity of the emotional experience and reduces the tendency to act upon the emotion. In contrast, suppression curbs emotional expression but does nothing to reduce the actual experience of the emotion. Furthermore, suppression impairs memory and increases the harmful physiological effects of the emotion. Practicing mindful awareness promotes teachers' tendency to reappraise emotional experience (Jennings, Frank, Snowberg, Coccia, & Greenberg, 2013).

It is important to understand that the executive functions take a long time to develop. The prefrontal cortex is the last part of the brain to mature, and children and adolescents often have difficulty with inhibition, especially if they are exposed to risk factors that impair normal development, such as maltreatment and trauma (Shonk & Cicchetti, 2001).

Obviously, anger can serve an important purpose when our life is truly threatened, because it triggers aggression. Resorting to aggression to protect ourselves or our loved ones is often considered justifiable. However, most of our anger arises in the midst of daily hassles that are not life-threatening, and often we regret our aggressive behavior, whether it be physical or verbal. Expressions of anger can damage our relationships with others and our reputation in our community. Excessively angry adults and children are not well liked by their peers. However, there are times when we are so angry, we no longer care about the damage we may cause. The experience of anger itself contributes to the tendency to disregard the effects of our anger (after all, when our life is *really* threatened, it's most adaptive to sustain our anger and aggressive tendencies as long as they may be necessary). Sometimes we become so angry we don't even know we're angry, even though we are shouting angry words. Scientists aren't yet sure why this happens. It could be that some people are naturally less aware of their anger than others, or perhaps there is a threshold of intensity past which we no longer realize we are angry.

Psychologist Daniel Goleman (2005) has suggested that our amygdala, a small organ in the limbic system of our brain, is the culprit.

The amygdala is like a warning system. It is constantly scanning our environment for threat. If the alarm goes off and our stress system goes into high gear, the amygdala "hijacks" our rational cognitive functions.

Dan Siegel (2010) has a fun metaphor for this tendency. Imagine your hand is a model of your brain. Your palm is the brain stem, your thumb is the limbic system, and the rest of your hand is the cortex. Place your thumb inside your palm and fold your fingers over it. The tips of your fingers are your prefrontal cortex, the seat of the executive functions, the brain functions that help us stop ourselves from reacting.

The amygdala is located near the brain stem, which allows it to quickly communicate with the rest of the body without the involve-

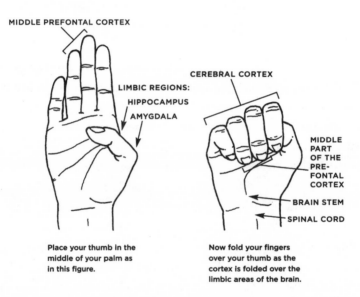

MIDDLE PREFONTAL CORTEX

CEREBRAL CORTEX

LIMBIC REGIONS:
HIPPOCAMPUS
AMYGDALA

MIDDLE PART OF THE PRE-FONTAL CORTEX

BRAIN STEM

SPINAL CORD

Place your thumb in the middle of your palm as in this figure.

Now fold your fingers over your thumb as the cortex is folded over the limbic areas of the brain.

ment of the higher-order brain functions. Thus, when we become highly emotional, we can lose our ability to self-monitor and self-regulate.

As Dan Siegel puts it, we "flip our lid." Using his hand metaphor, you can flip up your fingers so they no longer touch your thumb "limbic system." However, if we attend to the subtle signals of an emotional reaction before we flip our lid, our prefrontal cortex becomes engaged in the process. Our executive functions can allow us to maintain awareness and control over our emotional reactions.

As I mentioned earlier, I noticed this lid flipping phenomenon when I was supervising student teachers. I witnessed a teacher's angry reaction to a child's behavior, but when I spoke with her after class, she denied feeling angry. This was a big surprise to me. Even when I pointed out that her voice sounded angry, she denied it.

As a supervisor, this was troubling. I was supposed to be coaching these student teachers to manage the classroom and build supportive relationships with their students. If they didn't notice their anger and how it was interfering with their students' learning, how could I help them? My wish to answer this question took me on the quest that eventually led to my research and this book.

If we don't notice our anger, we can't regulate it. When we're aware of the sensations and thoughts associated with the angry reaction, we're more aware of the anger. When we're aware, we can be proactive.

In the heat of anger, our thinking becomes narrow, making it difficult to consider all the possible solutions to a particular problem. Once when I was teaching classroom management, a student came to me with a problem. Expressing a great deal of frustration, she said she had tried "everything." When I asked her what she had tried, she named two strategies. Considering that any given problem has myriad possible solutions, her thinking was obviously narrowed by her frustration. Mindful awareness can help us recognize our reactivity, calm down, and regain a broadness of thinking that will allow us to consider all the possibilities.

Anger has common physical sensations. Since its purpose is self-defense, heart and breathing rates increase, creating a sensation of heat. Tension in the jaw, neck, and shoulders arise from an impulse to jut out the chin, clench the fists, and prepare to fight. These are the felt bodily sensations of anger corresponding to the sixth sense—the "embodied mind"—of Siegel's wheel of awareness.

We can also notice our thoughts (the seventh sense on the wheel of awareness). Ekman (2007a) discovered that when we're in an angry state, there's a point at which our thinking becomes distorted. He called this the refractory period, because we see the situation in high contrast and become resistant to any information that does not support our angry state.

This tendency helps us survive by maintaining our heightened emotional state until it's no longer needed. It occurs with other negative emotions as well, and it is adaptive if our life is in physical danger. However, if this distorted thinking lasts very long, it can interfere with our functioning. We become biased in a way that can cause trouble.

For example, once I was observing a student teacher working in a class supervised by a teacher I'll call Ms. Skalinski. I noticed that a boy I'll call Sam was having difficulty staying on task. He clearly had self-regulation problems and took a great deal of the teacher's energy to manage. Finally he settled down with some seat work.

A girl named Jenna innocently got up to sharpen her pencil. As she turned the manual sharpener, she looked to see what the teacher was doing. Over the years, I've learned that this scouting behavior is a red flag. Children planning malicious deeds often scan the environment to see who is watching and determine whether the coast is clear. However, as I aimed my face in the other direction, pretending to take notes, she didn't notice I was watching her out of the corner of my eye.

Once Jenna felt confident that no one was watching, she walked over to Sam, sharp pencil in hand, and jabbed the pencil into his arm. Screaming in pain, Sam reflexively swiped his hurt arm at her, trying to defend himself, and hit Jenna in the face. She crumpled to the ground screaming, "He hit me!"

Ms. Skalinski, already frustrated with the boy, assumed that he was at fault. As she comforted Jenna, she angrily lashed out at Sam: "Why did you hit her?" Still whimpering, Sam said, "She poked me with her pencil!" Ms. Skalinski didn't believe him. She couldn't take in any information that contradicted her reason for being angry with him. She punished Sam and gave Jenna her sympathy. Considering Jenna's premeditation and malicious intent, her behavior was far worse than Sam's. He hit her reflexively, in self-defense.

Afterward, when I spoke to Ms. Skalinski and told her what had happened, she was flabbergasted. She couldn't imagine that the girl would do such a thing. She felt awful because she realized that the girl had taken advantage of her bias against the boy.

Sometimes dysregulated children become class scapegoats. Their classmates know they can be easily provoked, and they become targets. When we are unaware of how our anger is distorting our perceptions, we can be easily fooled by children who understand how to manipulate the social and emotional environment.

Let me take a moment here to be clear. I am not saying that anger is bad or that you should never express anger. Anger can be useful if it's channeled and expressed appropriately. Here's an example:

Ms. Sharma is an outstanding teacher. She is incredibly patient and rarely frustrated or angry. However, once when I was observing a student teacher she was mentoring, I saw her use her anger masterfully.

Ms. Sharma was in the playground with her kindergarteners, and Jusuf wanted a toy truck that Marco was using. He grabbed the truck and started to pull it away. When this didn't work, he hit Marco hard on the head. Ms. Sharma calmly walked over to the two boys. She comforted Marco and then sternly said to Jusuf, "It is my job to keep everyone safe. I cannot let you hurt others. Please sit down on the bench and calm down. Then we'll talk."

Her voice was firm, her tone matter-of-fact, but it was clear she meant business. She was clearly angry, but she consciously used her anger effectively. She didn't say or do anything hurtful. Later, when everyone had calmed down, she sat down with the two boys and they discussed the situation. Ms. Sharma helped the two boys communicate their feelings and explored alternative solutions to their conflict.

In contrast, Ms. Johnson, another teacher I regularly observed, had a temper that often flared and interfered with her teaching. Whenever she encountered a situation similar to the one with Marco and Jusuf, she tended to accuse, blame, and punish. Unaware that she was modeling these behaviors for her students, Ms. Johnson expressed wonder about why they were so aggressive toward one another. Her students had developed the habit of tattling, trying to engage her anger and direct it at a peer.

Once I witnessed Sarah and Emily having an argument over a box of markers. Openly annoyed by the disruption, Ms. Johnson quickly walked over to the two as her anger rose. "You are disrupting the class. You need to stop right now!" Her tone implied that their behavior was intentional. "She took my markers!" said Emily in defense. "No, she did!" accused Sarah. Since Ms. Johnson hadn't observed what had happened, she took the markers away from both of them. In a punishing tone, she said, "Since you both are disrupting the class, you will sit with your heads down for five minutes"—a rather harsh response to a minor disagreement and one that didn't help them learn to manage their conflict.

When we model anger, blame, and punish, it's no wonder our children act like us! We are responsible for creating the social and emotional tone in our classroom, and if we don't use our anger skillfully, it can be very damaging to our classroom environment.

In the preceding example, Ms. Sharma's response to the playground situation communicated that she cared about her students and understood that they were young and still learning how to get along. She clearly expressed her anger in a way that didn't hurt, but that firmly communicated that hitting was unacceptable. She recognized that when children are angry, they need time to calm down, and she coached the children through the problem-solving process, teaching them to express their feelings and constructively consider alternative solutions. She didn't blame either one, nor did she punish them.

Channeling anger in this way builds trust and respect. In contrast, angry reactions like Ms. Johnson's can easily trigger a negative, reactive cycle of revenge. While children easily recognize our anger, they rarely empathize with or understand our angry reactions. They haven't yet developed the necessary level of perspective-taking, and they may not have been taught the skills to behave appropriately in the classroom context. Consequently, our angry reactions may feel unfair to them.

When individuals feel unfairly accused and punished, they usually feel angry and want revenge. If we aren't careful, we can inadvertently teach children, through our modeling, that anger and revenge are socially acceptable means of gaining power over others. As we practice mindfulness and begin to recognize the signals of our anger, we can take a moment to calm down by taking a mindful breath or two and consider how best to respond to the situation, rather than overreacting. When we can do this consistently, we will be teaching our students a better way to manage anger and conflict by our example.

Earlier in the chapter we learned about scripts and how they can interfere with our ability to perceive a situation accurately. When we feel a strong emotion, we can take a moment to see if it makes sense under the current situation. Here's an example:

Ms. Garcia, a second-grade teacher who attended one of my mindfulness workshops, had a student named Monique who came to school late every morning. Since class had already begun, Monique's late arrival disrupted the activities already under way, annoying Ms. Garcia. Complicating the situation, Monique was embarrassed about arriving late. When young children have difficulty with self-regulation, they may act silly when they're embarrassed. This is exactly what Monique did. When her classmates looked at her as she came in late, she would stick out her tongue at them.

Once seated, she made a lot of noise, dropping her books, papers, and pencils when she was supposed to be getting settled into her schoolwork. Monique's behavior provoked giggles and silly responses from her peers, further disrupting the class. Her classmates would imitate her by dropping their things too. When this happened, Ms. Garcia's annoyance would grow into angry frustration. She responded to Monique's silly interruptions with anger, moving her to a corner of the classroom by herself. Rather than helping Monique self-regulate, this caused further embarrassment, resulting in more silly, disruptive behavior. During the first day of our workshop, Ms. Garcia identified Monique as her biggest behavior problem.

After a few days of mindful awareness practice and learning about her emotional patterns and scripts, Ms. Garcia became curious about her strong negative reaction to Monique. She realized that she had never asked Monique why she was late every day. The next day, Ms. Garcia sat down with Monique during recess and asked her why she was late. Seven-year-old Monique told her that her mother worked at night and was asleep in the morning when she had to get ready for school. Monique had to get to school without any adult help or supervision.

When Ms. Garcia heard this, her feelings about Monique changed dramatically. She realized that Monique was trying to make it to school on time and needed help, not condemnation. Ms. Garcia realized that she had a personal script that was creating her strong angry reaction to Monique's chronic tardiness. She recalled that when she was a young child, her parents has been very strict with her about punctuality. Once, when she was late for an event, she had been severely punished by her furious mother. This frightening experience created a strong script— "Thou shalt not be late!"—that she had projected onto the situation with Monique. The script interfered with her ability to perceive the situation clearly. She assumed that Monique was intentionally coming to school late and disrupting her class on purpose.

Once Ms. Garcia recognized her script through mindful awareness, she was able to overcome her inclination to react with anger to Monique's tardiness and changed her approach to the situation. She welcomed Monique when she came late, helped her get settled, and included her in the class activity, rather than sending her to the corner. Feeling accepted, Monique behaved better, as did the rest of the class. Ms. Garcia had solved her biggest behavior problem by simply recognizing one of her scripts, using mindful awareness to overcome her automatic tendency to become angry, and giving Monique respect and acceptance.

Fear

Remember: We feel fear when we perceive threat of harm, either physical or psychological. The automatic adaptive response that fear provokes is to run or to freeze. Depending upon the nature of the threat, we may feel anger right after feeling fear. If we perceive that the person threatening us is less powerful, our fear may turn to anger quickly.

For example, imagine that a student in your class is verbally threatening you. You may feel a brief sensation of fear, then feel angry at the student. It is inappropriate to threaten a teacher—a breach of ethical behavior—and that provokes anger. On the other hand, if your principal verbally threatens you, you are more likely to remain fearful for a longer period of time. However, when you get home and recount the situation to someone close to you, you may find that you feel quite angry, because it's safe to do so.

According to Ekman (2007a), fear reactions depend up on three basic factors: intensity (severity of the threat), timing (is the threat immediate or impending?), and coping (can anything be done to prevent the threat?). We feel the most fear when the threat is severe and immediate and there's nothing we can do to prevent it. When we are exposed to a severe, immediate threat but we can take action to alleviate the threat, we may not feel fear. We are so focused on managing the crisis that we don't feel afraid. If we feel impending threat that we cannot control, we may feel severe anxiety or panic.

Take a moment and recall a time you felt afraid. It might be easiest to recall a time when you worried about something threatening that might happen in the future. For instance, in these days of high-stakes testing, many of us share the concern that our students won't do well on the achievement tests and that this will reflect badly on us. In some cases, our jobs may be threatened.

When we feel extreme fear, we may notice our hands becoming cold and clammy. Our breathing may become more rapid, and we may feel trembling in our extremities. We may also notice our urge to get away or pull back from a situation. This is the automatic flight reaction manifesting in our bodies, creating a strong impulse to flee from the subject of our fear. This may express itself as thoughts about quitting or leaving the school where we're working.

It's good to recognize fear, both in ourselves and in others. If we notice fear among our students, there's a strong possibility that they're afraid of *us*. The fear should alert us to the possibility that our anger is provoking it. When we are afraid, we often become hypervigilant as a way to protect ourselves. This may help us avoid a threat, but it impairs our ability to learn. If our students' attention is entirely focused on protecting themselves against a threat, they are not attending to our math lesson. As we become more mindfully aware of the emotional climate we are creating in our classrooms, we become more tuned in to the possibility that our behavior is having a negative effect on our students' ability to learn, and we can change.

Sadness

The universal trigger for sadness is loss (Ekman, 2007a). Loss can take many forms, such as the loss of a loved one, loss of a relationship, loss of a job, or loss of the esteem of a colleague. Sadness can range from mild disappointment to severe agony. Sadness has the function of helping us conserve energy and signaling to others that we need help and care.

Take a moment to recall a time when you felt sadness or disappointment. Most of the time, when we think about a sad situation from the past, the sadness returns. As you recall this situation, tune in to the physical sensations of sadness. How does your body feel? When we feel sad, we typically experience a decrease in energy. We may feel a heaviness or hollowness in our chest. We may feel a burning sensation in our eyes that precedes tears.

Some of the saddest experiences I have had while teaching were in response to learning about the tragic conditions under which my students lived. When I began to apply a mindful approach to sadness, I noticed how the emotion impaired my ability to act in ways that might be helpful to these students. I realized that while my empathy for their situation was giving me a sense of how difficult their lives were, it wasn't motivating me to be helpful. Empathy involves experiencing the same emotion as the other, which can often be overwhelming. As I learned to manage my sadness, I was able to shift my empathy toward compassion—which involves the motive to help—and find ways I could be helpful.

Disgust and Contempt

The universal trigger for disgust is a potentially contaminated object or substance, often one associated with eating (Ekman, 2007a). The defensive function of disgust is to protect us from ingesting anything that might be harmful. However, disgust is not limited to eating.

We feel disgust when we see gore, or symptoms of an illness that maims or deforms. We also feel disgust in response to certain behaviors, such as sexual deviance. There are cultural differences in what we find disgusting. This is obvious when it comes to food. We may turn up our noses at foods that another culture would consider delicacies.

Take a moment to remember a time when you felt disgust. Again, as you access the memory of the emotion, you may begin to feel the associated sensations in your body. As you recall this memory of disgust, how does your body feel? When we feel disgust, our nose wrinkles and we squint. We may feel slightly nauseated. There may be an impulse to bend over. These are all signals that we have been exposed to something toxic that we need to eliminate.

For children, certain activities and things that most adults find disgusting can be humorous. For example, children may have a preoccupation with potty words or tell jokes involving human excrement. This is evidenced by the popularity of shows like *Beavis and Butt-Head*, *The Simpsons*, and *South Park* among children and youth. For adults, this tendency can be annoying, especially when we're trying to teach important subject matter.

Contempt is similar to disgust, but involves a degree of distain and condescension (Ekman, 2007a). Disgust can be directed at inanimate objects and substances, while contempt is reserved for people. We may feel contempt for a person who is doing something we find disgusting. While contempt involves a feeling of superiority, it's not uncommon for a person to feel contempt for a superior. For example, a student may feel contempt for authority, or a teacher may feel contempt for a principal or superintendent.

One danger associated with disgust and contempt is depersonalization. If we feel disgust or contempt for another person, we may have a tendency to feel entitled to treat that person badly. We may begin to think of them as less than human, as a monster or an animal. In this way, disgust and contempt can interfere with the relationships we build with our students.

As we learned in Chapter 2, research on teacher burnout has found that it tends to follow a three-step progression. The first step occurs when teachers become emotionally exhausted as they attempt to self-regulate under conditions of stress, as when their classroom is chaotic. If teachers become overwhelmed with emotional exhaustion, they may develop a tendency to depersonalize their students.

Disgust and contempt can be a way to cope with exhaustion. If teachers view a student or her or his behavior with disgust and contempt (e.g., "That little monster!"), they have an excuse not to treat her or him with care, respect, and compassion. When we begin to notice ourselves becoming disgusted with or contemptuous of our students, it's time to pay attention. We are engaging in a coping strategy that can be very damaging to our teaching and our students' learning.

Achieving Emotional Mastery

In summary, we have learned about the stress response and negative emotions. These natural physiological responses evolved to help us survive, but in today's world, these functions can wreak havoc on our well-being and our health. This is because what stresses us today is often not physically threatening, but psychologically threatening.

In many cases, the sense of threat that we feel arises from a script—a pattern of neural networks that respond habitually to a situation similar to one that provoked strong emotions in the past rather than to the actual circumstances of the situation at hand. We carry with us a whole database of these scripts, and they keep us from experiencing the moment objectively.

With time and attentive, mindful awareness, you can learn to recognize and let go of your scripts so that you can consciously respond to situations rather than automatically reacting. Your own negative emotions and those of your students have a critical effect on your classroom relationships and the creation of a learning environment. Next you'll learn some mindful awareness activities you can practice to help yourself recognize and respond constructively to scripts.

Skill-Building Practices

Body Scan

One way to get in touch with your emotions is to do a mindfulness practice called the body scan. This is a simple technique that involves directing attention to different parts of your body and noticing sensations. You can do this activity quickly and informally any time you feel the need to tune in to your body. This is a powerful way to bring yourself into the present moment. You can also do this practice more formally, either sitting in a chair or on a cushion on the floor or lying down. Many people enjoy doing this practice right before they go to sleep and report that it helps them sleep better.

As you either sit or lie on the floor or in your bed, begin by focusing your attention on your breath, just as you learned for breath awareness practice. Notice the sensation of the air moving into and out of your body from your nostrils and into your lungs. Notice the expansion and contraction of your chest and abdomen as you breathe.

Once your mind begins to settle, shift your awareness to your feet. Notice any sensations you find there. If you are sitting, notice the weight of your legs pressing on the floor through the soles of your feet. If you are lying down, notice the pressure of your heels on the floor or bed. Notice if there is any tension in your feet. You may also feel the sensation of your socks and shoes touching your feet. The aim here is not to try to relax the tension, but just to become aware of it. Once you notice the feeling, see if it changes as you bring awareness to that place.

Next bring your awareness to your calves. What sensations do you find in your calves? Can you feel the sensation of your clothing touching the skin of your calves? Is there any tension in your calves?

Now shift your awareness to your knees and thighs and explore the sensations you find in these parts of your body. Do you find any tension here? You may notice the weight of your upper body pressing your thighs and buttocks toward the seat of the chair or toward the floor.

Now bring your awareness up toward your torso. Beginning with your back, bring your awareness up your spine and see if you find any points of tension. Expand your awareness outward from your spine, feeling your entire back. If you are lying down, notice the weight of your body pressing your back down into the floor or bed. As you explore the sensations in your back, notice any tension.

Now move your awareness up to your shoulders. This is a place where many of us hold a great deal of tension. Gently explore the sensations in your shoulders. You may notice the feeling of your clothing hanging on your shoulders.

Next bring your awareness to the front of your torso. Notice any tension in your chest and abdomen. Again, notice the sensation of your breathing as your chest and abdomen rise and fall with each breath.

Now bring your awareness to your neck, another place where many of us hold tension. Explore your neck and notice any tension there.

Shifting your awareness upward, explore your head. You may notice tension in your jaw, around your ears, or in the muscles around your nose. Your eyes may be tense. Bring your awareness to your forehead. Is there tension there?

Once you've completed the body scan, spend a few minutes sensing your entire body. Is there a place in your body that was particularly tense? If so, go back to that place and give it a little extra attention. Notice if the sensations in this location change as you bring your kind awareness to it. Spend as much time as you feel comfortable, bringing gentle awareness to this place. Finally, end the practice by bringing your awareness back to your breath following each inhalation and exhalation.

Working with Difficult Emotions

The following practice is intended to give you skills to work through difficult, unpleasant emotions. There are many times throughout the day when you may notice yourself feeling an uncomfortable negative emotion. These emotional experiences may range from mild to intense. If the experiences are very uncomfortable and you're like most of us, you may have a tendency to avoid the feeling by distracting yourself with something else.

Rather than doing that, next time you notice that you're feeling bad, take a moment to study this feeling. First notice whether you are really physically threatened. If so, you may need to act quickly, and it might not be the right time for a reflective practice! However, if you're not in imminent danger, take some time to investigate the emotion.

Before you begin, remember that the purpose of this exercise is self-discovery, not self-criticism. You are observing a normal, human reaction to feeling a threat of some kind. What do you feel? Do a brief body scan. What parts of your body are feeling tense? Do you notice changes in the temperature of your body? Do you notice any sensations in your abdomen, head, neck, or shoulders? How about your extremities?

Explore these feelings and sit with them. Don't try to stop the feelings or change them; just be present for them in a curious, open-hearted, and compassionate way. Listen to the thoughts you have as you feel this emotion. Do you hear "all-or-nothing" kinds of statements? This is a signal that you have entered the refractory period in which your thoughts reinforce the feeling by not allowing contradictory information to be brought to consciousness. You might hear yourself think something like, "He always does that! He's trying to ruin my day!" See how that thought might reinforce your anger. If you can, just observe; don't engage in the negative thinking. Imagine you are hearing your thoughts from afar, as if you were listening to the radio or TV. Remember, you are not your thoughts.

For this practice, recall a time when you felt an uncomfortable emotion. For example, right now I am remembering a time when I was annoyed because a student was doing something I found incredibly irritating: She was tapping her pencil on her desk. The class was busy working and on task, and so, in retrospect, I recognize that there was really no threat at all. I was just in a particularly irritable mood. There was nothing I needed to do, but I felt very annoyed. As I recall this scenario, I notice that my head feels hot. In fact, my whole upper body is getting hot and tense. I also notice that I'm judging the student who is tapping the pencil. I'm beginning to feel dislike for her, for no real reason other than her behavior is annoying me. I hear myself thinking, "She's driving me crazy." As I observe this feeling, I notice that it begins to subside. Emotions don't last very long, and we can stay present for the entire process of becoming emotionally aroused and then observing the feeling subside.

This practice is helpful because it will enable you to learn how your emotions function. As you become familiar with the physical sensations associated with the negative emotions, you will begin to notice them during the early stages of an emotional reaction. As you learn about your emotional patterns and how your emotions affect your thoughts and perceptions, this awareness will allow you to regulate the emotion so that you can respond appropriately, rather than unconsciously reacting. It may help you to record these practices in your emotion journal.

As you record what happened to provoke your emotion, the physical sensations you notice, and the thoughts and the emotions that come up, you will gain mastery over your emotional life.

Understanding Our Scripts

As you learned in this chapter, a script is a conditioned emotional reaction to a trigger created in response to a past, emotional experience. A script is stored in your database of emotional memories that influence how you think, feel, and behave. As you practice working with difficult emotions, you will begin to notice the thought patterns that naturally arise from the feelings. These will provide clues to the scripts that underlie the emotional reaction.

Practice with difficult emotions prepares you to understand your scripts. This is a bit trickier, because your scripts are very deeply engrained in your body and mind. However, if you can explore the thought patterns that arise when you feel a strong emotion, you may notice a script behind the emotion.

For example, thinking back now to the pencil-tapping child, I notice that my thoughts about her annoying behavior are really irrational. I hear myself thinking that this girl is intentionally trying to drive me crazy. From an objective perspective, however, I realize that my thinking must be related to a script; in reality, she may not even realize she's making a noise with her pencil. Then I recall a time when my mother was irritated and punished me for similarly tapping a pencil. This experience created a program in my database that provokes a similar thought pattern when I witness a student doing the same thing.

As you keep your emotional journal, pay attention to these kinds of thought patterns. Over time, you will learn a great deal about your scripts and how to overcome them.

Chapter 4

The Power of Positivity

We've all had those miraculous moments in teaching when we're in sync with our students and things just flow. Moments when we're all in a groove, like a first-rate jazz combo. The students are buzzing with interest and enthusiasm, merrily engaged in the learning activity we worked so hard to plan. They're cooperating on the learning task, helping one another, and asking complex and interesting questions. Creative and novel responses to problems are arising spontaneously, and the thrill of learning is palpable.

These are the most rewarding moments—the times when we remember why we became a teacher. But when the stresses of teaching overwhelm us, these occasions can become rare. What if there were ways to make these learning moments come alive more consistently?

In this chapter, you will learn how to apply mindful awareness to cultivating and sustaining a positive classroom climate that promotes creativity, cooperation, higher-order thinking, problem-solving, and intrinsic motivation.

Like me, you probably became a teacher because you wanted to help children learn and grow. When a student has one of those "aha" moments and beams at us in gratitude, we feel a flood of positive emotions: joy, hope, pride, and inspiration. These positive emotions broaden our thoughts and perceptions and build the resources we need to continue our work. They reinforce our commitment to teaching.

However, sometimes we miss these delightful moments and find ourselves caught up in the pressures and demands of our work. Everyday hassles create the illusion that we have no time. They make us worry, "I have to get through this lesson or my students won't do well on the standardized tests in the spring. If they don't do well, I might lose my job." The truth is that, while the demands are real, the time we spend agonizing over daily hassles only takes time away from our ability to actually address them. When this happens, the minor aggravations of teaching overshadow and derail the real work of teaching: the artful orchestration of an engaging learning environment and effective instruction.

In this chapter, we focus on the positive, comfortable emotions that create the optimal conditions for learning. Our positive emotions are contagious. When we are feeling pleasant emotions, our students can't help but feel the same way. These positive feelings help our students broaden their thinking and build the important resources they need to be successful learners. In this chapter, you will learn how to apply mindful awareness to cultivating and sustaining positive emotions, both in your students and within yourself, and discover how this positivity can help create an emotionally rich and supportive learning environment.

Over the past two decades, scientists have discovered the power of positive emotions. We can also think of these emotions as "pleasant," because they usually are associated with pleasant thoughts and physical sensations.

Barbara Fredrickson and her colleagues (Fredrickson, 2001, 2013) developed the "broaden-and-build" theory of positive emotions. This theory proposes that positive emotions evolved to support survival by building an individual's resources through broadening the scope of awareness. Positive emotional experiences allow for a wider array of thoughts, responses, and perceptions.

Ekman identified "happy" as one of the basic universal emotions and Fredrickson explored the positive valence to uncover a wide variety of positive emotions manifested by a similar "happy" expression: the authentic smile. According to Fredrickson, the average person experiences 10 basic positive emotions on a fairly regular basis: joy, gratitude, serenity, interest, hope, pride, amusement, inspiration, awe, and love, the most commonly experienced positive emotion of them all.

In this chapter, you will learn how positive emotions change the way you think and behave. You will learn how experiencing positive emotions builds interpersonal and intrapersonal resources that make you healthier and more resilient and support your ability to build strong relationships with others. You will learn about the key emotions that generate a powerful motivation to learn and promote responses that make learning easier and more effective. Finally, you will learn how to cultivate, savor, and maintain these key positive emotions in your classroom to help your students thrive academically, socially, and emotionally.

What Is Positivity?

As you learned in the previous chapter, emotions are brief, automatic reactions to some change in the way we interpret or appraise a situation. These reactions occur within a variety of systems in our body. Our autonomic nervous system reacts first, to prepare us to respond to the situation. If we are angry, our body is prepared to fight. If we are afraid, we are prepared to freeze or run. Our hormonal and cognitive functions reinforce these reactions. Finally, our behavior changes to respond to the perceived threat. When we appraise a situation as bad for us, we experience negative (or unpleasant) emotions. When we appraise a situation as beneficial to us, we experience positive (or pleasant) emotions—that is, we experience positivity.

For many years, emotion researchers focused on negative or unpleasant emotions. As you learned in the last chapter, research supports Darwin's hypothesis that negative emotions are adaptive functions that prepare us to respond to a threatening situation by triggering us to fight, flight, or freeze. For example, when we see a snake in our path, our body reacts automatically by freezing or running the opposite direction. Our thinking reinforces our fear reaction: "Yikes! A snake! I better get out of here before it bites me!"

When emotion researchers turned their attention to positive emotions, first they applied the same theory that they had used to study negative emotions. They looked for the biological signatures for each emotion, such as changes in heart rate, skin conductance, and facial expression. Because this approach had been successful for studying negative emotions, scientists assumed it would work for the positive emotions as well.

However, they discovered that unlike negativity, positivity does not have dramatic and universal effects on the cardiovascular system. Positive emotions do not have discrete biological signatures beyond one facial expression: the authentic smile (as opposed to a fake smile). What, then, was the evolutionary benefit of having positive emotion? What do they prepare us for? How do they help us survive?

Over the course of several decades, Fredrickson and her colleagues have developed the broaden-and-build theory of positivity, testing it with a variety of inventive studies (Fredrickson, 2009). As we examine this theory and research and apply the findings to our work as teachers, you will see that when the combination of mindful awareness and positivity is artfully applied to teaching, it can transform our classrooms and significantly improve our personal and professional well-being.

The Effects of Positivity: Broaden and Build

When Fredrickson began her work, she hypothesized that positive emotions function to "undo" the physical effects of negative emotions. In several studies, Fredrickson and her colleagues confirmed this hypothesis. In one study, participants were shown an 83-second video clip of a man inching along the edge of a high-rise building (Fredrickson & Levenson, 1998). This video clip had been previously demonstrated to successfully induce the subjective experience of fear, as well as the biological signatures associated with the fear response.

After a short rest period, participants were then randomly assigned to watch one of four other video clips. One showed frolicking puppies, another ocean waves, another a screen saver, and still another a boy crying at the death of his father. These clips had been demonstrated to induce amusement, contentment, no particular emotion (neutral), and sadness, respectively. The groups shown the positive clips (puppies and waves) recovered from their previous fear reaction twice as fast as the group shown the neutral clip (screen saver), and a whopping three times faster than the group shown the sad clip (crying boy). This confirmed Fredrickson's hypothesis: The amusement and contentment "undid" the effects of the fear reaction.

While these findings were exciting, Fredrickson soon realized that the undo effect was just the tip of the iceberg. Positive emotions do much more. Negative emotions help us survive in the short term and therefore have immediate and sometimes dramatic effects on our bodies and minds. In contrast, positive emotions have more subtle, long-term effects. Positive emotions broaden our awareness and build resources that promote our resilience. Next, we will look at how these functions work and explore how they can improve our well-being. Then we'll explore the important role they can play in enhancing our teaching and classrooms.

Seeing the Forest, Not Just the Trees

To study the effects of positive emotions, scientists first needed a reliable way to trigger these emotions. They developed a variety of techniques, such as having research participants watch movies, look at photographs, or listen to music that reliably induced positive emotional states. Sometimes they used experimental situations that triggered emotions, such as giving study participants a small, unexpected gift, for example. After they induced the positive emotional state, they measured changes in the participants who received the intervention compared to those in a control condition. They eliminated extraneous variables, through testing, to ensure that it was, in fact, the emotion that created the responses that they observed.

Through such studies, scientists found that one simple effect of positive emotions is the broadening of visual attention. In one study, Fredrickson and her colleagues showed participants graphic images that could be viewed globally, based on overall shape, or more locally, based on individual details (Fredrickson & Branigan, 2005). In other words, this image contained a lot of details, but it also contained symbolic elements that were more global—communicating a unified concept that was more than the sum of its parts.

When study participants were induced to feel positive emotions, they were more likely to perceive the image from a global perspective.

When they were induced to feel negative emotions, they missed the big picture and focused on the details. They literally "couldn't see the forest for the trees." Other research has found that positive emotions literally broaden our visual search field. In other words, when we feel positive emotions, we are aware of more in our peripheral field of vision (Wadlinger & Isaacowitz, 2006).

Research has found that the attention-broadening effect of positive emotions makes people more attentive to the needs of those around them. Positive emotions increase trust and promote a variety of interpersonal bonds among people, which broadens social opportunities. Positive emotions break down "us versus them" barriers and reduce biases. This research has demonstrated that positive emotions change how we think, function, and act. Over time, these experiences build important and enduring resources that enable us to be resilient and help us thrive, both inside and outside the classroom (Fredrickson, 2009).

Building Blocks of Well-Being

The attention-broadening effect of positive emotions helps build a sense of well-being that promotes survival in the long term. Positive emotions enhance cognitive abilities and promote strong and enduring social relationships, good health, longevity, resistance to illness, agency, and efficacy. In other words, positive emotions directly contribute to improvements in our overall life satisfaction (Fredrickson, 2009).

An early emotion researcher, and one who inspired Fredrickson's work, was Alice Isen. She and her colleagues discovered that people experiencing positive emotions under certain conditions also experience very different thought patterns and behaviors (Isen, Johnson, Mertz, & Robinson, 1985). Under conditions of high motivation, positive emotion facilitates our cognitive processing. In other words, when a situation is either interesting or important to us, positive emotion helps us think better. Under these conditions, thinking becomes more efficient and thorough, yet also more flexible and innovative. Thinking is also more creative and open-minded, forward-looking, high-level, and efficient.

The implications of this research for educators are huge and far reaching. If we can consistently maintain a positive emotional climate in our classroom, and at the same time elicit interest and motivation in our students, it's likely that our teaching and our students' learning will improve dramatically. Practicing mindfulness helps us to be more aware of the subtleties of our own emotional state and the emotional climate of the classroom. And when we are mindful of our emotions and the emotional climate of our classroom, we are more likely to take actions that support and maintain that positive emotional climate. Furthermore, positive emotions are self-reinforcing. Thus, once you have mindfully and intentionally established a positive emotional climate in your classroom, research has shown that your students will help reinforce it (Marzano, Pickering & Pollock, 2011).

The positive climate will also promote prosocial behavior. For example, people experiencing positive emotions are more generous and helpful (Isen, 1987). When researchers induced positive emotions in study participants, those participants were more likely to help someone pick up dropped papers or donate to charity. Positive affect has been found to promote innovative approaches to problem-solving, conflict resolution, and team behavior in a variety of work settings. When people are induced to feel a positive emotion, they are more likely to think creatively about how to solve interpersonal difficulties and to apply perspective-taking to the situation. Finally, positivity makes people less defensive in stressful situations (Fredrickson, 2009).

Preventing Spirals of Negativity

As we saw in the last chapter, negative emotions help us survive by narrowing our perceptions to focus on actions that will ensure survival in the short term. The flood of hormones and neurotransmitters that prepare us to respond quickly to a threatening situation become toxic when high levels are maintained for long periods of time. So, recovery from these negative emotional reactions is critical to our health. However, sometimes we can get stuck in negativity spirals.

Here's an example. Let's say one of my students is particularly challenging. Most days I can manage my reactivity, but sometimes I lose it. Her behavior pushes my buttons and I overreact. Afterward, I regret my reaction. I may become self-critical and over-focus on my weakness.

Ruminative thoughts reinforce feelings of remorse and sadness. These may include thoughts like, "Why did I do that? I knew it wouldn't work. It just made things worse. Why can't I control myself?" Or I might focus on the student and ruminate in anger instead: "He's always interrupting and trying to interfere with my lessons! I wish he weren't in my class." Whether I ruminate in regret or anger, I am stewing in a broth of toxic chemicals that can impair my health over time. These negative emotions literally get under my skin and stay there.

Negative reactions can create negative cocreated spirals called power struggles. Students who push our buttons typically have problems managing their own emotion reactivity. They pose a challenge in a classroom setting because they are missing important social and emotional skills that they require to manage themselves and behave appropriately. When we overreact to these kids, we reinforce their reactivity. It is likely that they don't understand why we're upset, and they may feel that our overreaction is unfair. This leads to defensiveness or revenge, which further reinforces our perception that the student is disrespectful and intentionally trying to upset us.

Positive emotions can help us cope with such challenges by lifting us out of negativity. They are buffers against the downward spirals that negative emotions suck us into. The hallmark of resiliency is the ability to harness positive emotions when we need to counter the effects of hardship. If I can laugh off the situation and forgive myself and my students, I can quickly move on. In this way, positive emotions play an important role in building resistance to stress.

Noticing and Savoring Positivity

Remember Dan Siegel's wheel of awareness from Chapter 1? We can focus our mindful awareness toward inner and outer experience through eight senses. The hub is our awareness. The rim contains all the possible objects of awareness, that is, anything we can perceive through our eight senses: our five senses of perception; the bodily felt sense, or the embodied mind; "mindsight," or the awareness of our thinking; and the relational eight sense of attunement with others.

In Chapter 2, we explored how the wheel gives us important information about how to be more mindful of our emotions. Our internal bodily sensations give us clues about an impending emotional reaction, often before we are fully conscious of it. As I described earlier, when I get frustrated and anger is brewing in my system, I notice that my jaw becomes tense. I begin to feel "hot under the collar" and "raise my hackles"—my shoulders rise and my neck begins to stick out. I may also notice that I'm feeling "uptight" and that my fists are clenching. These physical reactions are part of the fight, flight, or freeze reaction that prepares me to react quickly to a real or imagined threat. If I notice these physical sensations, I can take action to self-regulate.

Positive emotions are much more subtle and easy to miss. Positive emotions have physical sensations reflected in our language. "Open-hearted" and "warmhearted" express the open and warm feelings we get in our chest area when we feel love, joy, and other positive emotions. To "pour your heart out" expresses the fluidity we experience when we put our positive emotions to work. Other positive emotional idioms include "jump for joy," "look on the bright side," and "have a soft spot." When we become more familiar with the physical sensations of positive emotions, we are more likely to notice that we are feeling positive and to savor the feeling.

There have been many situations where I have been flooded with positive emotions in response to my students' learning. One dramatic example occurred when I was teaching a small class of five children in a psychiatric hospital. Sammy was a five-year-old boy who had severe developmental delays and emotional problems as a result of abuse and neglect. He had language and motor delays, but he had a powerful urge to learn. My aim was to increase his vocabulary and to help him develop fine motor skills so he could hold a pencil and write.

Every day during class, I would introduce him to new words using picture cards and books. He was ravenous to learn and learned very quickly. He saw an older classmate spelling out words with plastic letters and wanted to know what they were, so I began teaching him the sounds associated with letters. Using a Montessori approach, I taught him the sounds of a few letters that can be easily combined into words. From my teaching experience, I had found that children can begin to sound out words before they know the entire alphabet, so I introduced him to the letters *c*, *a*, and *t*.

Before I actually showed him how the letters could be put together to form the word *cat*, he unexpectedly did it himself. He looked up at me and beamed, "I can write words!" He was thrilled that he had discovered the secret of making a word. It was such a delight to be part of this child's discovery—the overwhelming joy experienced by a child who had been abandoned to a crib without adequate food for most of his early childhood. I wanted to cry with joy.

As I think and write about this experience, I get goose bumps all over. My body tingles with joy. I can sit with this feeling and savor it, like a delicious piece of gourmet chocolate. When I do this, I am using positivity to build my resilience. It's like making a deposit in a bank account. Over time, small but regular deposits grow into substantial psychological and physical reserves that we can draw upon during challenging times.

You can teach your students to notice and savor positivity as well. When those moments of joy, pride, enthusiasm, interest, excitement, and love occur in your classroom, point them out. When your student beams with pride after successfully completing a challenging problem, you can say, "You really worked hard and solved the problem, and I can see you feel really proud. Doesn't that feel good? How does your body feel when you feel proud? Can you draw a picture of yourself when you are feeling proud?" Younger children have more difficulty focusing their minds on something, and drawing or writing help them with the reflective process.

You can also point out positive emotions in teaching content. There are many opportunities to learn about the power of positive emotions through poetry, literature, math, science, and social studies. You can read poetry that instills strong positive feelings and ask your students to write such poetry themselves. You can share stories that have positive emotional themes: the thrill of invention, the hope and joy associated with overcoming great odds, the awe of discovery.

You can even apply positive emotions to math content! There's a traditional Montessori elementary math activity that involves the Egyptians' discovery of the right angle. When I used to give this lesson, I would tell the children the story of how in ancient times the Nile River flooded the farmlands every year, destroying the farmer's property lines. This resulted in a lot of arguing about where one farmer's lands ended and another's began. One day a farmer discovered that if he measured a right angle from the far border of his property line, he could follow the straight line down to the river and know whose land was whose.

When I gave this lesson, I would present the story with dramatic flair, asking the children to act out the dilemma together. When we hit upon the idea of using the right angle, we would all jump for joy. Teaching content in this way not only promotes interest and engagement; it also teaches kids that there are practical reasons for learning abstract concepts. It also helps them remember the concepts. When we associate a positive emotion with information, we remember it better (Potts, Morse, Felleman, & Masters, 1986).

Common Positive Emotions and Their Uses

In this section, we will examine the causes and effects of the most common positive emotions and how they can support our teaching and our students' learning. Emotions, both positive and negative, are very contagious. By nature, most children and young adults are incredibly sensitive to the emotions in their environment. They haven't yet developed the filters adults use to protect themselves by screening out the emotions around them.

As we discovered earlier, this makes evolutionary sense. Compared to most other mammals, human infants and children are much less developed and rely more heavily, for their survival, on the adults who care for them. It follows, then, that children who are most sensitive to the emotional cues of their parents and other adults are the most likely to survive. A mother hears a threatening sound and immediately jumps up to run. The alert child who doesn't wait to be picked up and jumps into her mother's arms will be most likely to survive. Similarly, our students look to us for cues about how to feel about and respond to any given situation.

When we are mindful of the social and emotional dynamics of our classroom, we can apply this understanding to orchestrating situations that promote positivity. This will help relieve our stress and help our students become more ready to learn. By taking a moment to slow down and take stock of our own emotional tone and that of our students in a nonjudgmental way, we create the space to shift the emotional energy to serve our instructional goals and objectives.

Here's an example of why this works: It was a few weeks before standardized testing, and Mr. Dannifer was becoming anxious about how his students would perform. Each day, he became more and more edgy, and this was starting to affect his class. He was participating in our mindfulness-based professional development program for teachers, and I was his coach. During one coaching session, he told me about his growing edginess: "I'm really worried that my students won't do well on the tests coming up next week."

He asked me if I had any suggestions for improving his students' test scores. I invited him to reflect on how he was thinking and feeling about the impending tests. He said, "I have this knot in my stomach and my shoulders are tense. I notice that I'm really obsessing over the test."

"When you feel like that, how does it affect your teaching?" I asked.

He thought for a moment and said, "All this time I've been thinking that the kids were being resistant, and that's really frustrating. Now I see that it's me. I'm so stressed out over the tests that I'm becoming really impatient and crabby. The kids are resistant to my crabbiness and impatience, not the lessons."

During our discussion, Mr. Dannifer decided to let go of his worries about the test and spend some time rebuilding the emotional climate of his classroom. Later he told me that his students' behavior improved and that they did better on the test than he expected.

Next we will explore each of the most common positive emotions and learn what triggers them and what behaviors they promote. We'll see how we can best use each short-term emotion to help us maintain our stamina, our resilience, and our positive energy in the long term, and how each positive emotion can promote prosocial and learning behaviors among our students.

The Power of Love

You might be surprised to learn that love is the most common emotion (Fredrickson, 2013). In her research, Barbara Fredrickson has found that love has properties that set it apart from other positive emotions. She defines love as "positivity resonance" that occurs when two or more people share positive emotions (Fredrickson, 2013). Like all emotions, these love moments are fleeting—they are experienced entirely in the present. The more mindful we are, the more we are able to notice and savor these moments. Love is experienced by the eighth sense as represented on the wheel of awareness. By definition, it is the experience of attunement with another.

Of course, in our culture, we also define love in more durable terms, as a strong intimate commitment to another, with or without a romantic connection. For example, I can say I love my sisters and my son. I can also say I love my husband, but in a way that is more romantic. While I love them all, I wouldn't say that I share love moments, as Frederickson defines them, with all of those people at all times. Indeed, we share frequent "love moments" with many people in our lives with whom we are not so intimate. When my students and I laugh over a funny situation, or when I have an engaging discussion with a colleague and we share the excitement of discovery, we are experiencing small but important "love" moments that can make a big difference in our lives.

To cultivate and savor these important love moments, there are some important requirements. First, there needs to be a sense of safety. If we feel threatened in any way, our bodies and minds immediately respond by shutting down the possibility for feeling love. Like a castle that draws up the bridge and bars the door under siege, we go into survival mode and prepare to protect ourselves. We become wary and defensive. Our eyes scan our environment, looking to identify trouble before it gets us. This is not a condition open to a moment of shared positivity resonance!

The second precondition is physical connection or close proximity, which allows us to "sync up" or "get in tune" with another person. It's doubtful that anyone could experience love moments through social media. When we are in tune with someone, we experience the interpersonal mindfulness that I described in Chapter 1: We are on the same biological wavelength. Scientists have found that during these love moments, heart rate and other biological functions as well as gestures and facial expressions become synchronized (Fredrickson, 2013). We become, quite literally, tuned in to one another.

Eye contact is important to this experience. It helps us unpack our partner's emotions so we can better understand how he or she wants to connect. When we make eye contact, we can intuit what the other person is feeling by reading the expression on his or her face. We sense the other person's motives. The smile creates synchrony, a biochemical connection, and a sense of mutual care. Love arises when any of the other positive emotions is felt in the context of a safe relationship. In a sense, it is an amalgam of the other emotions. In this way, love reinforces the resources generated by the other emotions.

Here's an example of a real-life teacher who embodies love: Mrs. Reifler is a fifth-grade teacher at Wilcox Elementary School in East Los Angeles. She was featured in an online short video called "Shelter from the Storm." If you have a chance, search for it on Google, and you'll see an excellent example of a teacher who really loves her kids. She conveys a deep respect and a strong sense of care for her students, and they clearly feel safe in her classroom. If you watch the video, you can feel the resonance between Mrs. Reifler and her students. It's palpable, and the children's faces beam with happiness.

Love is our secret weapon. We can't easily compete with the fleeting but intense distractions of our hyperconnected, media-driven world. However, video games, iPads, email, texting, TV, and movies cannot provide the essential ingredient children really crave: connection and positive resonance with a caring adult. There is an innate human drive to connect in an authentic way and to make valuable contributions to our community. As we become more mindfully aware of opportunities to connect with our students, the positivity in our classroom will flourish.

The Effects of Other Positive Emotions

Joy

After love, the next most common emotion is joy. We feel joy when something pleasant and unexpected occurs. We may receive some good news or a pleasant surprise of some kind: a student brings us a bouquet of flowers from her garden, and another gives us the painting he made. Joy triggers the desire to participate in whatever is happening. As teachers, we know that joy is key to engagement, motivation, and experiential learning. When we enjoy teaching, our joy permeates our classroom. Our students are drawn to us because they want to share our joy.

Many of us adults have lost the spontaneous joy that children experience. Babies greet the world looking for joy. Early in development, they search out faces and smile, hoping to trigger a love moment with another. Among normally developing children, approaching the world with joy is a common experience. Children enjoy all sorts of play and learning activities. However, when they get to school, they often lose this joyful spontaneity. They get the message from their new environment that they must get serious. Thus, learning can become drudgery. It behooves us as teachers to keep finding ways to be joyful. We can do this by harnessing our students' natural tendency to enjoy new things. Of course, not all learning tasks are fun and exciting, but positive emotions like gratitude, interest, and pride can help motivate our students, even when the task at hand is challenging.

Gratitude

When we recognize and acknowledge that another person has played a role in an unexpected pleasant situation, we feel gratitude and often express thanks to that person (Park, Peterson, & Seligman,

2004). When someone thinks of our needs and helps us with kindness and consideration, it makes us want to do the same for others, and it builds in us new skills for expressing kindness and care.

Having regular experiences of gratitude is associated with healthy psychological and social functioning (McCullough, Emmons, & Tsang, 2002; Watkins, 2004). Frequently-grateful people experience more life satisfaction, vitality, and optimism. They also experience less depression and envy. Grateful people tend to be more supportive, helpful, forgiving, and empathetic toward others (McCullough et al., 2002).

There are many ways to develop a sense of gratitude. At the beginning and end of each teaching day, try counting the good things that happened that day. Studies have found a general improvement in affect after simple gratitude interventions, like a daily habit of counting blessings (Emmons & McCullough, 2003). Remembering all the things in our life for which we are grateful lifts our mood. We appreciate and value what we have, even small things. When we share our gratitude and appreciation with our students, we convey that we value them.

Several studies have demonstrated a connection between levels of gratitude and burnout among teachers and caregivers. For example, David Chan (2010) examined the relationship between dispositional gratitude and burnout among a group of high school teachers in Hong Kong. Researchers describe gratitude as "dispositional" when they are referring to a personality characteristic as opposed to a short-term response to a situation, or "situational gratitude."

As we have already discussed, burnout involves three primary dimensions: emotional exhaustion, depersonalization, and the lack of a sense of personal accomplishment or efficacy. Chan found that teachers who were naturally more grateful were also less burned out. He found a strong negative correlation between gratitude and emotional exhaustion and depersonalization. He found a strong positive correlation between gratitude and personal accomplishment.

Chan also tested an intervention designed to promote a sense of gratitude among teachers. The gratitude intervention increased satisfaction with life and positive affect, especially among the teachers who were low on dispositional gratitude. This suggests that if teachers practice gratitude on a regular basis, they may improve their overall well-being and prevent burnout, especially if they are among those who find it difficult to feel gratitude.

When we model gratitude for our students, it teaches them gratitude. Appreciation can become an important value in our classrooms. When I was teaching kindergarten, we had a ritual of sharing gratitude and appreciation with one another. I put a very special pink notebook in a heart-shaped basket and called it the "gratitude basket." I encouraged my students to write little notes of thanks and appreciation to one another using the basket. Sometimes I would use the basket to show my appreciation for a student who had helped me in some way. This activity encouraged the children to think about and show appreciation to one another. Little did they know it was also a writing activity!

Practicing gratitude may also enhance youth development in important ways, motivating young people to give back to their community and make important contributions to the world. One study involving 700 middle school students found that gratitude and social integration enriched one another. In other words, when a student felt gratitude, he or she would consequently feel more socially integrated, which would lead to greater and more frequent feelings of gratitude (Froh, Bono, & Emmons, 2010). Thus, gratitude may have the power to initiate upward spirals toward greater emotional and social well-being and positive youth development.

Froh and his colleagues (Froh & Bono, 2011) have developed a variety of activities to promote gratitude and grateful thinking among children and youth. These activities can easily be integrated into your teaching. For example, ask your students to write down five things each day for which they are grateful. Another idea is to ask students to write a letter to a benefactor whom they have never properly thanked and to read the letter to him or her in person (Froh, Kashdan, Ozimkowski, & Miller, 2009).

Interest

Interest arises when we are faced with novelty in a way that is safe—something mysterious or challenging but not too threatening or overwhelming. Interest triggers the urge to explore and learn, building lifelong skills. It's easy to see that the durable resources interest creates are the skills we learn when we engage in experiential learning.

When I taught preschool, I had a special velvet bag where I hid things related to my lessons that I wanted to show to my students. The bag was really special: It was made of purple velvet trimmed with gold. When I brought out the special bag, it would immediately draw their interest and their full attention. Finding small ways like this to stimulate interest can help motivate your students to engage and persist in learning activities.

Interest is a powerful motivator for learning, even when the task is difficult or arduous. For example, for my master's thesis I developed an early childhood anatomy curriculum and tested it with my class. Knowing how much many young children love Halloween, I decided to teach the anatomy of the skeleton in October. At a novelty store, I bought two skeleton decorations made of cardboard. The bones were connected with grommets. I laminated one skeleton to a piece of cardboard. I took the other skeleton apart and put the pieces in a container, creating a puzzle. I showed the children how to match the bones. They loved it. They were so interested in this activity that they asked me to teach them the names of the bones. To learn the names, we played Simon Says (e.g., "Simon says touch your patella") and sang "Skull, Clavicle, Patella, and Phalanges" to the tune of "Head, Shoulders, Knees, and Toes." To my surprise, soon my whole class had memorized the technical names of the major bones. If I hadn't encouraged and capitalized on their strong interest, I doubt I could have so easily taught this challenging material!

Hope

Hope is unique in that it typically arises under circumstances of threat. We may fear the worst but hope for things to improve. When we feel hopeful, we work toward a resolution by applying our creativity and inventiveness to turn things around. This builds optimism and resilience to adversity.

Cultivating a hopeful attitude around our students is critical in today's classroom. Expressing hope on a regular basis can prevent student discouragement and "learned helplessness." When parents and teachers do too much for a child, it sends the message that the child cannot do things for himself or herself. Most of the time we do this quite unintentionally. We're in a hurry and can't wait for Mia to put her shoes on, even though she can. We are unsure how much freedom to give our teen, so we give him too many restrictions. Children and youths need us to believe in them. They need a sense of hope that they can succeed and thrive.

Children and youths also need us to convey a sense of hope about the condition of our world today. Our students are exposed to distressing news about the many problems we face, such as climactic change, war, violence, and poverty. It is important that we convey that we are hopeful that human beings have the capacity to overcome these challenges and threats. Our hopefulness may help prevent our students from becoming depressed and overwhelmed.

Pride

We feel pride when we can take credit for an outcome that is valued by our society or community—that is, when we accomplish an important goal. When we or our students feel pride, we imagine other, bigger goals we might accomplish. This builds the motivation to achieve bigger and better things.

When we instill a sense of pride in our students, we help motivate them to take on challenges. We help them learn that with persistence, we can accomplish the most difficult tasks. We also help our students generate their own sense of intrinsic pride, rather than inculcate the need to please us and make us proud. Intrinsic pride has the power to motivate us to accomplish great things and to promote upward spirals of determination and perseverance.

Teachers can instill pride in their students through praise, complements, and expressions of appreciation. However, Carol Dweck (2007) has found that that the way we express these is very important. When a student accomplishes a difficult task, be sure to acknowledge their hard work. For example, you could say, "Wow, you finished that problem! I know it was difficult, but you worked very hard and accomplished it!" However, Dweck has found that empty praise that focuses on intelligence, talent, or ability—such as, "Wow, you're really smart!" "You have natural talent!" or "What a good student you are!"—can be harmful to students because it encourages a fixed mindset. Empty praise conveys the message that characteristics such as intelligence are fixed and unchangeable. It gives the message that the child needs to be smart, talented, and good all the time, which can lead to a fear of failure. On the other hand, by praising their effort, we send a message that they can accomplish anything with persistence and hard work. This type of praise promotes a growth mindset, the recognition that intelligence and other personal characteristics can be intentionally developed through conscious effort.

Generating and Savoring Positivity

A few years ago, a YouTube video titled "Merci!" went viral on Facebook. As the video begins, commuters are sitting on a train. They appear bored, sleepy, suspicious or distracted. A man who boards the train is trying to stifle a chuckle. After a while, he can no longer hold it back and begins to laugh out loud. At first the other passengers look around in concern, but quickly they are all chuckling along with him. Soon the whole rail car is roaring with laughter. If you haven't seen this video, you can likely find it by searching "laughter on a train" and "Merci!" As an experiment, watch the video and see how long it takes before you are laughing and smiling.

Fredrickson and others who research positive emotions have found that it's quite easy to spark positive emotional responses in most people. Paul Ekman (2007b) discovered that feeling happy is as easy as putting a smile on your face. When you engage the smiling muscles around your mouth and eyes, for whatever reason, there's a tendency to report that you feel happier. Putting a smile on your face can also reduce stress (Kraft & Pressman, 2012). If you're around people who are happy, it's very difficult not to join in their glee. Happiness is truly contagious.

This phenomenon has been demonstrated in several clever studies. One involved an experimental manipulation that asked participants to use a pencil in their mouths in such a way that smiling was required to perform the task (Soussignan, 2002). The participants were told that the study was designed to test alternative approaches to responding to questions for people who couldn't use their hands. While they held the pencils in their mouths, they watched several video clips designed to induce positive, negative, or neutral emotional responses. The participants who were randomly assigned to the smile condition rated the positive film clips more highly positive than the participants in the other conditions.

Another interesting study looked at the emotional reactions of people who had been injected with Botox (Davis, Senghas, Brandt, & Ochsner, 2010). Botox reduces the appearance of wrinkles by paralyzing facial muscles, making it difficult to smile. The researchers compared one group of participants who underwent Botox injections to a control group who received a different kind of injection that reduces the appearance of wrinkles but doesn't cause paralysis. Both groups were shown emotionally provocative video clips before and after the injections. Compared to controls, the Botox participants reported a significant decrease in the intensity of the emotional experience, especially in response to mildly positive video clips. These studies confirm Ekman's hypothesis that facial expressions contribute to real emotional experience.

Just think about what a difference your smiling face can make to your students' enjoyment of school. Taking a moment to share a smile with each student as you greet them in the morning can set the emotional tone for the day. You can also notice and point out moments of positive emotions to your students. For example, you may be reading a book about a character who receives a surprise gift. Before you continue the story, you can stop and ask them, "How do you think he felt when he received the gift?"

You can explore these feelings more by asking your students to write about a time when, like the character, they were surprised by a gift or a thoughtful gesture. You can ask them to describe what happened but also to remember how they felt and describe this too. Remembering an emotionally charged situation can reignite old feelings.

Describing good feelings can also help us notice them better the next time so that we can savor our positivity the same way we might slowly enjoy an exceptional piece of chocolate. Next time you are feeling a positive emotion, take a moment to really experience it in all its dimensions. What sensations do you feel? In what parts of your body? How would you describe these sensations? Notice how the emotion changes your thoughts and perception of whatever is happening around you. Then, take some time to savor this experience. Allow the good feelings to spread. Sit with the feeling and let it permeate your entire being. Fredrickson has found that we can improve our overall well-being by regularly noticing and savoring our positive emotions (Fredrickson, 2009).

Positivity and Classroom Climate

As we have discussed, children are naturally attracted to positive emotions. They need positivity like they need food and water. Love and the other positive emotions build important resources that last a lifetime. Through a strong, loving relationship with their parents, teachers, and other caregivers, children build all the important resources they need to thrive in the social domain (Selman, 2003).

The literature supporting this contention is vast. A child's secure attachment with his or her parents and/or caregivers is associated with the development of executive functions (Bernier, Carlson, & Whipple, 2010); "self-other" awareness (Trevarthen & Aitken, 2001); reflective ability and self-organization (Fonagy & Target, 1997); emotional expressiveness and communication (Tronick, 1989); and shared attention, which sets the stage for social cognition (Bruner, 1995). It has also been associated with the development of healthy peer relationships (Keller, Spieker, & Gilchrist, 2005), perspective taking (Selman, 1980), and forgiveness (Lawler-Row, Younger, Piferi, & Jones, 2006). Feeling loved and cared for supports children's resilience and protects them from mental health problems as they grow and develop (Keller et al., 2005).

Attachment theory proposes that an infant needs to develop a secure relationship with at least one primary caregiver for successful social and emotional development. This caregiver is typically a parent; however, other adults, especially teachers, can also fulfill this role with children to some degree as they grow and develop.

Applying attachment theory to the teacher–student relationship, scientists have demonstrated that a teacher's supportive relationship with a student can make an important contribution to that student's success. Indeed, we teachers make critical and long-lasting contributions to our students' social and emotional development (Birch & Ladd, 1998; Hamre & Pianta, 2001, 2006; Murray & Greenberg, 2000; Pedersen, Faucher, & Eaton, 1978; Pianta, Hamre, & Stuhlman, 2003).

We influence our students constantly, through the way we relate, teach, and model social and emotional concepts and manage the social and emotional dynamics of the classroom. Truly supportive relationships with caregivers are characterized by trust, responsiveness, and involvement. When teachers are supportive, they provide students with a sense of connection with the school environment and the security to explore new ideas and take risks—both of which are fundamental to learning (Mitchell-Copeland, Denham, & DeMulder, 1997; Murray & Greenberg, 2000; Watson, 2003).

Developing supportive relationships with students contributes to a healthy school and classroom climate, students' connection to the school, and important academic and socioemotional outcomes (Abbott et al., 1998; Darling-Hammond, Ancess, & Ort, 2002; Gambone, Klem, & Connell, 2002; McNeely, Nonnemaker, & Blum, 2002; Osher et al., 2007), and it also reduces problem behavior. Conducting a meta-analysis of over 100 studies, Marzano, Marzano, and Pickering (2003) discovered that teachers who had high-quality relationships with their students had 31% fewer behavior problems over the school year than teachers who did not.

When our students feel they have our support, they show higher levels of interest and motivation (Wentzel, 1998). Our expectations of our students' achievement influences how we engage with them. If we expect them to succeed, they are more likely to perceive themselves as people who are capable of succeeding (Jussim & Harber, 2005).

Studies of children across all age ranges have demonstrated that positive emotions build the intellectual resources kids need to succeed in school and throughout life. In several studies, researchers induced positive states and found that they resulted in faster learning and better intellectual performance than neutral or negative states did (Bryan & Bryan, 1991; Bryan, Mathur, & Sullivan, 1996; Masters, Barden, & Ford, 1979). Positive emotional states also improve working memory, a brain function critical to academic success (Potts et al., 1986).

When children are happy, they are more able to successfully engage in complex cognitive functions that require flexibility and integration, such as word association and memory, creativity, and problem-solving. Overall, studies involving children have shown that positive emotion facilitates memory, learning, and prosocial behavior, and that negative emotions impair these functions.

Creating and Sustaining a Positive Classroom

In this chapter, you learned about the power of positive emotions and how you can mindfully apply these emotions to orchestrate the optimal conditions for learning. These positive feelings will help your students broaden their awareness and build the resources they most need to be successful learners. By applying mindful awareness, you can become more conscious of the social and emotional climate in your classroom, and you can apply simple strategies to foster the positive dynamics that best stimulate your particular students' interest, attention, and motivation.

Start by bringing a greater intentionality to your classroom climate, purposefully setting the tone from moment to moment. As you start the class, take time to personally greet each of your students by getting down to their eye level and welcoming them by name. Remember details that are important to them. Notice the clothes they are wearing and give them a compliment if it's appropriate. As you do this, you will notice that your students will become your allies. If someone becomes disruptive, they will exert their peer pressure to help you get the class back on track.

Skill-Building Practices

In the preceding sections, you have learned about the amazing power of positivity. Now you can work on ways to generate and sustain positivity. You may be surprised to learn that there are some very easy ways to cultivate positive emotions within yourself. As you apply mindfulness to fully experiencing your emotions, you will also learn to notice and savor the moments of positivity that you may often overlook. By following a few simple steps, you can teach yourself to "look on the bright side."

Generating and Savoring Positivity

When you feel the need to cultivate positivity, you can focus your attention on your memories of positive experiences. As a simple exercise, sit comfortably and recall a time when you felt very joyful. Most likely you have many experiences you can draw from, but for this exercise, try to focus on just one. (If nothing comes to mind, think about something that you would like to have happen—something that would make you joyful.) Spend some time recalling the details of this experience. Where were you? Who were you with? Can you recall the weather? The sounds and smells? Try to gather as many details about the experience as you can. (If you are working with something imaginary, bring to mind as much detail about the imagined situation as possible.)

Once you feel you have enough details to generate a rich experience of the incident, take a moment and imagine you are stepping into this particular time and place, as if you were stepping into a movie. Now notice how you feel. Notice the sensations in your body. Where do you feel the joy? Do you notice any change in temperature or color? As you settle into savoring this joyful feeling, see if you can intensify it just a little bit. Imagine your joyful feeling has a dial controller and turn it up slightly. Then try turning it down a bit. Turn the dial up and down until the feeling of joy is just right, and then spend as long as you wish simply savoring the joy.

When you're finished, notice that the joy you experienced came from inside of you and that it wasn't dependent upon anything external. Recognize that you have the capacity to generate and savor positive feelings whenever you need to. You can practice this same savoring exercise for any other positive emotion you may need at a particular moment: gratitude, serenity, interest, hope, pride, amusement, inspiration, awe, love.

Positivity Journal

Keep a journal in which you write down the pleasant feelings you've experienced each day. Keeping a record of your positive experiences will build gratitude and appreciation for how much goodness you have in your life. When you take time to notice a student's smile or a parent's goodwill, you will begin to feel that your life is full of blessings. Tailor your journal to fit your emotional needs. For instance, if you notice that you're growing a chip on your shoulder at work, you can practice gratitude, and every day you can spend a few minutes reflecting in your journal on reasons you have to be grateful. If you're feeling down, you can spend time recalling and writing about joyful times.

Centering

Sometimes I find that my energy is scattered and it really helps me to spend a few minutes getting centered. Here's a simple technique to gather your energy and attention to help you feel more grounded and centered in the present. Stand with your feet about shoulder width and relax your knees, don't lock them. Bring your attention to a point in your abdomen about two inches below your navel and about an inch into your body. This is the actual center of gravity of your body. Focusing attention on this point is used in most martial arts to gather and generate vital energy. Spend a few minutes focusing on this point and feeling gravity connecting your body to the earth. This is a practice you can do inconspicuously any time you feel the need.

Mindful Walking

Another way to practice mindful awareness is to focus your attention on the act of walking. When you first start practicing mindful walking, find a place where you can walk in a straight line comfortably for at least five feet. Before you begin to walk, spend a few minutes getting centered by following the instructions above. When you feel ready, begin to walk slowly, one step at a time. As you walk, bring your focused attention to the soles of your feet. Notice as your weight shifts from the heel to the ball of the foot. Notice the sensation of the foot being lifted off the ground and the feeling of the heel of the other foot beginning the next step as it touches the ground. As you continue walking, keep your focused attention on the soles of your feet. If your mind wanders, as we did during breath awareness practice, notice that your mind has wandered and bring your attention back to the soles of your feet.

After you have practiced mindful walking this way for a few sessions, you can begin to increase the speed of your steps to a more normal pace. However, if you find you begin to lose your focus, slow down again. Find a pace that works well for you. Over time you can bring focused attention to your walking during your normal everyday activities.

Chapter 5

The Heart of Teaching

As we saw in the last chapter, our "secret weapon" is our warm, open heart and our caring presence. We can't compete with the constant stream of digital entertainment that our students are exposed to all day. However, we have something that no multimedia can offer but kids crave: the attention of a caring, warmhearted adult.

You have learned how to practice being mindfully aware of your own thoughts and feelings so that you can be fully present for your students. You have learned about positive and negative emotions—how they influence teaching and learning and how you can master them to improve your classroom environment and your relationships with your students. In this chapter, you will bring together all the skills and knowledge you have learned thus far in this book and apply them to creating a warmhearted classroom environment.

Acquiring this knowledge and mastering these skills creates the conditions for the emergence of compassion: recognizing the suffering of others, noticing and regulating your own thoughts and feelings in response to that suffering, cultivating the motivation to help, and taking wise action to help alleviate suffering where you can.

As we have discussed, the need to connect to a group of people who care for and respect one another has strong evolutionary roots. Today we may not need human connection as much to survive physically, we still need it to survive and thrive psychologically. Indeed, it could be argued that feeling connected to others and the desire to make a valuable contribution to our community is what motivates most human behavior (Glasser, 1998).

When I greet each student individually, I instill a sense of belonging. It sends the message that I notice my students and that I'm glad to be with them. Unifying classroom rituals such as morning circle or meeting time can promote a sense of belonging as the day begins. We can introduce simple mindfulness exercises as a daily ritual to help students feel connected to one another, reduce the stress of transitioning from home to school, and prepare their minds and bodies to learn. Some of these activities can be found at the end of this chapter and the next one.

We can motivate our students by providing opportunities to make valuable contributions to the classroom community—for example, by giving each student a classroom job. By skillfully using recognition and appreciation, we can reinforce students' feelings of pride and commitment to building a supportive community together. When we begin the school year by building this sense of community, it becomes a tool for reinforcing prosocial behavior.

We've explored how, as we develop greater awareness, a deeper understanding of our students begins to grow and we learn to recognize that what we once considered intentional misbehavior may be a sign of suffering. Perhaps Sheila can't attend to the lesson because she had no sleep. Her parents were fighting loudly all night, keeping her awake and worried. Stephan may be irritable because he's had no breakfast.

When we recognize our students' suffering and see them for who they really are, we offer ourselves to them as a compassionate witness. The expression of compassion forges deep human connections. Showing our students that we care and cultivating a culture of care and compassion in our classroom can dramatically improve their engagement and readiness to learn. It's not that we overlook Sheila's lack of focus or Stephen's irritability, but we show understanding and provide support rather than judging, criticizing, or simply ignoring.

To begin, we will investigate how we care for ourselves, because keeping our hearts warm and open requires that we remember to care for ourselves first. Next we will examine simple strategies for teaching care and reinforcing caring behavior among our students. We will also explore how we improve our listening skills. Finally, we will talk about compassion and how to generate compassion for those students and their families who are experiencing deep pain and suffering. We will end the chapter with two practices and two activities designed to help you develop and employ these skills.

Caring for Ourselves

Every time we board an airplane, the flight attendant demonstrates how to put on the oxygen mask in case the cabin pressure falls. We are instructed to put on our own mask before helping someone else, such as a child who needs our assistance. This is because if we don't take care of ourselves first, we might pass out from lack of oxygen before we have a chance to help. This philosophy applies to all caring activities. If we don't do a good job of caring for our own needs, we will have difficulty keeping up with the needs of others.

I have found that caring for myself is much more difficult than caring for others. I am often blind to my own needs and tend to overlook important aspects of my self-care. When I am not taking care of myself well, I start to feel overwhelmed and can become bitter and resentful.

Practicing mindfulness has helped me recognize this tendency by observing the scripts that creep into my mind: "No one appreciates all I do for them. No one cares about me." When I'm in a sour mood, my caregiving takes on a quality of martyrdom and it's easy to slip into guilt trips and blame. Once I began to realize what I was doing, I started to make self-care a priority. Now, when I notice myself feeling unappreciated, I ask myself, "What do I need?"

Over the years, I have found that I am not alone; this tendency to overlook self-care is common among teachers and other caregivers.

When I introduce the importance of self-care to groups of teachers in a mindfulness workshop, they often say, "But I don't have any time to take care of myself." The fact of the matter is that we have to make self-care a priority and set aside time for self-care activities. It takes time, self-awareness, and practice to find the balance of activities that best promotes our personal growth and development. Mindfulness can help us notice when we're out of balance.

I can reach for my smartphone and check my email first thing in the morning, or I can start my day with a 15- or 20-minute mindful awareness practice. Sometimes the emails trigger a sense of urgency, prompting me to think, "I have so much to do today!" But when I choose to practice mindful awareness, I start the day with a calm and focused mind instead.

It helps to spend some time assessing how we are spending our time and replace activities that are draining our energy with activities that nurture us. There are four primary domains of personal development that require self-care: physical, emotional, intellectual, and spiritual. The physical domain refers to our physical health and well-being. Caring for ourselves in this domain involves participating in physical activity to strengthen our body and improve our stamina. It involves eating right and getting enough sleep. Through practicing mindfulness, I have become very aware of how what I eat affects my well-being. I'm also very aware of the difference in my functioning when I've had enough sleep as opposed to times when I haven't. By mindfully monitoring my physical body and noticing my energy level, I can be sure to care for it properly.

The emotional domain refers to emotional health and well-being. We care for ourselves emotionally when we engage in activities that promote positive emotions, such as reading an inspirational book, laughing with friends, attending a concert or a game, or enjoying the company of our friends and family. Applying mindful awareness to our emotional state helps us recognize when our emotional life needs attention. We can notice ourselves becoming grumpy or blue and consciously choose to do something emotionally uplifting rather than wallowing in our bad mood.

The intellectual domain refers to our cognitive skills, our knowledge base, and our personal interests. Activities that nurture our intellectual life include doing puzzles and playing games for enjoyment, reading books that are intellectually challenging, and studying new subject matter, such as learning a language or taking a college course to learn something new.

The spiritual domain refers to our sense of meaning and connectedness to something greater than ourselves. While it includes any religious or spiritual beliefs we may have, it can also be experienced as a secular philosophical approach to what gives our life meaning—how we con-ceptualize our connection to and place in the larger world. Activities that nurture our spiritual life can include attending religious services, but can also involve any activities that instill a sense of meaning in our lives, such as finding awe in a gorgeous sunset, reading inspirational poetry, or singing in a choir. Practicing mindfulness is a powerful way to nurture our spiritual development in a secular way because it can provide access to direct spiritual experiences of meaningfulness and interdependence (Jennings, 2008).

While we all need nurture and self-care in these four domains, everyone has her or his own way of interpreting and filling these needs. Take a moment to complete the self-care self-assessment at the end of this chapter, which will help you learn about how you are cur-rently taking care of your needs and nurturing yourself across these four domains.

Once you complete the self-care assessment, complete the self-care plan using the form that follows so you can ensure that your needs are met. As you develop this plan, be careful not to overdo it. You only have so many hours in the day. When I plan self-care strategies, I have a tendency to be overly ambitious and unrealistic. For example, I might decide that I'll walk the 2 miles to work every day. But then it rains and I think that I'd prefer to drive rather than walk in the rain, and ultimately I feel bad and unmotivated because I haven't kept my commitment and I feel like giving up. In the end, I realize that maybe walking every day is unrealistic and that it's more about keeping active than walking a specific number of miles at a certain time of day.

When making a self-care plan, it helps to build in simple little self-care routines throughout the day. For example, when I'm in the shower, I take a moment to remember my intention for the day. Some teachers I know will take a moment in their car before they depart for work to consider and set their daily intention. If you regularly take public transportation, spending a few minutes doing breath awareness when you're waiting for the subway or in transit is a great way to give yourself some caring attention.

I used to spend most of my lunch "half-hours" doing catch-up work at my desk. I realized that I wasn't giving myself a break, so I created a new routine for myself. Weather permitting, I took my lunch to a nearby park, sat on a picnic bench, and enjoyed my lunch. I brought mindfulness into my eating, tasting each morsel and savoring each bite. I began to put more attention into the preparation of my lunches and looked forward to this time alone in the park. Doing this as much as possible made a dramatic improvement in the quality of my afternoon class session. I was able to give up the afternoon coffee that was getting me through the end of the day, and as a result I slept much better as well.

How Caring Helps Us

A growing body of research is demonstrating that by regularly engaging in practices that help us generate a sense of care and compassion for others, we can improve our own lives. Loving-kindness and compassion meditation practices (also called metta) are designed to orient us toward the cultivation of unconditional care and compassion for others. Research on these practices suggests that they increase positive and decrease negative emotional states (Hofmann, Grossman, & Hinton, 2011).

Furthermore, compassion practices may reduce stress and improve the body's immune response (Pace et al., 2009), and brain imaging studies have found that they may enhance brain functions in areas associated with emotional processing and empathy (Lutz, Brefczynski-Lewis, Johnstone, & Davidson, 2008). These practices have been used successfully in therapeutic settings to reduce depression, anxiety, and marital conflict and improve anger management (Hofmann et al., 2011).

One such practice that we call "caring practice" (basically another name for the traditional *metta* practice) can be found in the skill-building practices section of this chapter. This practice involves generating feelings of care for ourselves and others. As we generate feelings of care and kindness, we feel a warmth and openness in our heart. Taking time to do this practice may help us build the resilience we need to care for others on a regular basis. By generating feelings of care and kindness toward ourselves and others, we become habituated to this state and find that it comes to us more frequently. After a while, the practice becomes easier and more enjoyable and rewarding. It is a particularly useful practice when we are dealing with troubling interpersonal difficulties because it helps us keep our hearts open to others, even when we find their behavior challenging.

Ms. Winter, a teacher in one of my mindfulness workshops, once shared how caring practice helped her deal with her fear of a student's mother who had been expressing anger and hostility over her daughter's failing grades. Dreading the upcoming parent conference when she would have to face this parent alone, Ms. Winter decided to try engaging in caring practice, with this mother in mind, during the week before the conference. As a result of practicing caring, Ms. Winter began to notice that her fear was subsiding. She realized that the mother was worried about her daughter and that her anger was an expression of this concern, not personally directed at her. With this perspective in mind, Ms. Winter found it easy to generate feelings of care and kindness for this mother.

When the time for the conference finally arrived, Ms. Winter was calm and open-hearted. She listened mindfully to the mother and acknowledged her concern. The mother was very responsive, and together they worked out a plan to help the student improve her grades. This is an example of how a regular caring practice can improve our well-being and give us the inner strength and resilience to help others.

Ethics of Care

Once we are well on our way toward taking good care of ourselves, we can focus on how we care for others. The fact is, every single day we can and do make incredibly valuable contributions to the lives of individual students and to society as a whole. I believe that it's important to keep this altruistic vision alive. It's what keeps us going to work day after day. It helps us keep the spark of enthusiasm alive, our hearts warm, and our minds open. Ultimately, it will prevent us from burning out and becoming harsh and cynical.

However, caring can get complicated. It helps if we can understand the parameters of caring within the context of our professional role as a teacher. When I first started teaching, I was buoyed by idealism. I held a deep sense of care and concern for my students and was intensely committed to doing my best to meet their needs. However, after some time, this enthusiasm began to erode and I found that my impulse to care was being torn by conflicting needs: the conflicts between individual and group needs, among individuals and their needs, and between individual needs and institutional needs (not to mention the conflict between my needs and all these other needs!).

As teachers, we face these conflicting needs all the time. One student needs more time to complete an activity when the rest of the class needs to move on to the next step in the learning process. Two students argue over who gets to use the computer first. One student with a severe math phobia is afraid to take the annual standardized test, and because of institutional demands, we can't provide her with the support she needs: stress-free opportunities to work.

Overwhelmed by this plethora of conflicting needs, I forgot about my own needs. Over time, trying to manage these conflicts wore me out. In retrospect, I realize that I didn't understand the ethics of care. My tendency was to completely take on the burden of every need (except my own!), and when I couldn't meet all those needs, to feel overwhelmed, frustrated, and discouraged.

Sometimes when we feel overwhelmed by our students' needs, we may tend to dismiss them, especially if their needs conflict with the institutional needs we feel professionally responsible for fulfilling. Mindfulness can help us recognize when we are beginning to slip into this tendency and maintain the composure we need to accept the limitations of our role.

To care does not require that we meet every need that we recognize in others. Nel Noddings, emeritus professor of education at Stanford University, is an educational philosopher who has focused a great deal of attention on the ethics of care. According to Noddings (2003), care ethics decree that whether we can meet a student's needs or not, we can always respond in a way that honors our relationship with that student. Clearly, we cannot meet every individual need. However, we can always meet the need for relationship. When we cannot meet a specific need, we can communicate this in a way that still honors the need and supports the relationship.

For example, sometimes our students have problems that interfere with their ability to function in school. For a whole week Derek came to school with a chip on his shoulder. Whenever I greeted him, he gave me a sour look, and he was hostile to other students who tried to talk to him during lunch or recess. When it was time for math, he just sat there in front of his work looking glum.

"Do you need some help?" I asked.

"I hate math. I can't do it."

As he spoke, I noticed the bitterness in his voice, but also resignation. I took a deep breath. "Math can be challenging. I find it especially difficult when I'm feeling down."

He looked up at me with surprise on his face, as if he had expected a reprimand. "Yeah, I guess I'm having a hard time."

I offered to talk with him some more during recess. As he lingered in the classroom after the rest of the students had left the room, he looked down at his feet.

"Let's have a seat and talk," I said.

When I suspected that troubles at home were at the root of the problem, I decided to begin by sharing my own experience, hoping that it would help him open up. "When I was a kid, I found it really difficult to focus on school work when I was having trouble at home."

"My mom and dad are getting a divorce."

I sat quietly for a minute. "I'm sorry. I know that can be really hard."

We sat together quietly for a few minutes. While I couldn't meet his need for an intact family, I could meet his need for a caring relationship. I could feel that my compassionate presence was making a difference. As I sat, I brought my mindful awareness to the experience. I observed my urge to tell him that everything was going to be all right or to find a way to distract him from his feelings, but that would have felt dismissive. I knew that the best thing I could do for him was to be fully present and to give him my caring attention.

After some time, I said, "I know it's difficult to focus on school when things at home are troubling you. Just let me know when you need a break, and I can find something else for you to do."

He never took me up on this offer. After a day or two, his mood began to lift and he was able to better focus on his school work. I believe that just having the opportunity to share what was going on at home and to have a caring adult listen and understand helped him to move on.

Personal versus Institutional Needs

Mindfulness can help us sort out the way we perceive our students' needs. Most of us work hard to help our students achieve academically, because this is a need assumed by society and the school institution and therefore one demanded by our professional role. However, academic achievement is not necessarily an expressed need. In other words, the child and her or his parents may not prioritize this need in the same way that the institution does.

The school institution was created to fulfill a societal need for an educated public based upon certain assumptions about what will best prepare them for the future (e.g., the Common Core). Society cares about children's learning. Noddings (2010) calls this "virtue caring," because in our culture it is virtuous to care about the education of young children. However, virtue caring does not require the establishment of a caring relationship. It assumes responsibility for the recognition of need rather than being open and responsive to the needs an individual actually expresses. It communicates, "We know what's best for you, even if you don't."

When the needs a student expresses do not align with institutionally determined needs, we may hesitate to respond and may actually try to convince the child and her or his parents that the needs are illegitimate. Noddings (2005a) notes that when we approach a situation in this way, our efforts to care can misfire, and students who need a caring relationship the most often suffer the most.

For example, I once worked in a California district with a large number of Latino immigrants, most of whom were from Mexico. Many of their parents were migrant workers, and once the harvest was over in the late fall, many of them returned to Mexico to be with their extended families. Typically students and their parents left in late November or early December, missing several weeks of school before the winter holiday break. In this case, the students' need to maintain connections with their culture and extended family conflicted with the institutional need for regular school attendance.

The teachers and administrators often expressed dismay and annoyance. "How can we keep these kids on track academically when they go off to Mexico so early and miss so many days of school?" While this attitude is understandable, it was dismissive of the students' needs and showed little understanding for these families who had uprooted themselves from their extended families and their culture to make a better living. It was obvious that the parents were consciously choosing to prioritize maintaining family connections over school.

The school personnel did their best to convince the parents and their children that their need to go to Mexico so early was not legitimate because it conflicted with the school's need for attendance. The school valued the students' attendance and academic achievement over their connection with their home country and extended family. As a result, conflict arose between the school and the families and the children didn't get the support they needed to make the best of a difficult situation. They often returned feeling more distant and alienated from their teachers and peers. In this situation, it would have been more helpful to give the students extended homework to do when they were away than it was to complain and create tension with the parents.

Mindfulness can help us recognize and appreciate others' values and perspectives. It helps us suspend our tendency to judge so that we can be more helpful and caring. We can recognize the needs actually being expressed by our students and their families, rather than clinging to the institutional needs that seem to take precedence. This helps us build strong relationships with our students and their families because they know that we are listening and that we truly care about and respect their perspectives.

Mindful Listening

An important dimension of care involves the way we listen. In order to respond with care, we need to be attentive, listen with an open mind, and be receptive to our students and their families so we can under-stand and empathize with their experience and recognize their needs. This involves bringing mindful awareness to the act of listening. The listening process helps us attune to another. This is the interpersonal dimension of mindfulness and the eighth sense on the wheel of aware-ness that we looked at in Chapter 1.

As we listen, we gather our full attention and notice both the inter-nal and external dimensions of our experience. We notice the sound of the other person's voice—the tone, the volume, and so forth. We notice the other's facial expressions, and we listen to her or his words without automatically judging them and reacting to them. At the same time we notice our internal experience—our thoughts and feelings—without judgment.

We can practice mindful listening throughout the day. We can do simple things, such as taking a brief moment to give a student our full attention. We can get down to her or his level and make eye contact when the student is speaking. This communicates that we care about our students and that what they have to say is important. When we give our students our full, open-hearted, nonjudgmental attention, we are more likely to hear the needs they are expressing, rather than unconsciously imposing our own ideas (or the institution's ideas) of what the student should need.

I used to assume that caring for others required solving their prob-lems and fixing things for them. However, this tendency disconnected me from the present moment. Rather than truly listening and giving the other person my full attention, my thoughts would wander to the cause of their problem and how to fix it. I also noticed that this ten-dency to figure out and fix others' problems arose from my deep dis-comfort with simply being with a person who was suffering.

Being deeply and mindfully listened to is an incredibly powerful experience and is often all that another requires. Returning to the story I told earlier in this chapter, when I invited Derek to speak with me during recess, I focused my intention on listening to him mindfully. When Derek told me that his parents were getting a divorce, I noticed the sadness in his voice and posture. As I empathized with him, I began to feel very sad too. I observed my tendency to want to tell him that everything would be okay and to distract us both from this sadness. But when I realized that that would be dismissive, I sat mindfully with the sadness until it dissolved and then brought my full attention to him, silently offering him my care and concern.

Remember, we can't always meet our students' needs, but we can respond in a way that supports the relationship, and practicing mindful listening is key. This simple act of deeply listening is critical to building a caring relationship with our students. We can't meet all their needs, but we can listen to them with an open mind and an open heart. We can really hear the needs they are expressing, rather than assuming that we know what they need. With time, we may find that we can deeply attune to others and recognize ways to help them that we had never considered before.

I had the great fortune of doing my student teaching with a teacher who had a side practice as a marriage and family counselor. She really knew how to listen, and she taught me a great deal about the power of listening. Her training in counseling gave her skills that made her teacher-parent conferences truly unique.

Once a parent came to a conference very upset about an ongoing conflict her daughter was having with another girl. From this parent's perspective, her daughter could do no wrong and the root of the problem was the other child's bad behavior. She came to the conference visibly angry and ready to do battle with us. Donna was aware of this and opened the conference with a question: "Is there anything in particular you would like to discuss at this meeting?" This gave the mother an opening to blast us. She said the other girl was getting her friends to gang up on her daughter and asked why weren't we doing anything to stop it. She made some very derogatory statements about the other girl, her parents, and her friends. While she expressed these strong feelings, Donna gave the mother her full attention and listened quietly. Donna's facial expression conveyed concern, and every once in a while she would nod her head and say, "I see," or, "I hear you."

After a few minutes, the mother cooled off and stopped her tirade. For one moment, there was a pregnant silence. This gave Donna an opening. She took a deep breath and calmly said, "As parents, we all worry about our kids and want them to be happy. It's understandable that you're upset." The mother nodded and Donna asked, "Would you like to hear about what we're observing at school?" After the mother nodded again, Donna explained the social dynamic between the two girls and how they were equally responsible for their conflicts. The group of girls that they were both part of were taking sides with each of them on different occasions. Then Donna outlined some strategies that we had been using to improve their communication and cooperation skills and explained to the mother how she might help us reinforce these activities at home. The mother left the conference smiling and visibly relieved.

From this experience, I learned how mindful listening has the power to shift a conversation in a more positive direction. Donna gave this mother her full, caring, undivided attention, and it paid off. She maintained a positive relationship with the family and engaged the mother in contributing to problem-solving strategies.

Caring Routines

Now that we've explored the ethics of care and the importance of building relationships based upon responsiveness, respect, and listening, let's look at ways to create classroom routines that promote caring relationships. Establishing caring routines in our classroom makes caring the norm and builds habits among our students that can last a lifetime.

One year, one of my teacher education students was assigned to intern with one of the most skillful teachers I have ever observed: Ms. Chen. Ms. Chen's serenity and warmth infused the classroom, and her students responded with calm, joyful engagement. As I observed her class, I noticed a variety of simple routines she had established that contributed to the warmth in her classroom.

Just as I suggested earlier, Ms. Chen greeted every child individually. Unlike me, however, Ms. Chen made this into an art form. She seated herself by the door so that she was at her students' eye level. Smiling, she looked each one in the eye, shook her or his hand, and said something like, "Good morning, Julie. I'm so glad you're here today. It's going to be special." Usually she mentioned some personal detail, such as, "How's that new puppy doing?" In response, her students beamed.

After the greeting, each student put her or his belongings away and began the day by doing a classroom job. Each student was assigned a duty, such as checking the plants to see if they needed water, feeding the fish, or straightening books. Ms. Chen had organized these duties so that each child had the knowledge and tools to successfully complete the assigned chore. I watched in amazement as a group of 22 first-graders went about dusting shelves and picking up pencils off the floor. The process of greeting and completing chores took only about 10 minutes, and it primed the students with a sense of care for their environment that lasted throughout the whole day.

Next Ms. Chen began to sing a simple song that signaled that it was time for the morning meeting: "Come, my friends, and join me for circle time." As she began singing, the students joined her song and gathered in a circle marked by a piece of tape on the carpeted floor. As soon as everyone was settled, she began to sing a "good morning" song in Spanish. Each of the children in turn went around the circle and looked at each other child, singing, "Buenos días, ¿cómo le va?" Then Ms. Chen led them through the daily ritual of checking the calendar, talking about plans for the day, and one or two brief introductory lessons, all the while smiling brightly.

When morning meeting was over and it was time for students to begin working on an assignment, she used a mindful bell activity for transition. She directed them to listen carefully to the bell and, when the bell stopped ringing, to listen carefully as she whispered their names to excuse them to their desks. The room became silent and the children listened attentively as she rang the bell. After the sound of the bell subsided, she began to whisper each child's name, and they quietly tiptoed to their seats and began working.

This brief series of activities instilled a deep sense of care from the very beginning of the day. Ms. Chen demonstrated her care for each student by individually greeting them. They demonstrated their care for their classroom by engaging in their chores right away, and they demonstrated their care for one another by singing the good morning song in which they acknowledged and greeted one another.

Mind you, these rituals took time to establish. At the beginning of the school year, Ms. Chen had introduced these activities one by one and given her students time to practice them. She spent the first two weeks of the school year focused on establishing these caring routines while working on learning activities that were mostly review and didn't require much instruction or direction. She didn't really introduce much new content until she felt the class had "jelled," as she called it, and most of the students knew what to do and didn't need direction to complete the morning routine activities. As a result of Ms. Chen's preparation and care, the children in her classroom felt safe and secure. They knew what to expect, that they were cared about and cared for, and that they belonged, and they knew how to contribute to their school family. It was now safe to learn.

Teachers of the upper grades and in secondary school can also create caring rituals, although they obviously need to be designed to engage older students. I once observed a high school English teacher named Mr. Santos begin his class with a casual five-minute check-in to see how each student was doing. Smiling as he visually scanned the group, he gave them his undivided attention before moving into his lesson: "How's it going? What's new? What do you think about the game this Friday? Do we have a chance against the other team?" This brief interaction communicated that he recognized and cared about their interests.

Mr. Santos also masterfully connected his content to issues his students cared about. For example, for a lesson on metaphor, he asked students to bring in some of their favorite popular music to see if they could find any metaphors in the lyrics. Then he helped them understand how metaphor communicates meaning and related the lyrics to issues in modern society that are important to adolescents. For example, one student chose Jimmy Page and Robert Plant's song "Stairway to Heaven" and interpreted it as a quest for substance and meaning in a society where "all that glitters is gold" and you can even buy a "stairway to heaven" rather than earning it through good deeds.

These are just a few simple ways to instill care into your classroom daily routines. As you go through your day, you may find other opportunities to introduce caring as part of an activity or within the curriculum. For example, you might teach your students songs that convey care and compassion such as Bill Withers's "Lean on Me," so wonderfully performed by the cast of Glee. Or you might choose to read a book about a character who cares for another and discuss how each character felt. Two outstanding examples are Lois Lowry's "The Giver" and "Number the Stars" (Lowry, 1989, 1993).

Care and Limits

Caring attention takes the form of face-to-face interpersonal contact. When we look into our students' eyes, we can see the emotions on their faces. We see the spark of interest, the thrill of imagination, and the worry that we will judge them and won't accept them as they are.

If we keep our hearts open and warm, respect our students, and offer them our care, they will respond. If our students have been exposed to violence and trauma, it may take a bit longer. They may not trust us at the beginning, and they may test us. The key to dealing with these situations is consistency. Do not give up!

This doesn't mean that we let them walk all over us. When I was working with student teachers, I found that some wanted their students to be their friends and to like them at all costs. The teacher–student relationship is not a friendship. It is a professional caring relationship; caring is part of our job. It is our job to respect our students, listen to them, and recognize and understand their needs. However, as we have seen, we cannot respond to every need of every student. For our own well-being, it's best to maintain strong boundaries in our social relationships with students and their parents.

An important part of caring involves setting and protecting limits. We can set limits in a firm yet kind way that will help our students understand that when they are at school, they need to behave appropriately and that we are there to help them. This can be done in a very matter-of-fact way that need not be harsh or punitive. Our students need to know that we respect them and care about their needs, but that our responsibility to fulfill those needs is constrained by our professional role.

For example, we can't give our undivided attention to one student all the time. When we have a student who is demanding undue attention, we must set a limit. We can do this with kindness but also with firmness. We can say, "I cannot give you my attention right now because I'm helping someone else. I will be happy to help you when I can. Right now I want you to go back to your desk and try to figure it out for yourself." We will explore more specific strategies for managing students' demands for undue attention in the next chapter.

Compassion

Compassion is the capacity to empathize with another, to recognize his need, and to feel motivated to help. The motivation to help is what distinguishes empathy from compassion. Sometimes when we feel empathy for another, our strong emotions can overwhelm our capacity to help. If my bereaved student is crying and I begin to cry and fall apart emotionally, I won't be of much help. To act with compassion, I must compose myself, calm down, and appraise the situation so I can help.

Compassion can be both universal and relative. It's easy to feel compassion for those closest to us—our "in-group." That's relative compassion. Universal compassion involves acting with compassion toward everyone, under all conditions. This is much more difficult. Compassion becomes more challenging when we are under stress and faced with multiple, conflicting needs and demands. Under these conditions, our scripts can interfere with our compassion. As explained in Chapter 3, our scripts can distort our perceptions and influence how we act. We may limit our compassionate action to our in-group. As teachers, we need to be aware of this tendency and work to overcome it. In this section, we will examine how mindful awareness can help.

Sometimes we have students who are exposed to serious problems such as trauma and violence. Years ago, I had one such student I'll call Shane. Shane's mother was dying of breast cancer, and his 20-year-old sister was trying to care for him. While the sister was doing her best, she was dealing with huge amounts of grief herself and was not adequately prepared to give Shane the support that he needed.

Shane didn't know how to cope with his feelings. Understandably, he was emotionally volatile and had difficulty focusing on schoolwork. The other students knew about the challenges he was facing and tried to be supportive, but sometimes his angry outbursts hurt his peers and they began to shy away from him. I was often frustrated with him; it was a challenge to be compassionate while at the same time keeping his outbursts from hurting the other students.

At the time, I did the best I could. However, since then, I have learned about an approach that could have helped. This is a compassion practice developed by Joan Halifax, a Zen Roshi (or teacher) who is a leader in the field of hospice. She teaches nurses and other caregivers a process to help them act with compassion under stressful conditions. Halifax uses the acronym GRACE[1] as a quick reminder of the process (Halifax, 2014). With her permission, I have adapted her five-step model for teachers:

> *Step 1.* **G** is for "Gathering your attention." Take a pause and focus your attention on your body, the breath, and the sensation of your feet on the ground. As you bring your attention to the present moment, you can be a more helpful resource to yourself and your students. You will offer a fresh presence that is stable, discerning, and caring.

> *Step 2.* **R** is for "Recall your intention," that is, your reason for being a teacher. As you learned in Chapter 1, recalling your intention helps you align your behavior with your values and reignite your motivation. Your altruistic motivation primes you to act in caring and supportive ways.

> *Step 3.* **A** is for "Attune to yourself, your body, heart and mind, before you attune to those around you" and then attune to your students, to parents, and colleagues. Attuning to yourself first let's you touch in to your biases, and what is arising in your body and mind at this moment. Then sense into what your student is feeling (empathy) and how he or she might see the world (perspective taking). Take time to tune in to what is happening. Assumptions often come from scripts—cognitive biases that interfere with the ability to perceive what is needed. Your scripts bias your perception. At this step, the key is just to notice these scripts and let them go.

> *Step 4.* **C** is for "Consider what will serve your student or colleagues." This might include institutional expectations,

---

1 Reprinted from Journal of Nursing Education and Practice, Vol. 4, No. 1, Joan Halifax, "G.R.A.C.E. For nurses: Cultivating compassion in nurse/patient interactions," pp. 121-128, 2014. Used with permission of Joan Halifax.

environmental features, social constraints, conflicting needs, and consequences. At this step, you engage in a process of discernment to ascertain what will truly serve others.

Step 5. **E** is for "Enacting and ending." The entire GRACE process results in a principled, ethical, and compassion-based action: engaging or apply compassion in service of others. This step is the conclusion—the point when the action is complete and it's time to move on to another activity, letting go of any lingering feelings that may keep us from being fully present for the next situation.

Going back to my story about Shane, let's imagine a time when he triggers my anger by acting aggressively toward his peers. My angry feelings make it difficult to respond in a positive way. This time, however, I follow the steps in the GRACE process. I take the time to pause, gather my attention, and recall my altruistic intention. This helps me calm down and begin to attune with myself. I notice the feeling of anger and become aware of my scripts and biases. This recognition paves the way for me to attune to Shane and the other students as I consider all the factors in the situation. I recognize that aggression in childhood is a symptom of deep suffering. The entire process helps me shift my attitude and behavior toward Shane from judgment to compassion.

Acting with compassion involves discernment. I still need to stop Shane's aggressive behavior, but I can do so from a state of compassion rather than angry judgment. By responding kindly but firmly to stop Shane's aggression, I communicate that I care about him and the other students. In doing so, I also model compassionate responding for the other students, which helps them understand and help Shane, too.

The GRACE process allows us to slow down and be more mindful and aware in the process of interacting with students who need our compassion. In this way, we prime our internal resources, making way for compassionate action. With practice, the experience of compassion becomes embodied knowledge, like how to ride a bicycle. With experience, we train our sensory perceptions to become more attentive to the subtle details of multifaceted and rapidly changing situations.

Skill-Building Practices

Self-Care Assessment

I invite you to explore how you are currently caring for yourself. Consider a typical workday and write down a list of your usual activities. Then rate each activity according to your level of enjoyment on a scale of 1 to 4 (1 = not enjoyable at all, 4 = very enjoyable). Next rate each activity according to the degree to which the activity focuses on you or on others. For example, let's say you spend 20 minutes every morning making lunches for your family. It's a mundane activity, but you enjoy the feeling of doing something for your wife and children, so you give it a 3 for enjoyment. It's entirely focused on others, so you put "0%/100%" under "Self/Other."

Time Spent	Typical Work Day Activities	Enjoyment	Self/ Other

Total the hours that you spend during a typical workday doing things for yourself that you enjoy: _____ hours

Nurturing Activities Self-Assessment

In this section, you will discover the things you are doing now to nurture your well-being. In the section "Things I Do Now," write all the activities you can think of that you really enjoy that you do now. For example, you may enjoy getting a massage, working out in the gym, playing tennis, reading a novel, or just taking a walk in the woods. Next think about how each of these activities supports one or more of the four dimensions of your personal growth and development: physical, emotional, intellectual, and spiritual.

Activities that promote physical development include such things as exercise, relaxation, and massage. Those that promote emotional development include fun things with others that make you happy, such as attending a party with friends, seeing an inspirational film, or just sharing a meal with your family. You can promote your intellectual development by, for example, reading newspapers or intellectually stimulating magazines or books, attending courses, or having intellectual discussions with your colleagues. Activities that give your life meaning and help you connect to something greater than yourself give you spiritual meaning. These can be activities done in a religious context, such as attending services, but they can also be purely secular, such as reading an inspirational poem or practicing mindfulness.

Next think about things that you are not doing now but would like to do. Again consider how each of these activities supports the four dimensions. This is your self-care plan.

Things I Do Now:

Activity	Physical	Emotional	Intellectual	Inner Life

Self-Care Plan:

Activity	Physical	Emotional	Intellectual	Inner Life

Caring Practice

Caring practice (*metta* in Pali or *maitre* in Sanskrit, translated as "loving-kindness") is a way to cultivate the feeling of care for and connection with yourself and others. During this practice, you will generate feelings of care and goodwill toward yourself and others by offering wishes of well-being, happiness, and peace, first to yourself, then to others in your life, and ultimately to all beings. The ultimate aim of caring practice is to engender within yourself universal compassion: the desire or wish for well-being, happiness, and peace for all. For a comprehensive exploration of the philosophy and practice of loving-kindness, I suggest Sharon Salzberg's book "Lovingkindness: The Revolutionary Art of Happiness" (Salzberg, 1995).

It's best to begin this practice by spending a few minutes practicing focused attention, as you learned in Chapter 1. In focused attention, your primary focus is on the experience of breathing. Pay attention to the simple, ordinary experience of breathing, noticing the sensations of the breath as the air enters and leaves your body. Once your mind has settled and you are feeling relaxed and present, you can shift your attention to the caring part of the practice.

Each step of this practice can be done for as little as a few minutes or as long as you would like. Therefore, the entire practice can take from 10 minutes to as long as an hour. As you become familiar with the steps of the practice, find a time frame that works best for you and your situation.

Caring for Yourself

Caring practice begins with caring for yourself. Sometimes it can seem easier to love almost anyone other than to love yourself. But, as you have already learned in this chapter, you need to take care of yourself first. So begin by giving yourself permission to accept unconditional love and affection from yourself.

After your mind has settled, gently turn your attention to yourself. Silently repeat to yourself, "May I enjoy well-being, happiness, and peace. May I enjoy well-being, happiness, and peace." If saying this to yourself feels awkward, you can chose other words that feel more appropriate to you or simply generate and offer the feeling of well-being, happiness, and peace to yourself without words. Offer this unconditional love and care to yourself in whatever way feels best to you.

As you learned in Chapter 4, when you feel love, you open up and feel expansive and interconnected with others and all of life. There's a feeling of wholeness and strength. Savor this feeling as if you were drinking fine wine or eating the most delicious gourmet meal. If you find yourself slipping into feelings of self-doubt, fear, or anger, see if you can imagine that they are just passing clouds. They have no substance; with time they will pass, and the warm sun will shine through again.

When you begin to practice caring for the first time, do only this first part of the practice—offering love and care to yourself. During this practice it's important to be patient and gentle with yourself. Relax into it.

Caring for a Loved One

Once you have spent a few sessions focusing on the first part of this practice of caring for yourself, you can shift to the next step, which involves bringing into your awareness a person who is very dear to you and offering this feeling of unconditional love and care to him or her as you repeat silently, "May you enjoy well-being, happiness, and peace." Again, if you prefer, change the words or simply get in touch with the feeling of deeply caring for this dear person. Notice if your mind wanders. Thinking about this dear one may bring up thoughts of plans or memories of past experiences. If this happens, gently direct your mind back to the aspiration, "May you enjoy well-being, happiness, and peace."

Caring for a Neutral Other

Now you are ready to practice the entire sequence. First spend a few minutes focused on offering care to yourself and then to your loved one. Next bring another person to mind. This time, choose a person who is emotionally neutral. In other words, this should be someone you know but about whom you have no strong positive or negative feelings. It might be a person you see regularly—the clerk at the grocery store, the mail carrier, your neighbor. Once you've settled on one person and brought her or him to mind, offer this individual care in the same way you did for yourself and your loved one. As you keep this person in mind, silently say to yourself, "May you enjoy well-being, happiness, and peace," or simply focus on feeling unconditional care for him or her.

This practice stretches your ability to care for others. As you learned in the compassion section of this chapter, it's easier to feel care and compassion for those closest to us but more challenging to care for those outside our in-group. You may find your mind wanting back to the close loved one. When this happens, simply note your tendency and gently bring your attention back to offering the neutral person your care.

Caring for a Challenging Other

The next step in the caring practice can be somewhat challenging. This step involves offering the same unconditional care to a person you find difficult in some way. This may be a person who triggers negative emotions such as fear or annoyance. This person may be a coworker, a parent, or even one of your students whose behavior you find difficult or puzzling. It could even be a family member.

At first, choose someone who is only mildly difficult, not someone for whom you feel very strong negative emotions. Those strong feelings can make this exercise very difficult, and it is ideal to start out practicing at a level that is not too challenging. Offer this person the same friendliness and care as you did the others, saying silently to yourself, "May you enjoy well-being, happiness, and peace" or simply feeling the offering of care to this person.

This part of the practice takes time. It's important to be gentle with yourself and remember what Rilke said: "Perhaps all the dragons in our lives are princesses who are only waiting to see us act, just once, with beauty and courage. Perhaps everything that frightens us is, in its deepest essence, something helpless that wants our love" (Rilke, 2002, p. 39).

It's not uncommon to find this part of the practice extremely challenging. Negative thoughts and feelings may arise, making it difficult to extend care to this person. Don't be hard on yourself. Accept that this is a difficult practice. Take a break and go back to the first part of this exercise, when you directed love and care to yourself, for a few minutes until you feel better, and then shift back to the practice of offering well-being happiness and peace to this challenging individual.

There are a variety of commercially available audio recordings of guided caring (loving-kindness or metta) practices that you may find helpful as you learn this practice. See the Resources section of the book for more information.

Child Interview[2]

Sometimes you may have students in your class whom you just don't understand. Their behavior may be challenging or confusing. Or it may be that you feel the two of you are just not "clicking" for some reason. This exercise is designed to create an opportunity to connect deeply with one student in a very nonthreatening way.

Find a time when it's comfortable to speak with this student alone. Tell this student that you want to learn more about her or him and that you would like to ask some questions. Make arrangements to do this at a later time when you and the student will not be interrupted. Before you interview her or him, spend some time doing caring practice with a focus on this student.

Begin the interview by taking one deep breath to center yourself and gather your presence. Connect with the feeling that you generated during the caring practice. Silently remember to offer your care to this student ("May you enjoy well-being, happiness, and peace"). You can do this in any way that is natural. It only takes a second—a brief pause before you begin.

Make eye contact with the student and then begin to ask age-appropriate questions about her or his life. It's okay to ask the questions even if you already know the answers. The information is not the point of the interview (although you may learn something that may surprise you), but to create a safe opportunity to demonstrate your care and interest in the student's life.

---

2 This exercise is adapted from an assignment designed by Tom Peterson, Ed.D. used with permission.

For example, you might ask:

- "What do you like to do in your spare time?"
- "Who are the people in your family? Tell me about them."
- "Do you play a musical instrument?"
- "Tell me about your favorite TV show [or song, sport, etc.]?"
- "What's really important to you?"
- "Who do you most admire? Why?"

These are just a few examples. You can generate your own questions that are specific to the particular student. You can also follow up any of these questions to engage the student in a conversation. For example, if the student says he has a brother, you might say, "I have a brother too. Is your brother younger or older than you?"

Carefully record the student's answers on a piece of paper. This demonstrates that her or his answers are important and meaningful to you. When you're finished, thank the student for sharing with you. Over the next few weeks, notice if there are any changes in your relationship with the student.

Chapter 6

Orchestrating Classroom Dynamics

The demands of teaching can sometimes feel overwhelming, and it's easy to let ourselves get caught up in worries and concerns about what needs to happen in the future—even in the future hours or minutes. However, when we do this, we can miss important things that are going on in the now.

When I teach, I sometimes notice that my mind is so focused on thinking about what I need to do and how to do it that I'm not paying attention to what is happening in the present moment. It's as if my mind has carried me away and I'm no longer in the here and now. I become a "human, doing" rather than a "human being."

During the course of the day, my thoughts, worries, and plans loom large. I have expectations about how things ought to be and I become attached to them, rather than noticing and accepting how things actually are.

Under these conditions, almost anything that may be happening will fail to match what I think should be happening. This causes distress, making me emotionally volatile. This volatile emotional state can, in turn, affect my perceptions. I may become more sensitive to threat and more affected by my scripts.

In this state, I may imagine that a student's disruptive behavior is intentionally designed to interfere with my teaching when in fact it is the normal behavior of a child who needs help with his self-regulation. This tendency to take things personally impairs my ability to manage my classroom effectively. I am apt to lose my temper and say something that actually makes matters worse.

Practicing mindfulness can help bring us back to the present moment as we attend to our breath, our walking, our thoughts, our scripts, our emotional experience, and our bodily sensations.

Earlier in the book we focused on learning about regulating ourselves. We explored how to apply mindful awareness to our emotional experiences so we can recognize our emotions and our emotional patterns and proactively regulate how we behave and respond in the way we want, rather than automatically reacting in ways we don't.

We have also examined how to hone our attentional skills through practicing mindfulness. This helps us become more aware of internal and external phenomena. Mindfulness helps us notice the subtle changes in a student's posture that let us know he's feeling discouraged and could use some help. It helps us recognize "teachable moments" so we can optimize our instruction.

In this chapter, we will further explore how mindfulness can help us stay present so that we can better manage our classrooms. The self-management skills that mindfulness cultivates strengthen our capacity to create and maintain engaging and effective learning environments while promoting our resilience and preventing burnout.

Mindfulness helps us become more aware of the social and emotional dynamics of our classrooms and our own behavior so that we can better respond to individual student needs, promote student–school bonding, manage conflict, prevent misbehavior, and successfully employ intervention strategies with students who have chronic emotional and behavioral problems.

Once we have practiced mindfulness regularly for some time and have achieved a level of emotional and attentional self-mastery, we may begin to notice subtle shifts in the classroom climate. We may take things less personally and manage our emotions better, even during situations that used to trigger us.

As we manage our emotions better, we become more attuned to our students, our relationships with them improve, and we can handle the chaos and ambiguity that sometimes come with deep, joyful learning. Tension gives way to trust, and when children feel a sense of trust, they feel safe to take risks and explore the unknown—the foundation of learning.

Classroom Dynamics

There is a mistaken belief among many teachers that we can and must control our students' behavior. This belief is a setup for power struggles. The reality is that we cannot control our students' behavior, and attempts to control them often backfire, leaving us feeling frustrated, exhausted, and ineffective. While we cannot control their behavior, we can control myriad environmental elements critical to creating and maintaining an effective learning environment.

First and foremost, we can control ourselves. We can control how and what we communicate, how we behave, and where we position our bodies in space. We can set and reinforce classroom expectations and limits. In most cases, we have some degree of control over the physical environment, the sequence and timing of activities, and the way we transition from one activity to another.

Each of these elements has dynamics. My speech can be soft or loud, calm or harsh. I can move slowly or quickly. I can stand up, or I can sit down on a chair or the floor. The classroom can be bright or dark. I can arrange the furniture in ways that feel cramped or spacious.

I like to imagine that the art of arranging these elements is like musical orchestration. A composer skillfully combines sound elements and their dynamic qualities to create the beautiful sounds we call music. When we are mindful of the elements of the classroom that we can control, we can, like a composer, orchestrate these elements to create the optimal conditions for learning.

With this approach to classroom management, we focus our attention on learning rather than on control. Our goal is to create and maintain the optimal conditions for learning. When something interferes with this goal, we take time to mindfully observe and adjust the classroom elements and their dynamics rather than reactively trying to control our students.

Here's a very simple example: Mr. Brown was having a problem in his kindergarten class. "They won't stop running," he told me. "We created a class rule together about walking inside and I have been reminding them to walk when they are inside, but it doesn't seem to make any difference. They just don't listen." He was clearly frustrated. However, it only took a few minutes of observing his class to see what needed to change.

The furniture was arranged to create two very distinct "runways." Young children have a natural inclination to run in open spaces. Mr. Brown's students were not intentionally misbehaving; they were simply responding impulsively to the open space. I suggested that he move some tables around to block off these runways. The next time I visited, he told me how much the learning dynamics had changed. "They aren't running anymore. This really helps everyone stay more focused, and I'm not getting frustrated all the time."

Emotional Climate

The emotional climate is an important element that we can control to some degree. As we discussed in Chapter 2, when it comes to emotions, children have a strong innate tendency to follow an adult's emotional lead. If we are unhappy, exhausted, and irritable, our students will feel it and react accordingly. If we are joyful and enthusiastic, they are more likely to feel that way too. Mindfulness can help us be more aware of our emotional state and how it is affecting the emotional climate of our classroom.

Reducing Noise

When we want our students to do something, modeling the behavior we hope they will adopt works best. I have heard teachers yell, "Be quiet!" and then wonder why their students didn't respond.

One effective Montessori technique for quieting a noisy classroom involves writing the word "silence" on the board (Montessori, 1917/1973). At the beginning of the year when we were going over behavioral expectations and guidelines, I would tell my students, "When we're learning, sometimes it's important to be quiet so we can think. If it starts to get too noisy, I will write 'silence' on the board to remind everyone to be quiet." I would then show them what the word 'silence' looked like. Then I would say, "If you think it's getting too noisy, you can do this too. Here's a card with the word 'silence' written on it that you can copy if you don't know how to spell it."

This technique worked best when I was mindful of the noise level and used the procedure when the level was just beginning to rise, before it got too noisy. At this point, my students were focused enough to notice what I was doing, and they could settle down and refocus on their work rather quickly. If I waited a little too long, my students wouldn't notice what I was doing because they were too distracted by the noise. In this case, I would often go over to a few students and quietly point out that I had written "silence" on the board. Usually they would settle down eventually, but it took a little longer.

Occasionally a student would feel that the classroom noise level was making it hard to concentrate, and he or she would write "silence" on the board. The other students respected this and responded in the same way. The students appreciated having the opportunity to express their needs and to have the class respond appropriately. It's a simple way to promote students' sense of autonomy and independence while also creating an opportunity for cooperation.

Many teachers use a raised hand as a signal to initiate silence. The teacher instructs the students that when he raises his hand, it's time for everyone to be quiet and give him their full attention. They are taught to raise their hands when they notice him so that the signal spreads to everyone, even if they can't see the teacher at that moment.

Arranging Students and Furniture

Another dynamic we can control is how we arrange desks or tables and where each student sits. Overcrowding can create emotional discomfort. Some students are particularly sensitive to crowding and need a bit more space than others. Some students do well working close to their friends; others do not. When we mindfully observe our students as they are working, we can notice subtle signs that indicate the need for change.

It doesn't take long to notice the boy who needs to be moved closer to the front of the room where I can more closely monitor his activities, or the girls who need to be separated because they talk too much and don't get their work done. It may take some time, but eventually I can create an arrangement that allows everyone a place where they can all learn best.

Transitions

Transitions can be challenging times. It's tough to get a large group of students to move from one activity to another. There's nothing like having a class rudely interrupted by a bell in the middle of work time. A class of 25 is quietly focused on their work and the bell suddenly blares, creating a sense of urgency. Like a stampeding herd of elephants, they start running for the door. Bodies collide, books fall on the floor, and tempers flare.

Situations like this are particularly difficult for students with self-regulation problems or those who have been exposed to trauma or violence. While everyone can feel physically threatened by such chaos, these students feel it more acutely and tend to react with aggression (Dodge & Coie, 1987).

Some students have a particularly difficult time with transitions. They just don't like to change what they're doing. These students often get really engrossed in one activity, and to them it feels like an affront to be interrupted with a transition. They need extra support during transition times to help them shift their attention from one activity to another.

I find that it helps to be mindful of the time so that I can prepare for the transition. I can set the alarm on my smartphone to vibrate about 12 minutes before the transition time so that I can begin to prepare. When it buzzes, I start by scanning the classroom to see what is going on. I take a moment to bring my full mindful awareness to the present moment. (A description of this practice can be found in the skill-building practices at the end of this chapter under "Practicing Withitness.")

As I do this, I note the overall tone of the classroom and then zero in on specific students who may need my attention. Who is starting to get restless? Who is totally engrossed in their work? Is anyone experiencing frustration? Then I write a message on the board: "Coming soon: Lunch." Next I connect with each student who has difficulty with transitions. I gently tap each of them on the shoulder and point to the message on the board. This is a silent way to help them prepare mentally and emotionally to a change in activity.

Finally, I play some soothing music that the students know means a transition is coming. Soon the activity in the room begins to shift. Students finish up their work, put things away, and gather their belongings. When the bell rings, everyone is already prepared for the transition. Because we've practiced lining up and walking together, they all know when it's their time to get in line, so there's no mad dash to the door.

Mindful Communication

Like many new teachers, I had a challenging first year of teaching. I had no idea how to get my students to pay attention to my lessons, respond to my directions, and behave appropriately. I thought that if I was nice to my students, they would like me, want to please me, and automatically do what I wanted them to. However, much of the time, my students seemed to do whatever they wanted, ignoring my directions and attempts to direct their behavior. Day by day, my frustration grew, and I found myself becoming impatient and snapping at my students when they "didn't listen."

One day, a supervisor came to observe my teaching to evaluate my progress as a new teacher. After class, she gave me some important feedback: "Do you realize that after every direction you give to your students, you say, 'Okay?'? For example, earlier today, you said, 'It's time to do math, okay?' By saying this, you're giving your students the message that math is an optional activity. They didn't understand why you were frustrated when they didn't respond to your invitation to do math. You gave away your power."

This feedback blew me away. I was amazed that I was so unaware of what I was saying. I had no idea that I was habitually ending directions to my students this way. No wonder they were so unresponsive! I had inadvertently sabotaged my attempts to direct their attention to every learning activity. I wasn't giving my students clear, simple messages that conveyed what they were supposed to do. The "Okay?" conveyed that my students had the option to say no to me.

After the supervisor's visit, I began to monitor myself to break this bad habit. At first, I found that it was nearly impossible. I would hear myself say, "Okay?" after the fact, but I found it difficult to catch myself before it slipped out. However, after a few weeks of working on this, my ability to stop this bad habit improved, and I noticed an immediate improvement in my students' behavior and responsiveness. This was the first time I truly understood that I needed to develop greater self-awareness if I was going to succeed as a teacher.

This opened my eyes to the importance of what we say to students and how we say it. This is one of the classroom elements over which we have complete control—when we are mindful. However, much of the time, I would find myself operating on automatic pilot, totally unaware of what I was saying and how I was saying it in terms of tone, volume, and pacing.

When I began to supervise student teachers and had the opportunity to observe other teachers' classrooms on a regular basis, I discovered that the tendency to passively expect students to obey "suggestions" was not uncommon. I began to notice other dysfunctional communication patterns as well. Often these patterns were rooted in scripts. For example, the fallacious script underlying my "Okay?" pattern was the idea that if I was nice, my students would like me and therefore cooperate with my suggestion.

Another common pattern was based on a different fallacious script: "I must maintain complete control of the classroom at all times." When students are not behaving as desired, a teacher operating from this script may resort to coercion and threats.

For example, Mrs. Mosley was frustrated when her class began to chatter during a transition time. She demanded, "I want you all to be quiet now so we can line up and go to music class!" When they ignored her, she said, "Don't make me angry, or you'll regret it!" Her threatening approach put her students on the defensive. Some would comply out of fear or the wish to please. However, others ignored or refused to obey her out of defiance or a desire for power. In either case, her dysfunctional pattern interfered with the learning environment because she, too, gave away her power. When she said, "Don't make me angry," she communicated to her students that they could control her. When we fall into this pattern, some children will test the limits to see who's really in control, often triggering a power struggle.

At times, we may find ourselves slipping into a combination of ineffective patterns. We start by passively requesting a behavior, and when the students fail to comply, we become frustrated and shift into the controlling mode. This gives our students a very confusing message.

For example, imagine that Cecilia hasn't finished her math assignment. She's been distractedly doodling in the margins of her paper. "Let's finish up our math, okay?" I say sweetly. She ignores me and keeps doodling. "Let's finish up now, okay? You don't want to miss recess, do you?" Cecilia still ignores me. I give her two more reminders, but soon my sweetness turns sour. "Cecilia, finish up this math assignment now!" I snap.

Cecilia becomes defiant. "No, I hate math. Besides, I don't care if I miss recess!" Clearly I didn't realize that my first communication gave Cecilia the impression that she had a choice in the matter. She ignored me because she didn't think my comment required a response and thought that she had permission to keep doodling if she wanted to. I didn't communicate the clear message, "Cecilia, finish your math now." My mounting frustration and controlling reaction only triggered her defiance.

Imagine yourself during a break, sitting in the lunchroom at work, engrossed in an exciting novel. A colleague says to no one in particular, "Let's go out for a quick cup of coffee, okay?" You continue to read your book. You're ignoring him because you think he's making a general statement to everyone. You're reading a particularly exciting part and don't want to be interrupted. Soon your colleague begins to yell at you harshly, "Come with me for coffee now! Don't make me angry!" How would you feel? Confused? Defiant? Outraged? This is how our students feel when we don't make our expectations clear.

Often our students have underlying issues that make compliance with our demands difficult or even impossible. When I tried to get Cecilia to finish her math, I was so wrapped up in getting her to behave that I didn't consider that she might be having difficulty with the math problems. When I got to know her better, I learned that she had grown to hate math because she had moved many times and missed a lot of school. Her parents were migrant workers, moved often, and returned to Mexico for a long period of time during the Christmas holidays.

By the time she was in my class, she was behind, and the math problems I was expecting her to complete were too challenging. No wonder she reacted with so much hostility! If I had been more aware of her needs, I could have responded with more sensitivity: "Cecilia, I notice that you haven't finished the math problems. Do you need some help?"

Building a Community of Learners

As we discussed in Chapter 5, our students have a basic need to belong to and contribute to a community. We can foster a sense of community in our classrooms by modeling caring and other prosocial behaviors, instituting caring routines, and mindfully listening to our students. Practicing mindfulness helps us keep our minds open to opportunities for learning that promote community building.

When the need for community is satisfied, students bond with their teacher, class, and school, and they are inclined to behave in accordance with the community's values, reducing the need for adult intervention. They are more cooperative, helpful, and concerned for others, and there are fewer disruptive behaviors (Battistich, Solomon, Watson, & Schaps, 1997).

We can cultivate a community of learners by providing students with opportunities to collaborate with and help one another. When we are mindful of our individual students' strengths, weaknesses, needs, and interests, we can skillfully design learning activities that promote cooperation and helpfulness.

For example, high school English teacher Mr. Jacobs encourages collaboration by assigning short stories to groups of students to analyze together. He creates heterogeneous groups that include students with varying skills, abilities, and interests. He understands that having students work together in groups that are similar in ability has a negative effect on lower-level students' motivation and learning (Allington, 1980; Hiebert, 1983; Schell & Rouch, 1988).

To encourage participation, each student is given a specific task. One student examines the characters and writes a brief description of each one. Another is responsible for summarizing the plot. One is assigned to illustrate the story, and another is responsible for building a list of vocabulary words. When each group has finished its analysis, together they present their findings to the whole class, and each student has a role to play.

Collaborative learning gives students the opportunity to help others and to reflect upon the experiences and needs of others. This promotes empathy and perspective-taking. Creating groups of students with varying skills and abilities gives students opportunities to make contributions to the community in a variety of ways.

In the above example, the student who was weak on reading but strong on art was assigned to draw the illustrations. One student made such stunning drawings to illustrate her story that other students recognized the outstanding value of her contribution and hoped she'd be assigned to a group with them the next time.

Another way to build community among your students is through joint service learning projects. One year, my fourth-graders became very interested in recycling. We took a field trip to the recycling center and learned how various materials are recycled. My class became very interested in helping to promote curbside recycling in our town. We spent time thinking about how we might do this.

Together we decided to create a recycling fair on Earth Day that year. We set up the fair in the park next to city hall. Students created and installed banners promoting curbside recycling and passed out information to interested citizens as they passed by. That year, the city council voted to initiate curbside recycling citywide, and my students were thrilled. They felt so proud that together they had made a valuable contribution to their community.

Building Good Relationships

Research on effective classroom management points to the importance of teacher–student relationships (Pianta, 2006). We can set up great management systems involving guidelines and limits, but if our students don't trust and respect us (or think we don't respect them), we're in for some challenges.

When you ask people why a teacher made a difference in their lives, the typical response is that the teacher saw them for who they were and cared about them. Giving each student our full mindful attention for even a short period of class time gives him or her the message "I see you." By making these important moments of connection with our students, we let them know we value them as an individual—they're not just one lost among the many.

Because the most literal goals of teaching seem to encourage it, we naturally tend to signal to students that we value high academic achievement. It's our job to teach our students, and we want them to succeed. However, not all our students are high academic achievers, and we need to be mindful to also communicate that we value nonacademic attributes that our students exhibit, such as helpfulness, friendliness, creativity, problem-solving, and conflict resolution.

Consider this example: When Mrs. Black began practicing and applying mindfulness, she began to pay closer attention to the students who did not tend to be high academic achievers. As her level of awareness in the classroom increased, she realized that she was giving some students excessive praise when they did well on assignments and tests but overlooking some of her students' other accomplishments.

One day she noticed a student named Megan going around the classroom picking up pieces of paper after an art project. Megan, a quiet girl, was not usually one of the high achievers, but Mrs. Black now realized that Megan was often helpful in this way and made a point to recognize this valuable contribution to the school family: "Megan, you are really helping us keep our classroom in order. I really appreciate your help!" Megan beamed, and Mrs. Black noticed that other children began to help Megan clean up the classroom.

Rules and Procedures

In Chapter 5, you met Ms. Chen, who spent the first few weeks of school building community by establishing caring routines. Part of this process involved introducing rules and procedures. On the first day, she engaged her class in a discussion of schoolwide expectations: Be respectful, be responsible, be safe, and be prepared to learn. She offered examples of behaviors that exemplified each expectation. For example, she might say, "We walk down the halls quietly with no talking, together, in a straight line, keeping our hands to our sides. When we do this, we are being respectful of the students in the other classrooms who are working. We are careful not to bump into others so we can all be safe."

Notice that she carefully outlined all the details of the expectation: walking quietly with no talking, together, in a straight line, keeping hands to one's sides. Often we assume that children should know what to do, and when they don't, we become annoyed. However, not all children know or remember what's expected of them, so we need to be specific. It also helps to practice each behavioral expectation so that the students embody the behavior and it becomes routine. At the beginning of the school year, Ms. Chen had had her students line up and practice walking according to her expectations.

It's best to keep the expectations simple and stated in the positive. In Ms. Chen's school, all expected behaviors can be categorized as respectful, responsible, safe, or preparatory for learning. When a student is off task or doing something out of line, it's easy to point to the expectation. For example, when Jonah is leaning back on his chair, Ms. Chen might say, "Jonah, tipping back on your chair is not safe and I expect you to stay safe. Put the chair on the ground."

Teaching and practicing rules and procedures is key to establishing order. However, the way we reinforce these rules and procedures is even more important. It's best to be as consistent as possible. This can involve a lot of reminding and redirecting at the beginning, which requires a great deal of vigilance from the teacher.

We need to be mindful of what our students are doing and how we respond. If we notice that they need a reminder, we need to do so consistently, in a calm but firm manner. After a few weeks, the rules and procedures become routine. If we're not paying attention to what's going on, we may fail to notice when our students aren't following the procedures correctly and miss opportunities to remind them. On the other hand, we may also miss opportunities to acknowledge students for the behavior we want to see.

Careful preparation and consistent reinforcement can help us avoid the tendency to be reactionary—that is, to create rules and consequences in response to problems. For example, suppose that Ms. Frances is having trouble getting her fourth-grade class in after recess. She stands by the outside door and calls, "Room Three, it's time to come in!" No one responds. She resorts to walking around the playground rounding the students up, while some stand in line impatiently. By the time everyone is in line, they have all wasted a good 10 minutes of the afternoon and Ms. Frances is in a sour mood.

She barks, "We are wasting too much time coming in from recess. From now on, if you don't line up right away, you will miss recess the next day." The students roll their eyes at one another because they know Ms. Frances won't follow through with the threat. The next day, they are just as difficult to round up, and as they expected, no one loses his or her recess because Ms. Frances doesn't want to lose her recess break.

Ms. Frances's response is an overreaction that is ultimately ineffective. When teachers make rules with threats that they don't have the will to reinforce with real action, students learn that they don't mean what they say.

When we apply mindful awareness to such situations, we take time to calm down and observe what's happening before we take any action. When I find myself becoming frustrated, I notice the tension in my jaw and shoulders and take three deep breaths to relax. Then I seek out and watch the students who are ignoring me to see if there are any extenuating circumstances affecting their behavior. Once I've calmed down, I can analyze the situation and come up with an effective response.

For example, let's say that Mr. Brooks is having a similar problem with his fifth-graders. It is April, and the days are finally warm enough to enjoy the outdoors. Looking out across the playground, Mr. Brooks can easily see why his students are dawdling. He notices the growing tension in his neck and shoulders but takes a deep breath to calm himself and considers the alternatives.

He goes back into the classroom and gets a book. He comes back out, sits down on the grass near a tree, and begins to read. Surprised to see their teacher sitting on the grass reading a book after the bell has rung, his students begin wandering over to him and sit down.

Looking up, he says, "Oh, there you are! I thought you had decided that school was over for the day." His students laugh. "Well, how about if we find a way to do some of our afternoon work outside today?" His students cheer. Rather than fighting "spring fever," Mr. Brooks comes up with some learning activities that his class can do outside.

Later the next day, before recess, he discusses the problem with his class. "I know the weather is getting nicer and we all would like to spend more time outside, but we have test prep coming up, and when it takes so long for you to line up after recess, we're wasting a lot of time. I'm concerned that we'll get behind."

Together he and his class brainstorm and come up with an idea. They decide that once they've completed their test prep, they will have a "field day" and spend a whole day outside to celebrate. After they arrive at this decision, Mr. Brooks asks them, "So how can I help you line up quickly when the bell rings so we don't waste any time?" One student suggests that he blow his whistle five minutes before the bell so they'll have some warning before they have to go in. They successfully follow this procedure the next day.

I recognize that Mr. Brooks's solution might not work under all conditions and situations. I present this example because it contains important moments where mindfulness made a difference. At the beginning of this scenario, Mr. Brooks took a pause to bring mindful awareness to the rising tension in his body. Then he took a few deep breaths to calm down before considering ways to respond. When we are calm and present, we are more creative. Mr. Brooks's solution was quite clever. Rather than trying to fight for his students' attention, he did something unexpected that attracted their attention. He also demonstrated empathy, understanding, and acceptance of normal child behavior, one of the elements of interpersonal mindfulness that we explored in Chapter 1.

Once Mr. Brooks had his students' attention, he engaged them in problem-solving. Often we assume that our students understand the problem from our point of view. However, this is rarely the case. We usually need to explain the situation and our concerns in simple terms. Mr. Brooks did this calmly and without blame. He invited his students to help him think about possible solutions to the problem. This communicated to them that the whole class owned the problem and provided the opportunity for them all to buy in to the solution.

Spending a long day in a classroom full of peers can be very intense and exhausting for some students. Sometimes students need time to cool off or just take some time for themselves. It helps if we create a space to fill this need. For example, one class I observed had an area in the classroom identified as a "peace corner" (Lantieri, 2008). This is a place where students can go when they're feeling unhappy or just need a break. The children decorated the corner with pictures of their "peaceful places"—places they could imagine to help them feel more peaceful. There were pictures of the ocean, flowers, mountains, and houses full of happy families.

Conflict Resolution

We want our students to learn to get along with one another. However, this can be easier said than done. As kids are learning relationships skills, they can sometimes have difficulty resolving conflicts with others. Often the easiest response is to solve the problem for them by separating them or making an executive decision about the situation. While such solutions may be expedient, they don't teach conflict resolution and relationship skills.

When students have a conflict, other students can act as peer mediators. For this to work effectively, students need to be trained in some simple mediation skills. You'd be surprised how many conflict situations children can learn to work out for themselves if given the proper tools.

Teaching Students to be Peacemakers (Johnson & Johnson, 1991) is a curriculum that provides opportunities for students to practice role plays and specific procedures for negotiation and mediation until they can manage their own conflicts routinely. Once they have all learned these routines, the teacher can choose two different students every day to be mediators to help their peers resolve conflict peacefully.

For example, suppose two boys are arguing over who gets to use the classroom computer first. When their teacher, Ms. Wyckoff, hears the arguing, she asks one of the mediators to help the students with their disagreement.

Ellen, the chosen mediator, begins by telling the boys, William and Juan, that mediation is voluntary and that her role is to help them find a solution that is acceptable to both of them. She explains that she is neutral and will not take sides or attempt to decide who is right or wrong. She lets them know that it is her job to help them decide how to solve the conflict and that each person will have an opportunity to explain his or her view of the conflict without being interrupted.

Once the boys have agreed to the mediation process, they must also agree to the process rules. They must agree to solve the problem with honesty and without name-calling or interrupting. They must agree to keep the discussion confidential and to follow through with the agreements that come from the mediation process.

To begin, Ellen gives them each a die to roll to see who goes first. William gets the higher number, so he begins. "I got here first, so I think it's my turn to go. Besides, I need to look up some information for a report I'm working on." While William takes his turn talking, Juan and Ellen listen.

Then Ellen tells Juan it's his turn. "Well, I think we both got here at the same time and I have to look up something for my report too." Ellen restates what she has heard: "William says he was here first and that he needs to look up some information for his report. Juan says that he thinks that you both got here at the same time and he needs to work on his report too. Do either of you have an idea about how to solve this problem?" Juan says, "How about if we roll the dice and whoever gets the larger number can go first?" William agrees.

Before going forward, Ellen checks to make sure both of the boys understand the agreement. She says, "I heard Juan suggest that you both roll the dice and whoever gets the highest number can go first. I also heard William agree to this. Did I understand you both correctly?" The boys both nod their heads. Ellen hands them both a die. William gets the higher number, and Juan agrees to let him have the first turn at the computer.

Mindful Wait Time

One way to promote engagement and learning is to consciously create pauses throughout the day. We can create a sense of spaciousness in our classroom by slowing down the pace of our speech and punctuating our lessons with silence. Introduced well, this practice can improve classroom discourse.

The speed at which we can process information varies from person to person (Droit-Volet, Meck, & Penney, 2007). Some people process auditory information very quickly, while others tend to have more visual or sensorimotor strengths. In any case, when we have more time to process information, the quality of our thinking and learning improves. Younger children require more time to process than do older children, and adults often forget this as they zoom through content as if they were speaking to other adults. No matter what their ages, when we give our students just a little more time to process information, they learn better.

When I introduce this idea to teachers, I often hear concerns that they will be wasting valuable time doing nothing. It's important to recognize that during the pauses, you and your students are not "doing nothing." Your students may be considering several alternatives; they may be mulling a picture over in their mind; they may be making associations, comparisons, and contrasts. They may be trying to drudge up the right word from their vocabulary. When we give them this time, their processing becomes richer, deeper, and more abstract. When you rush through a lesson, you may deliver content more quickly and efficiently, but your students may not absorb the content very well, if at all.

The added bonus of these pause punctuations is that they give us as teachers a few moments to practice mindfulness. When this becomes an intentional part of our lessons, we can take the time to notice our body in space, the whole classroom, each student, and the small details that surrounds us, in the present moment. We give ourselves a short break—a micro-vacation from the constant activity of a busy classroom.

We can use the time to tune in to ourselves and our students. We can ask ourselves, "How am I feeling right now? How are the students feeling? What's happening right now? What do my students need? How can I explain this better?" By taking mindful pauses, we are modeling mindful behavior for our students and letting us all have some time to process the information we are exploring together.

Typically we pause after we ask a question and before we call on someone to answer. Most of the time, this pause is only about one second long. Students who process information quickly are at an advantage under these conditions. They tend to be the ones who always raise their hands immediately. While the speedy students are answering the question, the slower students are still trying to process the question, so they may not hear and comprehend the answer or be able to assimilate it into their existing knowledge. If the quick pace of the session continues, some students may feel left behind.

However, educational researchers have discovered that if the pause between the teacher's question and the student's answer lasts between three and five seconds, significant changes occur in student behavior (Rowe, 1987). Students are more likely to respond appropriately to the questions, answer the questions correctly, and offer longer and more complex answers. There are fewer "I don't know" or non-answer responses. Over time, many more students show higher levels of engagement (Honea, 1982; Swift & Gooding, 1983) and achievement test scores and school retention levels increase (Tobin & Capie, 1982).

Wait time has a positive effect on teachers as well. With conscious use of wait time, teachers' questioning strategies become more varied and flexible, and they ask follow-up questions that require more complex information processing and higher-order thinking (Casteel & Stahl, 1973; Rowe, 1972; Stahl, 1990; Tobin, 1987).

Robert Stahl (1990) identified eight categories of wait time. When we formally introduce wait time, these periods of silence are transformed from periods of awkwardness into valuable moments of silence. The first category is the type of wait time we've already discussed: the time between a teacher's question and the student's answer. The other seven are as follows:

Within-student's-response pause time. This is a three-second or longer pause that occurs when a student pauses or hesitates during the process of delivering a response to a teacher's question. Teachers tend to interrupt students when they are thinking through their answers and take time to pause. However, when given the time, students often follow these periods of silence by successfully completing their responses.

Post-student's-response wait time. This is a pause after a student has finished a response and other students are considering adding comments or reactions. This gives the other students time to think about what was said and to decide if they have anything to add.

Student pause time. This is a pause after a student has initiated a question, statement, or comment but doesn't complete the thought. It may seem strange to formalize this type of pause, but this situation arises more often than we might realize because the tendency is to ignore the question rather than allow for a pause. This happens to me a lot. I have a thought, idea, or question. I'm getting ready to tell someone, and my mind goes blank. I can't remember what I was going to say. When this happens to one of our students, we can give ourselves and the student a little time to recover, rather than just letting it drop.

Teacher pause time. This is a pause that the teacher intentionally initiates to consider what is happening, appraise the situation, and consider the best course of action. A particularly beneficial time for a teacher to pause is when a student has asked a question and the answer requires a complex answer. Taking time to consider how to frame the answer can improve student learning.

Within-teacher-presentation pause time. This is a pause that the teacher intentionally initiates during lecture presentations or other extended periods of content output. The teacher intentionally stops the flow of information to give students three to five seconds of silence to absorb the information and to consolidate their thinking. This type of pause requires no response from the students; it's simply processing time. Using silence this way, teachers can chunk their content into bite-sized pieces to help students absorb and process the information better.

Student task completion work time. This is pause time intended to allow students to complete an academic task that demands undivided attention. The length of the pause should be related to the time it takes to complete a task. The challenge involved in this type of pause is how to handle the variation in completion time among students. If students learn the value of pausing and some of them finish early, they can use the time to extend their thinking about the subject in some way.

Impact pause time. This is the use of pause time to create impact or drama. When we pause, we can create a mood of anticipation. A dramatic pause can generate feelings of suspense and expectation.

Wait time can be challenging. Many of us get so excited about sharing our own thoughts and ideas that we tend to interrupt students, leaving no space in the discussion for students to process information and respond thoughtfully. In the skill-building practices at the end of this chapter, you will learn more about how to apply wait time in your classroom.

Dynamic Instruction

Curious as to why some teachers were able to promote and maintain a high degree of on-task student behavior during instruction compared to others, Jacob Kounin (1970) observed teachers and coded their behavior and their students' responses. He noticed that when teachers responded to student misbehavior with frustration, it had a negative impact on classroom behavior management. He noticed that effective teachers were especially aware of everything going on in their classrooms and used proactive strategies to keep learning on track.

Kounin used his research findings to develop a classroom management theory focused on the teacher's ability to plan, organize, and deliver lessons while simultaneously applying flexible attention and proactive behavior. The effective interaction of management and teaching requires what he calls "lesson movement," achieved through five primary activities: withitness, overlapping, momentum, smoothness, and group focus.

Withitness

In Chapter 2, I introduced the idea of withitness, a term coined by Kounin (1970) to describe teachers' attentive and proactive behavior. This falls into Marzano, Marzano, and Pickering's (2003) "mental set" category of the most effective aspects of classroom management—basically the application of mindfulness in the classroom setting.

Kounin noticed that successful teachers were more "with it." They showed high degrees of awareness of individual and group social, emotional, and attentional dynamics and were able to influence and regulate these dynamics to proactively encourage on-task, prosocial behavior. While this sounds simple, it requires a high degree of cognitive flexibility and self-regulation to attend to individuals and the whole group simultaneously, to quickly appraise situations accurately, and to apply appropriate proactive responses.

In a study involving 80 first- and second-grade classes that each contained at least one emotionally dysregulated child, Kounin found that with-it teachers noticed subtle changes in students' emotions and behavior and responded proactively by letting students know they were aware of them, matter-of-factly reminding them of the task at hand, directing them back to the task if they got distracted, and offering a running commentary to monitor the class's progress (Kounin, 1970).

Developing "eyes in the back of our heads" is really developing heightened awareness of sounds. Tuning in to subtle changes in classroom noise lets us know that something needs our attention. For example, a teacher might notice that one student is beginning to fidget and recognize that this may be an indication that he is confused and needs help. By going to him and offering help before he becomes distracted, the teacher can help keep him and the whole class on track.

The practice of taking occasional pauses and broadening our attention to the whole class can help us develop our withitness. A detailed description of this practice can be found in the skill-building practices at the end of this chapter.

Overlapping

Kounin coined the term *overlapping* before the word *multitasking* came into common use. Basically they mean the same thing. A good teacher can present a new topic while at the same time maintaining an awareness of potential behavioral distractions and proactively setting up preventive strategies.

For example, suppose Ms. Gupta is engaging her high school English class in a discussion about Shakespeare's *Hamlet*. She asks, "What does Marcellus mean when he says that something is rotten in the state of Denmark?" Practicing wait time, she pauses for three seconds and spends this time visually scanning the classroom. She notices that Darnell is staring out the window, distracted. To draw back his attention, she gracefully moves toward him and repeats the question. He turns his attention toward her, reengaged.

Since Ms. Gupta moves about her classroom regularly as she teaches, it's not particularly obvious that she's focused on Darnell when she moves toward him. In this way, she can subtly attract his attention back to the lesson without interrupting the flow of her lesson or embarrassing him.

Overlapping requires a high degree of awareness, which will allow us to recognize the dynamics of a given situation and what strategies may be most appropriate. Juggling multiple demands without becoming anxious or tense also requires cognitive flexibility, presence, and calmness. When we engage in mindful awareness practice on a regular basis, we develop a greater capacity to remain calm under pressure. When we see things as they are in the present moment, without unchecked emotional reactivity, we can handle the demands of teaching better.

Momentum

The term *momentum* refers to the flow of a lesson. Imagine you are riding on a surfboard and catch a wave. To ride it into the sand, you need to stay balanced and resilient, bending your knees in response to the bumps in the wave.

Similarly, good teachers can ride the waves of their classroom. They can accept that a classroom full of children can become chaotic and that that's not necessarily a bad thing. Lessons don't always go according to plan, and a certain amount of spontaneity is appropriate in order to respond to students' interests and needs. Teachers' ability to keep their balance, fluidly adapt, and continue despite distractions and disruptions requires awareness, emotional composure, and persistence. A regular mindful awareness practice helps us cultivate these qualities.

Smoothness

Skillful teachers can maintain the smoothness of their lesson. They aren't tempted to go off on a tangent or become distracted or diverted by extraneous comments or questions. They know their content so well that they can manage a discussion that expands students' thinking and contributes to their understanding of the lesson's primary concepts. They don't get rattled by a challenging or irrelevant question. When we practice mindful awareness on a regular basis, our cognitive functions improve, especially our ability to focus and shift our attention, making it easier for us to stay on track when we're teaching.

Group Focus

When we can engage the whole class simultaneously, we have mastered group focus. This often involves the skillful use of affect, such as by building interest, suspense, excitement, or enthusiasm.

For example, let's say that Mr. Ba is teaching a lesson on fractions. "A fraction is part of a whole," he says as he walks around his class.

Hidden on a shelf is a large bakery box. Mr. Ba stops his lesson, points to the box, and says, "What's on the shelf over there?" All eyes turn to the shelf. Suspense builds as Mr. Ba walks to the shelf, picks up the box, and brings it to the front of the room. "Can anyone guess what's in this box?"

Students guess that it's something from a local bakery.

"Shall I open it to see?" he asks, adding to the anticipation.

"Yes!" they shout in unison.

He has their attention now. He slowly lifts the lid, revealing a sheet cake, and everyone sighs in delight.

"Would you like some of this cake?" he says—and of course they all say yes. But before he begins to share the cake, he turns it into a lesson on fractions.

"Okay," he says. "How about if I get one really big piece and you all get a bunch of tiny pieces? Would that be fair?"

"No!" they shout.

"So, how do I make this fair?"

After a long wait time, he calls on a student who says that every piece should be equal.

"How do I make sure every piece is equal?" he says.

He asks another student to count how many people are in the room. There are 23 students in his class; including him, there are 24. "That means each of us gets one piece of 24 equal pieces, right?"

He shows them how to write 1/24 on the board and proceeds to demonstrate how to cut the cake up evenly. He starts by cutting it in half, writing "1/2 + 1/2 = 2/2 = 1" on the board. Then he makes two more cuts, making four pieces, and writes "1/4 + 1/4 + 1/4 + 1/4 = 4/4 = 1." He continues cutting the cake until there are 24 pieces and then gives each student a piece. Throughout the lesson, Mr. Ba has held his students' group attention as he has creatively introduced fractions.

Responding to Challenging Behavior

In this chapter, we have examined how to apply mindfulness to how we orchestrate classroom dynamics. In this section, we will focus on how mindfulness can help us respond to challenging behavior. Mindfulness can help us recognize the reasons underlying a student's behavior, our emotional response to the behavior, and how to regulate it. We will look at a variety of approaches that can reduce inappropriate behavior and promote prosocial behavior.

Nonjudgmental Awareness

Nonjudgmental awareness is an important aspect of mindfulness that involves accepting things as they are in the present moment. Often when people first begin to practice mindful awareness, they feel that it's impossible not to judge. It's true that this practice is difficult. Often we'll notice that we're judging and then condemn ourselves for judging! However, the practice of mindful awareness involves noticing our tendency to judge. We don't try to stop ourselves from judging, but we notice that it's happening. As we observe ourselves engaging in judgment, we become more aware of it from moment to moment, our mind settles, and eventually our tendency to judge subsides.

For example, we may notice that a student is not paying attention and immediately think, "He never listens" or, "He's trying to make me angry."

Associated with these thoughts are feelings of frustration. When we start to notice these thoughts and feelings, we can take a moment to reflect and calm down. We can accept the fact that we are feeling frustrated and are judging. As soon as we accept this, our judgment begins to fade.

Two feelings go hand in hand with judgment: guilt and shame. Being judged, either by others or ourselves, triggers these self-conscious emotions. Sometimes teachers unconsciously use guilt and shame as management techniques. I believe that this tendency results from what I call the "default mode."

When I was a child and I did something my parents didn't like, I was punished with words intended to shame me or make me feel guilty. Sometimes, if my behavior was particularly egregious, my mother or father would spank me. Having grown up with this approach to discipline, my tendency is to use shame and guilt as a discipline technique as well. When I'm operating on autopilot, I do this without thinking. This is my default mode.

There's plenty of evidence that this guilt and shame approach doesn't work (Gettinger & Kohler, 2006; Levine, 2005; Maines & Robinson, 1995). Rather than encouraging children to behave, it promotes resentment, distrust, and retaliation. These self-conscious emotions reinforce feelings of inadequacy and do nothing to promote learning. By observing our judgments and tendency to judge, we can soften this tendency and begin to move away from guilt- and shame-based approaches to behavior management.

Reasons for Misbehavior

We've been exploring a variety of approaches to preventing behavior problems. Inevitably, however, we will at times need to intervene and stop inappropriate behavior. Before we intervene, it helps if we can determine the reason for the behavior. Practicing mindful awareness can help us make an objective assessment of why a student may be acting inappropriately. It can help us see what is really happening in the present moment, without judgments, preconceptions, biases, or expectations.

Sometimes students misbehave because the environment is inappropriate for their developmental stage. For example, we can't expect a class of kindergarteners to sit for a long period of time listening to a visiting parent talk about her trip to Italy. If older children are asked to sit in chairs or desks that are too small for them, they will become uncomfortable and have difficulty focusing on learning.

Students also act out when they're bored. Boredom can result from learning activities that are too easy or too difficult. When the activity is too easy, some students will finish quickly. If they have nothing to do to channel their energy, they may become disruptive. If the activity is too challenging for some, they may resist trying and become similarly bored and possibly disruptive.

Providing differentiated instruction can prevent students from becoming bored in either case (Tomlinson, 2001). Mindful awareness can help us provide access to the curriculum for all students, no matter what their level of ability. When we mindfully observe our students, we become very familiar with how best to reach them. We can teach the same skills or concepts but individualize the assignments and the expectations.

As we learned earlier, sometimes students misbehave because their physical needs have not been met. Some children become downright cranky when they're hungry because their blood sugar drops, making them physically uncomfortable. When children don't get enough sleep, they can become irritable and have difficulty controlling themselves. Illness can also affect behavior. I once had a student who developed frequent ear infections, and I always knew when he was starting to come down with one because he became very distracted and irritable.

These common causes for misbehavior can be easily remedied by taking simple steps to change the environment or the way we teach, or by making sure our students' physical needs are met. However, sometimes we have students with difficult temperaments or unmet emotional needs that contribute to problem behavior and require careful intervention strategies. Next we will examine each of these issues and ways that mindfulness can help us help our students.

Temperament

Each of us is born with certain temperamental characteristics. Some of us are particularly sensitive to our environment. Loud noises and crowded rooms may make us especially uncomfortable. Some of us handle change better than others, and some of us are just naturally more self-regulated than others. When some of us get upset, we have a hard time getting over it.

Each of these temperamental characteristics can be particularly challenging in the classroom environment. Sensitive students need help adapting to situations that are overstimulating. Students who don't handle change well need help during transitions, and those who are easily upset need help with self-regulation. When we observe our students mindfully, we can notice these sometimes subtle temperamental qualities and how they are influencing our students' behavior. Rather than automatically assuming that their behavior is intentionally designed to upset us, we can empathize and provide support to prevent misbehavior.

Consequences versus Punishment

There's a tendency for many of us to punish our students for misbehavior. When I use the term *punishment*, I am referring to a behavior that is intended to stop misbehavior by hurting. Often this involves name-calling or other words that blame or shame. After all, many of us were punished as children, and this may be a natural tendency for some. However, research has shown that punishment often has unintended side effects. It can negatively impact students' attitudes toward school, their perceptions of teachers, and their interactions with peers and adults (Martens & Meller, 1990). Rather than improving behavior, it can result in resentment, distrust, and the urge to carry out revenge.

When we are confronted with inappropriate student behavior, a more effective alternative is to deliver a natural or logical consequence (Webster-Stratton, Reid, & Hammond, 2004). A natural consequence is something that occurs naturally as a result of a particular behavior or action. For example, suppose Jorge refuses to eat his lunch. Later he says he's hungry, but lunchtime is over. His teacher calmly says, "I'm sorry you're hungry. Lunchtime is over. Tomorrow you can eat lunch during lunchtime."

A logical consequence is something that we decide will happen as a result of a particular behavior. To be effective, a logical consequence needs to be related to the behavior, enforced with firmness but kindness and respect, reasonable, and helpful—it must help a student behave better in the future. If any of these elements is missing, it is most likely not a logical consequence but a punishment.

For example, if a student refuses to do his spelling assignment during the spelling lesson, the assignment can become homework. If the student complains, the teacher can calmly state, "The spelling assignment must be done today. Since it wasn't finished during class, you can complete it at home. Next week, you can do the weekly assignment during class time."

Applying mindful awareness to our management activities can help us recognize whether or not we're using a consequence or a punishment. If we find ourselves feeling the urge to retaliate by shaming or inducing guilt, the response is a punishment. Sometimes it's difficult to acknowledge this feeling because it's not professional to want our students to feel bad. However, the wish to hurt others is a natural tendency when we are feeling angry or hurt ourselves. If we ignore this feeling, we may not notice the way we're communicating and think we're delivering a logical consequence when we're actually engaging in punishment. As we develop the habit of bringing mindful awareness to how we're feeling, we can stop, calm down, and make sure our words communicate a consequence rather than a punishment.

For example, Ms. Vega was frustrated because Anthony was talking to his neighbor again, distracting the class from her lesson. "Anthony," she said, "it's difficult to teach when you're talking. Move to the chair by yourself until you can stop yourself from talking." While her words expressed a logical consequence, the tone of her voice was harsh, turning her statement into a punishment. Her tone also had a demeaning, critical tone, implying that Anthony's behavior was childish. She may not have realized it, but her words were intended to shame and hurt Anthony, not to provide guidance.

Sometimes a response is a punishment because it is excessive. Mr. Randall caught Peter drawing on his desk. "Peter, we respect property at school," he yelled. "Today you will stay after school and clean all the desks." Having Peter clean up the mess he made would have been logical and reasonable. Having him clean all the desks was excessive.

If the response is unrelated to the behavior, it is a punishment rather than a consequence. For example, Jim pushed other students in line, and his teacher Ms. Van der Sel had him write on the board 100 times, "I will not push in line." This response was both unrelated and excessive.

When we establish rules and procedures at the beginning of the year, we can also set out related logical consequences. Three basic categories of logical consequences appropriate for the classroom are:

1. Loss of privileges. A student loses her privilege of being leader of the line when she doesn't line up when it's time to do so.
2. You break it, you fix it. A student who pours glue on a table is asked to clean it up.
3. Take a break. Instead of being spoken to in a degrading manner, as in the story above, Anthony is calmly asked to take a break from sitting near other students until he's ready to focus his attention on learning.

Unmet Emotional Needs:
Assessing the Motive Behind the Behavior

Today, more and more children are coming to school unprepared to adapt to the learning environment, and many have serious behavior problems as early as preschool. Growing numbers of young children are even being expelled from preschool or kindergarten due to these problems (Gilliam, 2005). Often these children come from homes that lack the resources needed to help them learn to self-regulate their attention and behavior.

Such children have difficulty focusing their attention on a task, getting along with others, following instructions, and sitting still. Furthermore, many have been exposed to trauma that can impair important developmental processes critical to learning. Children exposed to trauma tend to be hypervigilant—their brains are wired to be on high alert. They constantly scan their environment for signals of threat, and this unconscious preoccupation uses a lot of cognitive resources, leaving little for learning activities.

Students with these problems may feel overwhelmed and overstimulated by a classroom full of active peers. Because of their inability to self-regulate, they may act out in ways that disrupt the classroom and irritate and annoy their teacher and the other students. Under these conditions, punitive measures don't work and actually tend to reinforce dysregulated behavior.

What these students need are very clear expectations presented with concrete examples and boundaries and limits reinforced with kind but firm communication. When teachers follow this approach, all children respond better. However, children with self-regulation difficulties benefit the most, especially over time (Hamre, & Pianta, 2001).

Adlarian psychologist Rudolph Dreikurs (Dreikurs & Stoltz, 1964) believed that children have an innate need to feel self-worth. Building upon his work, Jane Nelsen (2011) wrote that misbehaving children are discouraged children who have mistaken ideas about how to belong and to feel connected to their community. Dreikurs, Grunwald, and Pepper (1998) have applied these ideas to classroom management.

When the need for belonging is unmet, children may resort to inappropriate behaviors as a way to meet this need. Dreikurs and Soltz (1964) classified these behaviors by their mistaken goals: attention, power, revenge, and displays of inadequacy. To be effective, teachers must address the mistaken goals rather than just the misbehavior.

When students feel a lack of self-worth and belonging, they tend to make bids for undue attention. They seem to need to be the center of attention at all times. When students feel that their attention-seeking doesn't bring them the sense of self-worth and belonging they need, they may begin to vie for power with adults and other students. When these attempts at gaining power fail to give them the self-worth and belonging they need, they may begin to feel disliked and unappreciated, leading to the tendency to carry out revenge. When revenge fails, students become discouraged and give up trying.

Let's look at each of these mistaken goals and their associated behaviors and explore how applying mindful awareness can help us recognize and respond to them appropriately. In Chapter 3, we explored how to apply mindful awareness to recognizing and regulating negative emotions. These skills are essential to working with challenging student behavior.

Recognizing our emotions can even help us assess a student's mistaken goal underlying the behavior. If we feel annoyed, the behavior is likely attention-seeking. If we feel threatened, the behavior is likely a bid for power. If we feel hurt, the behavior is likely an attempt at revenge, and if we feel discouraged, the student is likely engaging in displays of inadequacy (Dreikurs, 1968).

These feelings not only can become important clues to the motive underlying a student's behavior, but they can also help us respond appropriately. They are strong signals that give us a "heads-up" that we need to pay attention to the behavior, be careful not to react automatically, calm down, reflect, and consider the alternatives before we do anything that might reinforce the behavior or aggravate the situation.

The awareness of these feelings can also help us shift from a negative emotional state to a state of compassion. At first, I may feel extremely annoyed or hurt. With practice, I can recognize that the strong feeling is an indication that my student is suffering and needs my care and compassion rather than my anger and punishment. Recognizing that pain and suffering are at the root of the behavior helps me shift my emotional state and respond in a way that is helpful.

Attention

Students who feel a lack of self-worth often resort to seeking undue attention. Everyone needs attention, but students who feel a lack of self-worth seem to need it all the time. They demand attention from their parents and teachers when it's inappropriate. Often they demand attention when their teacher is trying to help another student. They may do things to show off, ask irrelevant questions, or just be generally disruptive, with the mistaken belief that if others are paying attention to them, then they have value.

It's easy to recognize bids for undue attention because they usually provoke feelings of annoyance or irritation. Once I had a student named Karla who exhibited the need for constant attention. Unless I sat with her and helped her, she refused to do anything. She would constantly whine that she needed my help when I was helping other students. This behavior really got on my nerves. Annoyed, I felt like snapping at her to leave me alone.

However, since I understood that my annoyance was a signal that her behavior was a bid for undue attention and that this desire was rooted in her lack of self-worth, I recognized that the best response was no response. I took three deep breaths to calm my annoyance, ignored her demands, and continued helping the other students. At another time when I wasn't so annoyed, I calmly told Karla, "When you feel you need help, I want you to try to figure things out for yourself. Then if you really need help, you can come to me and ask. I don't respond to students who call out."

Applying mindful awareness to the situation helped me notice when Karla was doing something that deserved my attention. For example, when she finished a task without my help, I was sure to say, "Karla, I noticed that you worked very hard on that assignment and finished it all by yourself. You must be proud." Rather than giving her empty praise, I was careful to frame the positive feedback in a way that acknowledged her effort and independence and helped her to value herself and her efforts. The aim of this feedback was to help her build a real sense of self-worth based upon her intrinsic self-motivation.

Power

When students don't think they are getting the attention they deserve, or if they feel that attention is not providing the sense of self-worth they crave, they may come to believe that they need power in order to be valued and resort to engaging in power struggles. Many teachers find students' bids for power incredibly challenging, and they may sometimes fall into a power struggle with such students.

For example, suppose that Ms. Ortega notices that Colon hasn't begun working on his assignment. He is sitting at his desk doodling on a piece of paper. She tells him, "Colon, put that away and get out your book. We're working on the history assignment now."

Colon looks up and glares at her. "No."

Ms. Ortega repeats her instruction more firmly, and Colon replies, "No, I don't want to. I don't need to do anything you tell me to do!"

Ms. Ortega beings to lose her cool. "Watch the way you are talking to me. Get started on the assignment or you're going to be in big trouble."

The power struggle escalates as Colon snaps, "You can't make me."

Ms. Ortega's voice becomes shrill and her face is flushed and contorted in anger as she shouts, "You had better shape up or you will be kicked out of this class!"

"Make me," Colon sneers.

"Okay, that's it. I've had enough of your disrespectful behavior. March right over to the principal's office now," she roars.

Colon kicks over a chair on his way out the door.

In this power struggle, neither Ms. Ortega nor Colon wins. Ms. Ortega is relieved to have Colon out of her class, but this respite is only short-lived. Colon will be back. Ms. Ortega has lost valuable instructional time, and while Colon may be happy to get out of work, he's not learning anything by sitting in the principal's office, except now he knows how to get out of class by engaging in defiant and disrespectful behavior, and his sense of self-worth has not been reinforced in a positive way. Furthermore, he is likely to feel less valued and even more resentful.

There is no way a teacher can win a power struggle with a student, because a student with power issues can do anything while our behavior must remain professional. Since we can't win, it's better to sidestep these situations than to attack them head on. The most important objective is to remain calm.

This is easier said than done, but here's where the application of mindful awareness can really help. Once we realize that we absolutely cannot overpower such students, we can recognize our strong emotions, the student's bid for power, and the suffering that is motivating this behavior. This helps us calm down so that we can dodge a confrontation.

Let's rerun the example above. This time, let's imagine that Ms. Ortega has been practicing mindful awareness regularly and that her emotional awareness and self-regulation have improved.

Ms. Ortega notices that Colon has not begun his assignment. Rather than broadcasting her instructions to him so that the other students can hear her, she goes over to Colon and quietly asks him to take out his history book. He says no, but instead of beginning a battle with him by repeating her instructions, she moves away.

She notices that the heat is rising in her face and that her jaw and shoulders are starting to tense. She's familiar with these sensations and recognizes that she's feeling threatened, clueing her in to an impending power struggle. She takes three long, slow breaths to calm herself and remembers that Colon's power issues are a result of his unmet need for a sense of self-worth. His behavior is rooted in suffering and is not personal. This helps her remain objective so that she can consider alternatives.

Depending upon her understanding of Colon and his issues, Ms. Ortega can respond in a variety of ways to avoid a confrontation. In a calm, matter-of-fact voice, she can restate the expectation that the history lesson is to be completed by the end of class and then walk away. She can calmly acknowledge that it's up to him to do his work and communicate the consequences of not doing it. She can offer him an alternative, or an incentive. Sometimes humor or doing something unexpected can shift the emotional energy in a way that diffuses power struggles, but adults need to be careful to avoid sarcasm, which can shaming or embarrassing.

Ms. Ortega can take time to consider reasons for Colon's behavior. Perhaps something happened before the class session that has upset him. Perhaps something troubling is going on at home. At a later time, Ms. Ortega can address these possibilities with him, when they are both calm and not under time pressure.

Revenge

When students feel as if their efforts to achieve self-worth and belonging by trying to gain power and control over others are thwarted, they may feel that the situation is unfair and may carry out revenge. They may lash out at their teachers and other students by hitting, kicking, scratching, or destroying property. When students behave like this, teachers tend to feel hurt, outraged, disappointed, or disgusted.

It's important to recognize that carrying out revenge is a symptom of severe suffering. These students act out and hurt others because they feel deeply hurt and alienated. What they need most is understanding and assistance. Mindful awareness can be particularly helpful because we must override our natural tendency to defend ourselves and others by lashing out at these students.

Raheem is discouraged in his efforts to feel valued by his teacher and his peers. He sees himself as inherently bad and unlikable. Others dislike him because of his unpredictable and hostile behavior, reinforcing his belief. While Raheem needs encouragement more than most, he is least likely to receive it. When his parents and his teacher punish him and his peers reject him, it reinforces his belief that he is bad and unlikable.

During class one day, Raheem grabs Sandra's assignment and tears it to shreds. His teacher, Ms. Rome, is horrified, and Sandra begins to cry. Understanding Raheem's problem, Ms. Rome takes a deep breath before she does anything. She knows she needs to respond calmly or she will risk reinforcing Raheem's mistaken beliefs.

Recognizing that they all need time to cool off, she tells Raheem to take some time out, carefully monitoring her voice to make sure there's no edge to it. "Raheem, I expect you to respect others' work. It is my job to be sure other students' property is not destroyed. When you did that, I felt very angry, and I see that Sandra is very upset too. I want you to take some time to calm down and then we'll talk about this."

When taking a breath reduces but does not eliminate our strong feelings, it's best to acknowledge them. Our students see what we're feeling on our face, so we might as well be honest. Otherwise we risk eroding their trust. However, the way we communicate our feelings is important. Ms. Rome does not lash out in anger. She does not attempt to hurt Raheem in any way. She uses an "I" message to communicate her feelings in response to his behavior (Gordon, 2003).

Ms. Rome has a peace corner in her classroom where students can go when they need to calm down (Lantieri, 2008). Raheem sits there quietly for some time, wearing headphones and listening to soothing music.

When the class has left for recess, Ms. Rome has a talk with Raheem and learns that Sandra made a silly remark that triggered his anger. Together they explore alternative responses to this remark, and later that day Ms. Rome coaches Raheem as he tells Sandra that he didn't like what she said.

Over the course of the school year, Raheem begins to build trust in Ms. Rome. He begins to believe that she cares about him and begins to respond to her help and direction more quickly. Soon his peers begin to follow her lead and they begin to play with him more often. Slowly, Raheem's behavior problems improve.

Discouragement

When students fail to achieve a sense of self-worth and belonging through attention, power, and revenge, they may become discouraged and give up trying. Feeling that they have no place in the world, they often experience deep despair. Students can also become discouraged if they have been taught that they are worthless from an early age (Dreikurs et al., 1998).

These students act as if they want to be left alone. They can be quiet and withdrawn and have a tendency to withdraw further if attention is focused on them. They act helpless and give up easily. Often they won't even attempt a task. Sometimes these students become invisible to their teachers and peers because they demand so little attention.

When our students display inadequacy to this degree, we may feel despair, frustration, and hopelessness. We may react by giving up on the child or trying to help too much. Mindful awareness can help us notice these feelings and tendencies so that we can consciously shift our approach to these students. We can recognize that the students' displays of inadequacy are a sign of deep suffering, and we can commit ourselves to refusing to give up on them.

These students need kind and firm encouragement. It's best if we focus on their strengths and avoid any criticism or expressions of pity, demonstrating that we understand their discouragement but that we have faith in them and won't give up on them. We can encourage incremental progress by chunking tasks into small parts and helping them accomplish very small goals, one at a time.

As we discussed in Chapter 4 in the section on pride, it's important to praise students' work, not their skills or abilities. Often discouraged children have a fixed mindset; they believe they are inherently and permanently worthless and incapable (Dweck, 2007). They are in great need of the kind of encouragement that promotes a growth mindset.

For example, we can say, "You worked very hard on that and finished one page," rather than, "Look, you did it! You're so smart!" To these children, such praise will ring hollow. They won't believe it, and it won't help you build trust. With regular encouragement, I have seen children like these change dramatically. It's a slow process that requires consistency and diligence, but the efforts can pay off.

Skill-Building Practices

Practicing Withitness

As you learned in this chapter, knowing what's going on in your classroom is critical to your ability to orchestrate social and emotional dynamics that are conducive to learning. Practicing mindful awareness can help you develop this skill. It involves paying attention in the present moment to everything that's happening with calmness and curiosity. Every day, take a few moments to practice this skill. Over time, it will become automatic. Wait for a time when the class is quietly engaged in an activity. Currently, you may like to use this time to check your email or go over your plans for the next lesson. Rather than doing these things, take a few moments to practice mindful awareness. Find a place to stand in your classroom where you have a good view of the entire class. Feel your feet on the ground. Feel the weight of your body pressing on the floor. Get in touch with your center and practice feeling grounded.

Now gently relax your eyes and let your gaze slightly settle downward. You can let your vision become unfocused. You don't want to close your eyes, but you want your attention to move from your eyes to your ears. Now, listen to the sounds in the room. You may hear the clock ticking and the sound of pencils writing on paper. You may notice the sound of clothing rustling as your students shift in their seats. Now try to hear sounds outside your room—the sounds of children playing outside, people walking down the hallway, traffic going by. Stay with this mindful awareness of sound until you notice a shift in your class. You may notice that some students are finished and are beginning to move to free-choice activities. Notice the sounds of your classroom as your students begin to change what they are doing. At this point, you may need to intervene, but maybe not. See how long you can stay in this state of mindful awareness before you absolutely need to become involved. You may begin by lifting your eyes and visually scanning the classroom. While you do this, see if you can maintain your mindful awareness.

Mindful Wait Time

In this chapter, you learned about the value of "wait time." Wait time involves waiting three seconds after asking a question during discussion time. If possible, it's best to begin the school year employing regular wait time. However, you can initiate the practice at any time during the school year. You can explain to your students, "We know that students learn better and teachers teach better when we give ourselves time to think about a question before answering it. I will wait about three seconds after I ask a question before I call on anyone to answer. This will give you time to think about how you'd like to answer. I will also give myself some time before I respond."

Each time you do your three-second wait time, use this time to mindfully take a nice, deep breath. If you are standing, notice the weight of your feet on the ground. Allow your awareness to broaden so that you can take in the entire class. Scan the class, noticing each student as they raise their hands, and choose a student you may not have called on much lately. As she delivers her answer, listen mindfully and spend time considering it. Do you have a follow-up question for her? How can you respond to her answer in a way that encourages higher-order thinking and problem-solving? After practicing mindful wait time for a few days, you will notice that both the quality of your students' answers and the quality of your own questioning will improve.

Introducing Mindfulness to Students

Below are three simple mindful awareness activities you can introduce to your students. These activities are appropriate for any age level and intended to promote self-awareness; foster cognitive, emotional, and behavioral self-regulation; and reduce stress. Ultimately, the aim is to prepare your students' minds to learn.

When you first introduce an activity, do it during a time when you feel relaxed and have no extra pressures to deal with. This will allow you to take the time to apply your own mindful presence to teaching these activities. Before presenting a lesson, take a brief moment to center yourself. As you bring mindful awareness to each teaching moment, you are providing a scaffold that will support your students' mindfulness, making it easier for your students to engage with you. I also suggest that you aim to make these activities part of the daily routine. Weave them into the fabric of your day. Regular, daily practice will help strengthen students' self-awareness, self-regulation, and cognitive skills. It will also create regular spaces in the day for everyone to calm down.

Mindful Listening

This is a common mindfulness-based practice that is found in many mindfulness education curricula. All you need is a special bell that you use exclusively for this activity. I recommend a Woodstock Percussion Zenergy Chime, which is usually available on Amazon at a low cost.

Mindful listening is very useful for transition times. You can use it at the beginning of each mindfulness activity session to help students focus their attention. For example, you could use at the beginning of class and then again after lunch. You could also close the day with this exercise before dismissal. Once your students become used to this practice, they will ask for it if you forget. Many teachers have found that students derive a lot of value from this exercise and even ask substitutes to do it when their regular teacher is absent.

Tell your students, "We're going to do a listening activity that will help our minds relax and become more focused. First, let's all sit up nice and tall in our seats with our hands folded in our laps (or on the desk). In a few minutes, I'm going to ring this chime, and we're going to listen to the sound until it disappears. I find that I can focus my attention on my hearing best when I close my eyes. You can try that, but if you aren't comfortable closing your eyes, you can lower your gaze to your hands." When everyone is ready, ring the bell. Once the ringing has stopped, you can say, "Now I will begin the lesson."

After you have practiced this for a couple of weeks, you can extend the listening time a bit. Tell your students, "Today we're going to listen a little bit longer. When the sound of the bell fades, see what else you can hear." After the listening exercise, ask the students what they heard. You may be surprised to hear some of their responses. Younger children have much better hearing than adolescents and adults.

Mindful Walking

This is another activity that is very helpful for getting your students focused during a transition from one activity or lesson to another. If possible, introduce this activity in a place where you have lots of space, like the gym or the playground, with your students in a circle. Tell your students, "Today we're going to practice paying attention to how we walk. I will show you how." Demonstrate walking slowly and describe how your weight shifts from the heel to the ball and then to the toe of your foot. "Pay attention to the feeling of the weight of your body on the soles of your feet." Have the students all face the same way and begin slowly walking in a circle. After a few minutes, stop and ask them how that feels. They may notice that it's not so easy to walk slowly. Once they have mastered slow, mindful walking, you can use this exercise during transitions to and from lunch, recess, and so on.

Mindful Eating

This is a simple mindfulness practice that comes from mindfulness-based stress reduction (MBSR). The purpose of this exercise is to bring mindful awareness to the sensory experiences involved in eating as well as greater awareness of what is being eaten.

You will need a few boxes of raisins—enough for each student to receive one raisin. Before you start, have your students wash their hands. Before you pass out the raisins, say, "Today we're going to do an exercise that will help us focus our attention on our sense of taste using a raisin. I'm going to pass out one napkin and one raisin. Keep the raisin on the napkin on your desk until I tell you to pick it up." Once everyone has their napkin with the raisin on top, you can begin.

"First, pick up the raisin and put it in the palm of your hand. Just hold it and look at it. Examine it carefully. In your mind, think about how you would describe the raisin. What color is it? How would you describe the texture? What does it feel like against the skin of your palm? Pick up the raisin with your other hand. How does it feel in between your fingers? Is it sticky? Rough? Smooth? Soft? Hard? Gently squeeze it. How does it feel? Put the raisin up to your nose and smell it. How does it smell?

"Now gently put the raisin into your mouth, but do not eat it. Can you feel it against your tongue? What does the texture feel like now? How does it taste? How does the taste compare to the way it smelled? Move it around in your mouth and notice every aspect of the raisin. Now take a small bite of the raisin and notice what you taste. Now how does the raisin taste in your mouth? Slowly finish chewing the raisin and swallow it. How did it taste? Describe the experience of the raisin."

Take a few minutes and have your students write about their experience of tasting the raisin. Use your creativity! You could ask them to write a poem about the raisin or simply describe the experience. This is a great way for them to develop their vocabulary of adjectives. This exercise can be done with any food. You can also apply the same kind of mindful awareness to other activities, such as art projects or exploring nature. In this way, you can enliven your curriculum with mindful awareness. This may promote interest and enhance memory by reducing the stress students sometimes associate with content matter.

Bell Activity

This activity is an adaptation of a Montessori activity called "Walking on the Line." It promotes focused attention, coordination, and motor planning. Below is a description of the basic exercise. Then I describe a series of extensions that increase in difficulty and involve interpersonal cooperation and coordination. This activity can be done with 10 to 12 small hand bells. However, if you don't have access to these, you can use cups of water. The aim of the exercise is to not let the bells ring (or the water spill). The intention of the activity is to promote mindful awareness of the eight senses described in the section in Chapter 1 on the wheel of awareness: the five senses of sight, smell, hearing, touch, and taste; internal bodily sensations; "mindsight"; and relational sense.

Invite your students to stand together in a circle, then ask for several volunteers to step forward into a smaller circle. Give each volunteer a hand bell (or cup of water) and instruct them to walk together in a circle, trying not to let the bell ring (or the water spill). To do this, students must engage all eight of their senses. They must anticipate the sound of the bell, see where the bell is in space, touch the bell, and manage its weight. They may notice bodily sensations of anticipation or nervousness about possibly ringing the bell or spilling the water. They may notice their thoughts about how to best hold the bell without letting it ring. They may also notice the interpersonal attunement among them—the flow of the activity as everyone works together toward one goal.

Depending on the age of your students, you can orient them to this activity by introducing some of these ideas. For younger children, I recommend saying very little—perhaps only asking a few questions about what the experience was like. For older children and adolescents, you can introduce the idea of mindful awareness and the senses.

Also depending on the age of your students, you can move to greater levels of difficulty. If you have enough bells for all the students your class, invite everyone to take a bell and stand in a large circle. Spend a brief time with everyone walking in a circle trying not to let the bell ring. Next, have them face inward and notice who is on the opposite side of the circle. Ask them to walk carefully across the circle to the place on the opposite side of the circle without ringing their bell and without bumping into anyone.

Another way to extend the activity is to take one bell and begin passing it carefully around the large circle, trying not to let it ring. You can increase the difficulty by adding more bells to the circle so that several are being passed around the circle simultaneously, with some moving in opposite directions. If there is time and you want to add yet another level of difficulty, ask for a small group of volunteers to stand outside the circle. Begin by asking the inner circle to start passing around the bells, and then instruct the volunteers to walk in and out of the circle while the bells are being passed around the circle.

Chapter 7

Mindfulness and School Transformation

You never change things by fighting the existing reality. To change something, build a new model that makes the existing model obsolete.

—Richard Buckminster Fuller[3]

In his book *A Mindful Nation* (2013), Congressman Tim Ryan (Ohio, District 17) illustrated how a peaceful revolution is quietly transforming America as individuals are taking up the practice of mindful awareness and it is becoming integrated into sectors of our society ranging from health care and education to the military. *Time* magazine echoed this understanding in a cover feature on mindfulness titled "The Mindful Revolution" (Pickert, 2014).

Moreover, the quiet revolution sweeping across the United States is mirrored in similar activities throughout the world. The *Time* article noted that today there are close to 1,000 Mindfulness-Based Stress Reduction (MBSR) instructors offering trainings in every state and more than 30 countries around the globe (Pickert, 2014). It appears that we may be experiencing a "tipping point," defined by Malcolm Gladwell as "the moment of critical mass, the threshold, the boiling point" (Gladwell, 2000, p. 12).

This cultural tipping point has the potential to transform (as opposed to reform) education. To "reform" means to change or

---

3 The Estate of R. Buckminster Fuller attributes this quote to several lectures by R. Buckminster Fuller

improve the condition of an existing structure or form. In contrast, to "transform" means to change the very nature of the structure or form itself—a metamorphosis.

As Fuller says in the quote above, transformation results in "a new model that makes the existing model obsolete." In this chapter, we will explore how mindfulness has the potential to transform the way we think about seemingly intractable problems. While educators and policy makers have struggled over school reform for decades, the skillful application of mindful awareness may help catalyze the transformation education urgently needs.

In this chapter, I will introduce the organizations and individuals who form the vanguard of the mindfulness-in-education movement, pioneers who are transforming our classrooms, schools, and whole districts. We will survey the numerous evidence-based programs and the research that is demonstrating that mindfulness reduces stress and improves well-being for students and teachers. We will see how these programs are also improving learning environments and student outcomes.

A Catalyst for Transformation

Be the change you wish to see in the world.
—Gandhi

Transformation begins with the individual. By regularly practicing mindful awareness and applying mindful awareness it to our life and work, we begin to recognize that we are not victims of circumstances and that we have the power to change ourselves, our classrooms, and our schools for the better. Gandhi's words remind us that we are the agents of change.

Mindfulness can provide the insight we need to envision a completely new model of education that we can begin to realize *now*, in our own lives and classrooms. As teachers, we are important role models for our students and their parents. We are in a unique position to "be the change."

We can base our vision for this new educational model on the hopes and dreams we have for our children. Recently I heard Congressman Ryan give a talk at the Contemplative Sciences Center at the University of Virginia. He said that we all want two things for our children: We want them to care about others and we want them to pay attention. He pointed out that parents and teachers are always telling children, "Pay attention" and "Be nice." But he went on to ask, "How often do they teach them how to do those things?"

He pointed out that mindfulness may be the simplest, safest, and most effective way to promote the attention and kindness we want for our children. As William James noted, "The faculty of voluntarily bringing back a wandering attention, over and over again, is the very root of judgment, character, and will" (James, 1950, p. 424). This is mindfulness, and, as James continued, "an education which should improve this faculty would be the education par excellence."

Rather than simply training our children's minds to absorb and regurgitate facts so that they can do well on standardized tests, mindfulness has the potential to promote other valuable cognitive skills, such as creative thinking, perspective-taking, and innovative problem-solving. These skills are critical to our collective capability for addressing the challenging problems we face today.

Practicing mindful awareness also supports the social and emotional dimensions of development by promoting an ethos of caring and compassion. Furthermore, it provides us with the tools to become more aware of our emotional experiences and to better regulate our emotions, skills that are critical to building successful social relationships with others.

Indeed, my colleagues and I have argued that mindfulness adds value to social and emotional learning (SEL) by cultivating the capacity for self-awareness and self-regulation, two essential dimensions of SEL (Jennings, Lantieri, & Roeser, 2012).

Mindfulness can be described as a developmental resource for the understanding of our inner lives—the engine that drives spiritual development, in the secular sense of the word (Jennings, 2008). Mindfulness promotes a sense of belonging and connecting. As we experience present-moment, nonjudgmental awareness, we can more readily recognize our common humanity and our interdependence on one another and on all of life, not as a philosophical abstraction but as direct experience of interconnection. The act of caring for one another, for living things, and for our planet becomes an ethical mandate because we recognize our oneness.

The practice of mindful awareness promotes awakening. As we hone our attentional skills, we develop insight. We begin to see subtle details that we never noticed before, thus awakening in ourselves a deeper understanding of situations, interrelationships, and systems.

For example, when I observe a classroom mindfully, sometimes I notice subtle but significant forms of learning that I would otherwise have missed. The little girl in the corner, intently concentrating on folding a piece of paper, could be perceived as a child "off task." When I take the time to let my preconceptions dissolve and view the situation through a mindful lens, I realize that she is engaging in deep concentration as she attempts to make an origami bird. While she may be off task in the traditional sense, she is learning something significant—to generate and utilize her deep powers of concentration to accomplish a challenging and intrinsically motivated task. By regularly practicing mindful awareness I can recognize my strong urge to interrupt and redirect her, and I can take a moment to breathe. Applying mindfulness to our teaching is about giving ourselves and our students some "space" by accepting them for who they are and recognizing the inherent value and meaning in their motives and actions rather than trying to fit them into a mold formed by institutional expectations.

Mindfulness promotes a wholesome way of living. When we become deeply aware of our habitual patterns of behavior, thought, and emotion, we begin to take responsibility for these aspects of our experience and to better understand how they affect others. We no longer see ourselves as victims of circumstances. We recognize that we have an infinite number of choices for responding to any given situation. Our old self-destructive patterns fall away, and we begin to take better care of ourselves.

Preparing Our Children for an Uncertain Future

Throughout history, the role of education has been to prepare children for adulthood. Today our world is changing so rapidly that it's difficult to know what it will be like even a decade from now. While we cannot predict the features of the world our children will inherit, we do know that the pace of change will most likely continue to accelerate (Thomas & Brown, 2011).

Therefore, we can be fairly certain that our students will need to be adaptable, creative, resilient, courageous, innovative, persistent, open-minded, open-hearted, and cooperative. They will need to learn how to think outside the box, so to speak, so that they can find new ways to approach the seemly intractable problems that loom ahead.

In 1946, the *New York Times* reported that Albert Einstein had sent a telegram to several hundred prominent Americans requesting their support for a nationwide campaign to promote a new way of thinking. In the telegram he said, "A new type of thinking is essential if mankind is to survive and move toward higher levels" ("Atomic Education Urged," 1946). Mindfulness may hold the key to transforming our modes of thinking.

Ironically, the change in thinking may be most possible when we stop anxiously striving for solutions. When we feel pressured to solve a problem, often our emotions get in the way. As we discussed in Chapter 3, negative emotions can distort and limit our thinking. When we mindfully experience the fullness of the present moment, a multitude of possibilities arise spontaneously, without effort. When we widen our perspective, our mind makes connections that we didn't realize existed before.

MIT professor Otto Scharmer calls this process of accessing potentiality "presencing." In the context of his "Theory U," a change management method, he describes it as the capacity to allow the future to emerge spontaneously (Scharmer, 2009). According to Scharmer, we have collectively failed to solve our problems because of a blind spot that blocks our ability to recognize the inner source from which transformational change can emerge. When a team of individuals connects in this inner space, it begins to operate at a higher level as "as an intentional vehicle for an emerging future" (Scharmer, 2014).

I believe that through practicing mindful awareness, we cultivate a connection with this source. In the present moment, we experience the fullness of this future potentiality and can set our intention, like a compass, to align our actions with the future we envision. When we aren't fixated in a mental construction of reality that exists in our memory of the past or our hopes and fears for the future, anything is possible. From this state of calm but clear awareness comes unexpected ingenuity.

With this new understanding, we can shift the focus of education from the accumulation of knowledge to the cultivation of understanding, wisdom, meaningfulness, and a sense of shared humanity. We can generate a deep sense of care and compassion for our fellow human beings around the globe. We have all the tools at our disposal to change the way we live to be sustainable and morally and ethically just. The skillful application of mindful awareness can help us cultivate the collective will. As we recognize our interdependence, we can see that we have no choice but to broaden our narrow focus beyond our individual wants and needs.

The Challenges Ahead

After reading this book, you may wish to go out and immediately begin teaching mindfulness to your students. I encourage you to be thoughtful about how you proceed. Public schools serve everyone. A school becomes what's called *in loco parentis*, meaning that it takes on parental responsibility for students and must respect the cultural sensitivities of the families it serves. So how we introduce the practice of mindful awareness in the schools is critically important.

Schools today are looking for practices that have been scientifically tested to show results, so we must really know what we're talking about. That means we need to be prepared with hard science, not just goodwill and good ideas, recognizing that our beliefs and our personal experiences alone are not adequate to make the case for a mindfulness-based approach in education. This book will help you make a strong case. In the following sections, I review programs and approaches that have scientific evidence of efficacy in improving teaching and learning.

Pioneers

Several organizations and individuals form the vanguard of the mindfulness-in-education movement. In this section I describe their innovative work of formulating ideas and growing capacity to transform education. These include Naropa University's contemplative education program; Calm Classrooms; the Inner Resilience Program of New York City; the South Burlington Vermont School District's Wellness and Resilience Program, a districtwide initiative; and the Skills for Life initiative in two districts in Ohio.

Naropa University

Naropa University is a unique institution founded in 1974 by Tibetan Buddhist teacher Chögyam Trungpa Rinpoche. His vision was to create a university that would combine Eastern contemplative approaches with traditional disciplines of the West.

Inspired by Nalanda University, founded in Northern India in the fifth century CE, Naropa University takes its name from Naropa, the 11th century abbot of Nalanda University. At the time, Nalanda was a model of interdisciplinary education. Scholars came from around the world to study, debate, and share their respective traditions.

Since its founding, Naropa University has been a pioneer in contemplative education—the application of mindfulness and other practices to teaching and learning. From its beginning, Naropa University has recognized that insight, wisdom, and deep understanding of the world are critical components of education.

In 1990, Naropa University professor Richard Brown founded the Contemplative Education Early Childhood Education Program. In 2001, the program expanded to offer a low-residency, two-year contemplative education master's degree that is designed for classroom teachers at all levels, pre-K through higher education. The program is designed to be delivered to a cohort community that is formed during the three-week summer residency program offered for two consecutive summers. The remaining coursework is delivered in online classes.

The program integrates holistic Western educational theory and philosophy with Eastern meditative practices such as mindfulness. Students learn how to integrate mindful awareness and other contemplative practices into instructional methods and subject matter.

Calm Classroom

The Calm Classroom (CC) program is based on the work of Herbert Benson, the Harvard Medical School professor and pioneer in mind-body medicine who developed the relaxation response (RR) method in the 1970s (Benson & Klipper, 2009).

The CC K–12 curriculum introduces a set of techniques that involve mindful breath awareness, concentration, relaxation, and stretching. The techniques are very brief, lasting between 30 seconds and two minutes, and are designed to be practiced several times a day, especially before or after a transition time. The program is designed to increase students' attention spans and decrease stress-related problems, including anxiety and disruptive behavior.

Calm Classroom was designed as a schoolwide intervention. Teachers introduce the techniques to students, but over time the students learn to lead the class during practice time. The practices are introduced and practiced by the entire school staff and are used to help students self-regulate during disciplinary activities.

An early study compared high school students who were taught RR versus a typical health curriculum three times per week. Students who learned RR reported significant increases in self-esteem (Benson et al., 1994).

Benson and his colleagues (2000) conducted a study to examine the effects of practicing the program on middle school students' academic and behavioral outcomes across a three-year intervention period. The study found that students who were exposed to two or more semesters of classes that included these practices had higher grade point averages, better work habits, and higher cooperation scores than students who had less exposure to the program practices.

Inner Resilience Program

On September 11, 2001, thousands of New York City school children ran for their lives. Children, teachers, parents, and administrators were faced with an unparalleled tragedy. In response, former NYC school administrator Linda Lantieri developed the Inner Resilience Program (IRP) to help New York City teachers in Ground Zero cope with the resulting trauma (Lantieri, Nambiar, & Chavez-Reilly, 2006). Not long afterward, she began to develop a mindfulness-based curriculum for students in response to requests from teachers, parents, and administrators (Lantieri, 2008).

IRP provides skills, tools, and strategies to help teachers develop their "inner lives," strengthen their resilience in the face of trauma, and model and teach these skills for their students. Teachers learn self-care, mindfulness-based stress reduction techniques, and yoga during residential and daylong retreats, after-school workshops and institutes, and technical assistance and training at their local school sites.

A randomized, controlled trial involving 57 New York City teachers working in Grades 3 through 5 found significant improvements in self-reported stress, attention, mindfulness, and relational trust among teachers who received the program compared to the control group of colleagues who did not (Simon, Harnett, Nagler, & Thomas, 2009).

For this study, teachers were provided with guidance on how to introduce the IRP mindfulness-based activities to their students (857 students were in the entire study, including the control group). Compared to third-grade students of control teachers, third-grade students of treatment teachers reported significant improvements in measures of autonomy and a sense of influence. The program also had a significant positive impact on reducing third- and fourth-grade students' levels of frustration.

Districtwide Initiatives

Another pioneer in the mindfulness in education transformation movement is the South Burlington School District in Vermont. During the 2008–2009 school year, the district initiated the Inner Resilience Pilot Project, offering the Inner Resilience Program (IRP, described above) to a group of 41 teachers, administrators, and staff from the district's three elementary schools.

The South Burlington IRP consisted of a 10-month series of workshops and retreats that introduced stress reduction and emotion regulation skills designed to improve teachers' personal and professional well-being. Activities included deep breathing, mindfulness meditation, and other contemplative practices.

A program evaluation comparing scores on self-report measures completed by educators before and after the program found significant reductions in stress and increases in mindfulness (New England Network for Child, Youth & Family Services, 2009).

Participating educators also completed monthly reports wherein they were asked to chart their progress. These showed a significant increase in their personal "health promotion scores," which included their perceptions of calmness, happiness, and satisfaction with their work. The evaluation also found that 87% of the participants felt that IRP had had a "serious" or "moderate" effect upon their personal lives, and 90% said the same about their professional lives.

After the educators had been introduced to IRP, the 28 teachers and 4 counselors that were part of the group began introducing activities to groups of students. At the end of the school year, a majority of them reported that they felt it had had a significant positive effect on the students. They reported an increase in their students' ability to calm themselves. Furthermore, 75% of the 84 students in five of the IRP classes said that the program activities had been beneficial.

Since the original pilot project, the district has initiated the Wellness and Resilience Program (WRP), which has expanded the district's services to include the integration of evidenced-based programs for students, such as the Learning to BREATHE program (described below in the section "Evidence-Based Programs for Children and Youth") and a lecture series for both educators and parents.

A growing number of other districts and schools, both public and private, are building programs modeled on the South Burlington program by integrating mindfulness with a compassionate approach to transform their school culture and climate, with promising results.

For example, the Skills for Life (SFL) Program aims to transform two academically challenged school districts in Youngstown and Warren, Ohio. The project is in the process of delivering a comprehensive curriculum to teachers and students that integrates a research-based social and emotional learning program called The 4R's and the Inner Resilience Program's mindfulness and stress management activities.

A recent implementation evaluation study found that participants enjoyed the program and that their knowledge of program topics had improved (Jones, Cash, & Osher, 2013).

Evidence-Based Programs for Children and Youth

In 2005, the Garrison Institute published a report that aimed to map the field of contemplation in educational settings (Garrison Institute, 2005). At that time, the report found only a few mindfulness-based programs for children and youth and virtually no research to study their efficacy. These days, new programs are springing up so quickly that it's difficult to keep up.

While there are now a rapidly growing number of programs being developed and presented to students and teachers in schools all over the world, the programs I chose to review for this book meet a high standard. I intentionally set my standards high because I want you to have the knowledge you need to make the strongest case possible when you speak to school leaders, colleagues, and parents.

These programs have been successfully integrated into schools in the US, Canada, and/or the UK; have a clearly articulated curriculum that can be easily accessed and replicated; are based in developmentally appropriate practice; and have some preliminary evidence of efficacy that has been published in a peer-reviewed journal.

Two important caveats: (a) Much of the research reported here is promising but preliminary. Due to space restrictions, I do not describe the limitations of each study. However, many are limited by small, selective samples; the lack of a control or comparison group; lack of random assignment; and biased reporters. (b) The research results reported here are probabilistic, such that evidence in support of a program's efficacy may change over time.

In the Resources section at the end of the book, I list many of the other mindfulness-based programs available to students and teachers that have not yet met my criteria. Included in this section is the URL for the Garrison Institute's searchable database of mindfulness-based programs available for children and teachers in both school and clinical settings.

Holistic Life Foundation

Children and youth in underserved urban communities are often chronically stressed due to exposure to violence and a lack of resources. This puts them at risk for stress-related problems, including behavioral difficulties and poor academic performance. A mindfulness-based approach may help these youth by promoting resilience and self-regulatory skills.

Brothers Ali and Atman Smith learned yoga and mindfulness from their parents and met their friend Andy Gonzales in college. They thought that together, yoga and mindfulness might help the struggling inner city kids growing up in the neighborhood made famous by the HBO series *The Wire*.

The Holistic Life Foundation's program combines yoga postures, fluid movement exercises, breathing techniques, and guided mindfulness practices. The movement activities are designed to enhance muscle tone and flexibility, and students learn breathing techniques designed to help them calm themselves. Each class includes a didactic component where instructors talk to students about identifying stressors and using mindfulness and breathing to reduce stress. At the end of each class, students lie on their backs and close their eyes while the instructors guide them through a mindful awareness practice. The program has been offered in a variety of settings in school and outside school.

Drs. Tamar Mendelson of Johns Hopkins and Mark Greenberg of Penn State University, along with their colleagues, conducted a randomized, controlled trial of a 12-week school-based version of the HLF program. Students assigned to HLF attended the program during school hours four days per week for 45 minutes per session. Researchers assessed stress responses, depressive symptoms, and peer relations before and after the program. The results suggest that the students, teachers, and administrators liked the program and that it resulted in reductions in students' problematic responses to stress, including rumination, intrusive thoughts, and emotional arousal (Mendelson et al., 2010). ("Rumination" in this case refers to a symptom associated with anxiety in which one compulsively goes over something that happened in the past.)

Inner Kids

Developed by Susan Kaiser Greenland (2010), the Inner Kids program teaches the "new ABCs"—attention, balance, and compassion. Through direct instruction, games, and other activities, the program aims to develop awareness of inner experience (thoughts, emotions, and physical sensations), awareness of outer experience (other people, places, and things), and awareness of how these two blend together.

The program has been offered to children and youths from preschool through 12th grade. Programs for young children typically meet twice a week for 30 minutes for a period of eight weeks. Programs for older children meet longer, 45 minutes twice a week for 10 to 12 weeks.

Each class session is divided into three sections. The program usually begins with a practice that focuses on the development of breath awareness or awareness of the body in space. Each session involves play and discussion to help children understand their experiences and apply them to their lives. An important part of the program is teaching children about community service and compassionate action. The class usually ends with a period of lying down and a "friendly wishes practice"—a secular version of the loving-kindness or *metta* practice adapted for children. These introspective practices become progressively longer over the duration of the program.

A school-based version of the Inner Kids program was evaluated in a randomized, controlled study involving 64 children ages seven to nine (Flook et al., 2010). Students were randomly assigned to either the Inner Kids program or a control group, which received a silent reading period instead. The students assigned to Inner Kids received the program for 30 minutes, two times per week, for eight weeks. Teacher and parent reports of students' behavior that exhibited their executive functioning were collected before and after the eight-week program.

Compared to the control group, the students in the Inner Kid group who were less self-regulated at baseline showed greater improvement in behavioral regulation, metacognition, and overall global executive control compared to control students. These findings suggest that the program had a greater effect on students who began the study with poor executive functioning.

Kripalu Yoga

Kripalu Yoga in Schools (KYIS) was developed to empower adolescents to learn social and emotional skills such as stress management, emotion and behavior regulation, self-appreciation, self-confidence, and relationships skills. The program is typically delivered in 24 lessons based within three thematic modules. The intention for each lesson is to create a safe space during the regular school day for adolescents to develop mindful awareness and compassion for themselves and others. Lessons incorporate warm-up activities, breathing exercises, yoga postures, deep relaxation, and mindfulness practice. These activities are designed to cultivate awareness of the mind-body connection.

A pilot study of the KYIS curriculum was conducted to examine the feasibility of integrating yoga and mindfulness into regular high school programing and to test the efficacy of the program in improving well-being (Noggle, Steiner, Minami, & Khalsa, 2012). The study involved 51 juniors or seniors who registered for physical education (PE).

The students were assigned by class, via cluster randomization, to either yoga or PE-as-usual. The KYIS program was presented two to three times per week for 10 weeks. Students were asked to complete self-report questionnaires before and after the program.

The students who received PE-as-usual showed decreases in all the primary outcome measures, while the students who received yoga maintained baseline levels or improved. Students who received yoga showed improvements in mood disturbance and anxiety. Students rated their satisfaction with the program fairly high.

Learning to BREATHE

Many schools in both Canada and the US have adopted the Learning to BREATHE (L2B) (Broderick, 2013) program, a mindfulness-based program for adolescents and pre-adolescents designed to promote emotional awareness and improve emotional regulation, attentional focus, and stress reduction.

Developed by Patricia Broderick, the program meets the National Education Health Standards (NEHS) and can be flexibly delivered in a way that fits into a school's class schedule. Each lesson takes approximately 45 minutes to complete and can be offered once per week or offered in different ways depending upon the school schedule.

L2B is based on six themes, which are based off the acronym BREATHE[4] and presented sequentially:

B: Body – body awareness
R: Reflections – understanding and working with thoughts
E: Emotions – understanding and working with feelings
A: Attention – integrating awareness of thoughts, feelings, and bodily sensations
T: Tenderness/Take it as it is – reducing harmful self-judgments
H: Habits for a healthy mind – integrating mindful awareness into daily life
E: Empowerment/gaining the inner Edge – an outcome of the other six themes

The program involves interactive group activities and discussions designed to illustrate the lesson's theme as well as in-class practices and home practice options. Practices include body scanning, mindfulness of thoughts and emotions, mindful movement, and loving-kindness practice.

A number of pilot studies have found that L2B promotes feelings of calmness, relaxation, and self-acceptance and improves emotion regulation, emotional awareness, emotional clarity, and emotional regulation efficacy (see Broderick & Metz, 2009, as one example).

The most recent study involved the presentation of L2B to general education high school students. Students who received the program

---

4 Republished with permission of New Harbinger Publications, Inc., from *Learning to Breathe: A Mindfulness Curriculum for Adolescents to Cultivate Emotion Regulation, Attention, and Performance* by Patricia C. Broderick, Myla Kabat-Zinn, and Jon Kabat-Zinn, June 2013; permission conveyed through Copyright Clearance Center, Inc.

were matched to a group of classmates who did not. Compared to the comparison group, L2B students reported lower levels of stress, negative affect, and psychosomatic complaints. They also reported increased levels of efficacy and emotion regulation (Metz et al., 2013).

Mindfulness in Schools Project

Educators and mindfulness instructors of the Mindfulness in Schools Project developed a curriculum called ".b" (pronounced "dot bee"), which stands for "Stop, Breathe, and Be." The curriculum has been used in a wide range of contexts. The program ".b for Teens" (ages 11 to 18) is presented as an eight-week course as part of a class or to small groups. A program for younger children called "paws .b" is currently being piloted in the UK.

The curriculum involves nine lessons, each of which teaches a mindfulness skill using media and metaphors designed to engage young people. The instructor begins each lesson with a brief presentation punctuated by visuals, film, and sound. Instructors demonstrate and students practice related exercises such as breath awareness, body scanning, and mindful walking. The eight lessons[5] are:

1. Puppy training: Playing with attention
2. Taming the animal mind: Cultivating curiosity and kindness
3. Recognizing worry: Noticing how your mind plays tricks on you
4. Being here now: From reaching to responding
5. Moving mindfully
6. Stepping back: Watching the thought-traffic of your mind
7. Befriending the difficult
8. Putting it all together

Researchers at Exeter and Cambridge Universities in the United Kingdom tested the effectiveness of an eight-session .b mindfulness curriculum in a study involving 522 secondary school students assigned

---

5 Used by permission of Mindfulness in Schools Project.

to the intervention group or control group (Kuyken et al., 2013). The results of the study indicated that .b reduced depression and stress and improved the well-being of students in the .b intervention group. The students reported that they enjoyed the program, and 20% were continuing to practice mindfulness at least once a week three months after the end of the program. Students who practiced the mindfulness skills more reported greater improvements in well-being and greater reductions in stress three months after the end of the program.

MindUp

The MindUp program (Hawn Foundation, 2011), now available for the elementary grades from Scholastic, covers four units: "How Our Brains Work," "Sharpening Your Senses," "It's All about Attitude," and "Taking Action Mindfully." The program combines mindful awareness practices, social and emotional learning activities, and positive psychology concepts and exercises.

MindUp includes a daily mindful listening practice called "Brain Breaks" and other mindfulness activities focused on honing the senses and movement. It teaches children how to generate positive emotional states such as happiness, caring, and compassion and promotes perspective-taking. Finally, it teaches children how they can take mindful action in the world. The program includes suggestions for integrating activities into the general curriculum and a large library of children's books that provide examples of the unit themes. The program aligns with state standards, including Common Core.

MindUp is now included in the curricula of most of the elementary schools in the southern mainland of British Columbia, Canada. Developed by the Hawn Foundation, the program was first introduced in BC in the early 2000s when actress Goldie Hawn and her family were living in Vancouver. Recently, the program was adopted by the entire city of Newark, New Jersey.

Kimberly Schonert-Reichl, a professor of education at the University of British Columbia, conducted a series of studies of MindUp and found that students who participated in the program were more optimistic and self-confident, and teachers reported that they demonstrated more social competence compared to students who were not exposed to the program. More recently, schools in Vancouver have been adding a mindfulness-based stress reduction program to their professional development options for teachers (Schonert-Reichl & Lawlor, 2010).

Transformative Life Skills

Described as "an immersive experience in dynamic mindfulness," the Transformative Life Skills (TLS) program was developed by the Niroga Institute in collaboration with Jennifer Frank, a professor at Penn State University. The program combines mindful yoga, breathing techniques, and meditation to help children and youth deal with life challenges with greater confidence and peace.

The curriculum refers to these three core practices as the ABCs: acting, breathing, centering. The Action component of TLS integrates mindful movement and yoga postures designed to promote awareness of the body and breath. The Breathing component is intended to help individuals manage stress. The program teaches calm breathing techniques designed to reduce the effect of the fight, flight, or freeze response and restore executive functions of the brain. The Centering component of TLS involves practicing mindfulness—bringing awareness to the present moment.

The curriculum is composed of four units of 12 lessons focused on a particular theme and yoga posture. The four units cover (a) the stress response, (b) physical and emotional awareness, (c) self-regulation, and (d) healthy relationships. Typically, students receive three lessons per week, allowing them to complete one unit per month. The program aims to provide students with the skills to continue to support their own well-being when the program is over.

TLS has been successfully used with children, adolescents, and adults in a variety of settings, including schools, juvenile detention centers, and prisons. The full curriculum is available for free on the Niroga website (www.niroga.org). Niroga offers regular training for individuals who wish to use the curriculum.

A pilot study of TLS found that the program reduced stress and improved well-being among a sample of 49 high-risk high school students enrolled in an alternative education program (Frank, Bose, & Schrobenhauser-Clonan, 2014). Students completed self-report assessments of stress, well-being, and hostility before and after the program. Pre-post comparisons of these measures found significant reductions in anxiety, depression, hostility, and general psychological distress. They also found reductions in rumination (anxious thoughts), intrusive thoughts, and physical and emotional arousal associated with the fight, flight, or freeze response.

Evidence-Based Programs for Teachers

There are numerous mindfulness-based programs for teachers cropping up around the world. Many are designed to prepare teachers to teach mindfulness-based curricula. For example, Mindfulness in Schools offers a Teach .b Certification Course to individuals who wish to teach the .b program to children and youth. The Niroga Institute also offers a professional development program to prepare teachers and others to teach the TLS curriculum.

Some professional development programs have been designed specifically for teachers—not to prepare them to teach mindfulness to children or youth, but to enhance their own development, help them reduce stress, and promote resilience as a means of improving their teaching.

Mindfulness-Based Stress Reduction (MBSR) has been successfully adapted to support teachers' well-being. A study of an MBSR course specifically adapted for teachers found that the participating teachers reported significant reductions in psychological distress and burnout and increases in self-compassion. The teachers also demonstrated improved performance on a computer-based cognitive measure of affective attentional bias—that is, the tendency for perception to be affected by emotion (Flook, Goldberg, Pinger, Bonus, & Davidson, 2013).

The study examined teachers' classrooms using an observational measure of classroom quality called the Classroom Assessment Scoring System (CLASS; Pianta, La Paro, & Hamre, 2003). The classrooms of the participating teachers showed significant improvements in classroom organization.

In 2000, the Mind and Life Institute held a dialogue between His Holiness the Dalai Lama and a group of prominent scientists to explore ways to foster emotional balance and decrease "destructive emotions." As documented in Daniel Goleman's book *Destructive Emotions* (2003), the distinguished scientists included Paul Ekman, a trailblazer in the field of emotion research; Mark Greenberg, a founder of the field of social and emotional learning; and Alan Wallace, a former monk, well-recognized meditation teacher, and author.

At this meeting, Paul Ekman was inspired to develop and test an intervention that blended emotion skills training from Western psychology with Eastern contemplative practices. Paul and Alan Wallace created an eight-week program called Cultivating Emotional Balance that was tested in a series of studies conducted at the University of California, San Francisco, and San Francisco State University (Kemeny et al., 2012). Mark Greenberg served as an adviser on these projects. While the program was not specifically designed for teachers, teachers were chosen as participants in the studies, because researchers recognized that teachers have to cope with a great deal of emotional stress and that their emotions can and do affect their students, both negatively and positively.

Next we'll discuss two programs designed specifically to support teachers' development that integrate mindfulness and emotion skills instruction. Both of these programs evolved from the Cultivating Emotional Balance program.

CARE for Teachers

Building upon previous research applying a mindfulness-based approach to reducing stress and promoting well-being (Brown, Ryan, & Creswell, 2007) and on our most current understanding of the neuroscience of emotion, the Garrison Institute in Garrison, New York, initiated the development of a new program that aims to support teacher social and emotional competence (SEC) in order to improve classroom climate and student outcomes.

I led a team of former teachers and teacher educators in the development of the Cultivating Awareness and Resilience in Education (CARE) for Teachers program. The team consisted of Richard Brown of Naropa University (described earlier); former teacher and child therapist Christa Turksma, currently one of the developers and trainers of the Promoting Alternative Thinking Strategies (PATHS) social and emotional learning program; and me. With the help of a team of scientific advisers, we set out to develop a program that would help teachers manage stress and enliven their teaching and, as a result, promote improvements in their relationships with students, their classroom management, and their students' social and emotional learning.

The CARE program blends instruction and experiential activities with time for discussion and reflection. When it is offered in the field as a professional development program, CARE is presented during the school year in four all-day sessions spread out over six to eight weeks in the fall, with a fifth session booster in the spring. It is also offered every summer at the Garrison Institute in the form of a five-day intensive retreat. The extended field-based program includes phone-coaching sessions for participants. Between sessions, facilitators speak with participants by phone to provide ongoing support to help them practice and apply the new skills they have learned.

The CARE intervention involves three primary instructional components: (a) emotion skills instruction, (b) mindfulness and stress-reduction practices, and (c) listening and compassion exercises. As discussed earlier in this book, emotional exhaustion is a primary contributor to teacher burnout and can interfere with performance. To promote emotional resilience, CARE introduces emotion knowledge and skills by combining direct instruction with experiential activities. The aim is to help teachers understand, recognize, and regulate their own emotional responses and to more effectively respond to the emotional responses of others (students, parents, and colleagues).

The program involves reflective practices and role-play activities that help participants recognize emotional states and explore their individual "emotional landscape"—their habit patterns, triggers, and reactivity profile. These skills help teachers learn to reappraise emotionally challenging situations and to respond with greater clarity and sensitivity to their students' needs and the emotional climate of the classroom, resulting in more consistent, assertive, compassionate, and effective classroom management.

As part of the CARE program, teachers learn how to balance their work and personal lives in order to continually renew the inner strength they need to do their jobs well. To support self-regulation of emotion and attention, to reduce stress, and to help teachers be more aware of what is going on in their classrooms and more fully present and engaged with their students, CARE introduces a series of mindful awareness practices. These practices are introduce sequentially, beginning with short periods of silent reflection, extending to longer periods of mindfulness practice, and finally including activities that bring mindful awareness into everyday activities such as standing, walking, and role plays of challenging situations.

To promote compassion and listening, CARE introduces caring practice and mindful listening. As discussed in Chapter 6, caring practice (also called *metta* or loving-kindness practice) is a guided reflection during which one mentally offers well-being, happiness, and peace—first to oneself, then to a loved one, next to a neutral colleague or acquaintance, and finally to a person one finds challenging (such as a difficult student, parent, or colleague). Mindful listening practice involves listening with full attention, without the need to judge or respond. A common tendency while listening is to anticipate how to respond in order to provide a helpful suggestion or answer. As a result of this practice, teachers learn that simply being present and listening can be supportive in and of itself.

CARE program components increase in complexity across sessions and are augmented by individual reflective writing and group discussion. Teachers are given a CD of recorded guided practices that they can use on their own at home and a series of homework activities designed to help them apply and practice the CARE skills.

The results of a study funded by the US Department of Education's Institute of Educational Sciences found that teachers who participated in the CARE program experienced improvements in well-being, efficacy, and mindfulness compared to a control group (Jennings, Frank, Snowberg, Coccia, & Greenberg, 2013). Teachers assigned to receive CARE reported dramatic improvements in physical symptoms that are often associated with stress, such as headaches and stomach aches. They also showed significant improvement in their ability to regulate their emotions using reappraisal (rather than suppression), as well as improvement in their sense of efficacy in student engagement and instruction. Their sense of urgency decreased. They felt less time pressure. Two dimensions of mindfulness, observing and nonreacting, showed significant improvement in comparison to the control group.

Program evaluations have found that the program is attractive to teachers and has succeeded in helping them deal with the emotions of teaching. The results also suggest that CARE improves teachers' ability to provide social, emotional, and academic support to their students and to more effectively manage their classroom dynamics (Jennings, Snowberg, Coccia, & Greenberg, 2011). Research on CARE is ongoing, examining whether improvements found among teachers will translate into improvements in classroom climate and student academic and behavioral outcomes.

SMART in Education

Another program that evolved from the Cultivating Emotional Balance project is Stress Management and Relaxation Techniques (SMART) in Education, an eight-week, 11-session program that involves after-school or evening sessions for a total of 36 contact hours. With the support of the Impact Foundation, this program was developed by Margaret Cullen, a licensed therapist, MBSR instructor, one of the developers of CEB, and a primary facilitator for CEB research.

The program is available through Passageworks in the United States and the University of British Columbia, Okanagan Campus, in Canada. Margaret Cullen is continuing to develop the program under the name Mindfulness-Based Emotional Balance, which now includes self- and other-compassion components as well.

Similar to CEB and CARE, SMART involves a variety of pedagogical approaches and activities designed to promote mindfulness. It also aims to promote self-compassion and forgiveness. The program is designed to help teachers build these resources so they can manage their stress more effectively and more quickly recover from emotionally challenging situations (Benn, Akiva, Arel, & Roeser, 2012).

SMART utilizes five primary teaching activities to introduce mindfulness and self-compassion: guided mindfulness and yoga practices, group discussions of mindfulness and yoga practices, small group activities to practice skills using scenarios, lectures and guided home practices, and homework assignments.

Mindfulness activities and practices from the SMART program include the body scan; focused attention meditation on the breath; open-monitoring meditation, which involves the practice of developing moment-to-moment awareness of all facets of experience (Kabat-Zinn, 1994); forgiveness; and loving-kindness practice. The program also includes two lectures on how to apply mindfulness to emotion regulation and stress reduction.

Participants are given homework assignments and practices to help them develop and apply mindfulness and self-compassion to their work as teachers. They are then invited to report back to the group about what they have learned from these assignments. For example, teachers are invited to keep a diary for one week in which they record their emotional experiences, emotional triggers, and how they manage stress in the classroom. In subsequent sessions, participants discuss these diary entries and together explore how mindfulness might help them manage their emotions more effectively.

Robert Roeser and his colleagues have conducted several randomized, controlled studies of SMART. A recent peer-reviewed article reported on the results of two field trials involving 113 elementary and secondary school teachers from Canada and the US who were randomly assigned to receive SMART or be in a wait-list control condition. Researchers collected data before, immediately after, and three months after the SMART group received the program. A larger majority (87%) of the teachers completed the program and reported that they found it helpful. Compared to controls, teachers randomly assigned to the SMART group showed improved mindfulness, focused attention, and working memory as well as self-compassion. They also reported reduced occupational stress and burnout immediately after the program and after three months (Roeser et al., 2013).

Conclusion

In this chapter we explored how each of us can make a valuable contribution to transforming our classrooms, schools, and districts. We begin this process by focusing on our own classrooms. We can't change all the problems our schools face alone, but if each of us applies mindfulness to how we relate to our students, their parents, and our colleagues, the cumulative effects will be transformative. By approaching our work with an open-hearted, present-moment, nonjudgmental awareness, together we can make an enormous difference in our classroom environments and our students' learning.

We have an opportunity to make a difference at the school level as well. By applying mindfulness to our own classrooms, we become role models for others. We can educate our colleagues about the mindfulness-based approach and begin to share resources and practices that will help us grow a strong, supportive community of learners including students, teachers, administrators, and parents.

In this chapter, we have observed that transformation is already under way: A growing number of individual teachers, schools, and districts are embracing a mindful approach to education that integrates mindfulness and compassion into the school curriculum in the form of evidence-based programs for students, professional development programs for teachers, and initiatives to promote a mindfulness-based approach to teacher education.

An easy way to get involved in this movement is to connect with others who are doing similar work. You can find links to a number of such organizations' websites in the Resources section of this book, along with bibliographies and links to free audio recordings of guided mindfulness practices and useful mindfulness apps.

Resources

This section is intended to help you find resources to support your developing mindful awareness practice and to learn ways to apply it in your teaching. It begins with a bibliography with sections on general mindfulness, education, parenting, emotion and children's books. The next section contains lists of mindfulness-based programs for children and youth and teachers along with contact URLs. Finally, there is a section where you can access free audio recordings of well-known mindfulness teachers' guiding practices. An overall resource for accessing all things mindful is Mindful Magazine (www.mindful.org), which is published online and in print. The website has a resources section with links to a vast array of mindfulness resources (http://www.mindful.org/resources).

Bibliography of Mindfulness Books

General Mindfulness

Anh-Huong, N., & Hanh, T. N. (2006). *Walking meditation.* Boulder, CO: Sounds True.

Baraz, J., & Alexander, S. (2010). *Awakening joy: 10 steps that will put you on the road to real happiness.* New York, NY: Bantam Books.

Bauer-Wu, S. (2011). *Leaves falling gently: Living fully with serious and life-limiting illness through mindfulness, compassion, and connectedness.* Oakland, CA: New Harbinger.

Begley, S. (2007). *Train your mind, change your brain: How a new science reveals our extraordinary potential to transform ourselves.* New York, NY: Ballantine Books.

Bloom, P. (Ed.). (2010). *The power of compassion: Stories that open the heart, heal the soul, and change the world.* Charlottesville, VA: Hampton Roads.

Boorstein, S. (1997). *It's easier than you think: The Buddhist way to happiness.* New York, NY: HarperCollins.

Boorstein, S. (2008). *Happiness is an inside job: Practicing for a joyful life.* New York, NY: Ballantine Books.

Boyce, B., & the editors of *Shambhala Sun* (Eds.). (2011). *The mindfulness revolution: Leading psychologists, scientists, artists, and meditation teachers on the power of mindfulness in daily life.* Boston, MA: Shambhala.

Brach, T. (2004). *Radical acceptance: Embracing your life with the heart of a Buddha.* New York, NY: Bantam Books.

Brach, T. (2013). *True refuge: Finding peace and freedom in your own awakened heart.* New York, NY: Bantam Books.

Bush, M. (Ed.). (2011). *Contemplation nation: How ancient practices are changing how we live.* North Charleston, SC: CreateSpace.

Chödrön, P. (2000). *When things fall apart: Heart advice for difficult times.* Boston, MA: Shambhala.

Chödrön, P. (2002). *The places that scare you: A guide to fearlessness in difficult times.* Boston, MA: Shambhala.

Chödrön, P. (2003). *Comfortable with uncertainty: 108 teachings on cultivating fearlessness and compassion.* Boston, MA: Shambhala.

Chödrön, P. (2004). *Start where you are: A guide to compassionate living.* Boston, MA: Shambhala.

Chödrön, P. (2010). *Taking the leap: Freeing ourselves from old habits and fears.* Boston, MA: Shambhala.

Csikszentmihalyi, M. (2008). *Flow: The psychology of optimal experience.* New York, NY: Harper Perennial.

Doidge, N. (2007). *The brain that changes itself: Stories of personal triumph from the frontiers of brain science.* New York, NY: Penguin.

Goldstein, J. (2003). *Insight meditation: The practice of freedom.* Boston, MA: Shambhala.

Goldstein, J. (2013). *Mindfulness: A practical guide to awakening.* Boulder, CO: Sounds True.

Goldstein, J., & Kornfield, J. (2001). *Seeking the heart of wisdom: The path of insight meditation.* Boston, MA: Shambhala.

Goleman, D. (1996). *The meditative mind: The varieties of meditative experience.* New York, NY: Tarcher.

Gunaratana, B. (2011). *Mindfulness in plain English*. Somerville, MA: Wisdom.

Hanh, T. N. (1992). *Peace is every step: The path of mindfulness in everyday life*. New York, NY: Bantam Books.

Hanh, T. N. (1999). *The miracle of mindfulness: An introduction to the practice of meditation* (M. Ho, Trans.). Boston, MA: Beacon Press.

Hanh, T. N. (2008). *Breathe, you are alive: The sutra on the full awareness of breathing*. Berkeley, CA: Parallax Press.

Hanh, T. N. (2010). *You are here: Discovering the magic of the present moment*. Boston, MA: Shambhala.

Hanson, R. (2013). *Hardwiring happiness: The new brain science of contentment, calm, and confidence*. New York, NY: Harmony.

Hanson, R., & Mendius, R. (2009). *Buddha's brain: The practical neuroscience of happiness, love, and wisdom*. Oakland, CA: New Harbinger.

Hart, T. (2014). *The four virtues: Presence, heart, wisdom, creation*. New York, NY: Atria Books/Beyond Words.

Hart, T., Nelson, P. L., & Puhakka, K. (Eds.). (2000). *Transpersonal knowing: Exploring the horizon of consciousness*. Albany, NY: State University of New York Press.

Kabat-Zinn, J. (2005). *Wherever you go, there you are: Mindfulness meditation in everyday life*. New York, NY: Hyperion.

Kabat-Zinn, J. (2006). *Coming to our senses: Healing ourselves and the world through mindfulness*. New York, NY: Hyperion.

Kabat-Zinn, J. (2007). *Arriving at your own door: 108 lessons in mindfulness*. New York, NY: Hyperion.

Kabat-Zinn, J. (2009). *Full catastrophe living: Using the wisdom of your body and mind to face stress, pain, and illness*. New York, NY: Delta Trade.

Kabat-Zinn, J. (2009). *Letting everything become your teacher: 100 lessons in mindfulness*. New York, NY: Delta Trade.

Kabat-Zinn, J. (2011). *Mindfulness for beginners: Reclaiming the present moment—and your life*. Boulder, CO: Sounds True.

Kornfield, J. (1993). *A path with heart: A guide through the perils and promises of spiritual life*. New York, NY: Bantam Books.

Kornfield, J. (2001). *After the ecstasy, the laundry: How the heart grows wise on the spiritual path.* New York, NY: Bantam Books.

Kornfield, J. (2008). *The art of forgiveness, lovingkindness, and peace.* New York, NY: Bantam Books.

Kornfield, J. (2009). *The wise heart: A guide to the universal teachings of Buddhist psychology.* New York, NY: Bantam Books.

Langer, E. J. (1990). *Mindfulness.* Boston, MA: Da Capo Press.

Langer, E. J. (2009). *Counterclockwise: Mindful health and the power of possibility.* New York, NY: Ballantine Books.

Levine, S. (1991). *Guided meditations, explorations and healings.* New York, NY: Anchor Books.

Levine, S. (1998). *A year to live: How to live this year as if it were your last.* New York, NY: Bell Tower.

Merton, T. (2007). *New seeds of contemplation.* New York, NY: New Directions.

O'Hara, P. E. (2014). *Most intimate: A Zen approach to life's challenges.* Boston, MA: Shambhala.

Ryan, T. (2013). *A mindful nation: How a simple practice can help us reduce stress, improve performance, and recapture the American spirit.* Carlsbad, CA: Hay House.

Salzberg, S. (1999). *A heart as wide as the world: Stories on the path to lovingkindness.* Boston, MA: Shambhala.

Salzberg, S. (2004). *Lovingkindness: The revolutionary art of happiness.* Boston, MA: Shambhala.

Salzberg, S. (2010). *Real happiness: The power of meditation: A 28-day program.* New York, NY: Workman.

Santorelli, S. (2000). *Heal thy self: Lessons on mindfulness in medicine.* New York, NY: Harmony/Bell Tower.

Senge, P., Scharmer, C. O., Jaworski, J., & Flowers, B. S. (2005). *Presence: An exploration of profound change in people, organizations, and society.* New York, NY: Currency.

Siegel, D. J. (2007). *The mindful brain: Reflection and attunement in the cultivation of well-being.* New York, NY: Norton.

Siegel, D. J. (2009). *Mindsight: The new science of personal transformation.* New York, NY: Bantam Books.

Siegel, D. J. (2014). *Brainstorm: The power and purpose of the teenage brain.* New York, NY: Tarcher.

Smalley, S. L., & Winston, D. (2010). *Fully present: The science, art, and practice of mindfulness.* Philadelphia, PA: Da Capo Lifelong Books.

Stahl, B., & Goldstein, E. (2010). *A mindfulness-based stress reduction workbook.* Oakland, CA: New Harbinger.

Teasdale, J., Williams, M., & Segal, Z. (2014). *The mindful way workbook: An 8-week program to free yourself from depression and emotional distress.* New York, NY: Guilford Press.

Tolle, E. (2003). *Stillness speaks.* Novato, CA: New World Library.

Tolle, E. (2004). *The power of now: A guide to spiritual enlightenment.* Novato, CA: New World Library.

Tolle, E. (2008). *A new earth: Awakening to your life's purpose.* New York, NY: Penguin.

Tsoknyi Rinpoche, & Swanson, E. (2012). *Open heart, open mind: awakening the power of essence love.* New York, NY: Harmony.

Wallace, A. (2006). *The attention revolution: Unlocking the power of the focused mind.* Somerville, MA: Wisdom.

Williams, M., & Penman, D. (2012). *Mindfulness: An eight-week plan for finding peace in a frantic world.* New York, NY: Rodale Books.

Zajonc, A. (2008). *Meditation as contemplative inquiry.* Great Barrington, MA: Lindisfarne Books.

Education

Bersma, D., & Visscher, M. (2003). *Yoga games for children: Fun and fitness with postures, movements and breath.* Alameda, CA: Hunter House.

Broderick, P. C. (2013). *Learning to breathe: A mindfulness curriculum for adolescents to cultivate emotion regulation, attention, and performance.* Oakland, CA: New Harbinger.

Chanchani, S., & Chanchani, R. (2007). *Yoga for children: A complete illustrated guide to yoga.* New Dehli, India: UBS.

Cohen Harper, J. (2013). *Little flower yoga for kids: A yoga and mindfulness program to help your child improve attention and emotional balance.* Oakland, CA: New Harbinger.

Flynn, L. (2013). *Yoga for children: 200+ yoga poses, breathing exercises, and meditations for healthier, happier, more resilient children.* Avon, MA: Adams Media.

Hanh, T. N., & the Plum Village Community. (2011). *Planting seeds: Practicing mindfulness with children.* Berkeley, CA: Parallax Press.

Hart, T. (2003). *The secret spiritual world of children: The breakthrough discovery that profoundly alters our conventional view of children's mystical experiences.* Novato, CA: New World Library.

Hart, T. (2009). *From information to transformation: Education for the evolution of consciousness* (Rev. ed.). New York, NY: Peter Lang.

Hoobyar, H. (2013). *Yoga for kids: The basics.* North Charleston, SC: CreateSpace.

Johnson, A. N., & Webb Neagley, M. (Eds.). (2011). *Educating from the heart: Theoretical and practical approaches to transforming education.* Lanham, MD: Rowman & Littlefield.

Kaiser Greenland, S. (2010). *The mindful child: How to help your kid manage stress and become happier, kinder, and more compassionate.* New York, NY: Free Press.

Kessler, R. (2000). *The soul of education: Helping students find connection, compassion, and character at school.* Alexandria, VA: Association for Supervision and Curriculum Development.

Krishnamurti, J. (2008). *Education and the significance of life.* New York, NY: HarperOne.

Langer, E.J. (1998). *The power of mindful learning.* Boston, MA: Da Capo Press.

Lantieri, L. (2008). *Building emotional intelligence: Techniques to cultivate inner strength in children.* Boulder, CO: Sounds True.

Lichtmann, M. (2005). *The teacher's way: Teaching and the contemplative life.* Mahwah, NJ: Paulist Press.

MacDonald, E., & Shirley, D. (2009). *The mindful teacher.* New York, NY: Teachers College Press.

McHenry, I., & Brady, R. (Eds.). (2009). *Tuning in: Mindfulness in teaching and learning.* Philadelphia, PA: Friends Council in Education.

Miller, J. (1994). *The contemplative practitioner: Meditation in education and the professions.* Westport, CT: Bergin & Garvey.

Murray, L. E. (2012). *Calm kids: Help children relax with mindful activities*. Edinburgh, UK: Floris Books.

O'Reilley, M. R. (1998). *Radical presence: Teaching as contemplative practice*. Portsmouth, NH: Boynton/Cook.

Palmer, P. (2007). *The courage to teach: Exploring the inner landscape of a teacher's life*. San Francisco, CA: Jossey-Bass.

Rawlinson, A. (2013). *Creative yoga for children: Inspiring the whole child through yoga, songs, literature, and games*. Berkeley, CA: North Atlantic Books.

Rechtschaffen, D. (2014). *The way of mindful education: Cultivating well-being in teachers and students*. New York, NY: Norton.

Reddy, R. (2014). *The art of mindfulness for children: Mindfulness exercises that will raise happier, confident, compassionate, and calmer children*. North Charleston, SC: CreateSpace.

Saltzman, A. (2014). *A still quiet place: A mindfulness program for teaching children and adolescents to ease stress and difficult emotions*. Oakland, CA: New Harbinger.

Saltzman, A., & Willard, C. (Eds.). (2014). *Mindfulness with youth: From the classroom to the clinic*. New York, NY: Guilford Press.

Schoeberlein, D., & Sheth, S. (2009). *Mindful teaching and teaching mindfulness: A guide for anyone who teaches anything*. Somerville, MA: Wisdom.

Srinivasan, M. (2014). *Teach, breathe, learn: Mindfulness in and out of the classroom*. Berkeley, CA: Parallax Press.

Vallely, S.W. (2008). *Sensational meditation for children: Child-friendly meditation techniques based on the five senses*. Asheville, NC: Satya International.

Weaver, L., & Wilding, M. (2013). *The 5 dimensions of engaged teaching: A practical guide for educators*. Bloomington, IN: Solution Tree Press.

Wenig, M. (2003). *YogaKids: Educating the whole child through yoga*. New York, NY: Stewart, Tabori and Chang.

Willard, C. (2010). *Child's mind: Mindfulness practices to help our children be more focused, calm, and relaxed*. Berkeley, CA: Parallax Press.

Parenting

Bardacke, N. (2012). *Mindful birthing: Training the mind, body, and heart for childbirth and beyond.* New York, NY: HarperOne.

Hawn, G., & Holden, W. (2012). *10 mindful minutes: Giving our children—and ourselves—the social and emotional skills to reduce stress and anxiety for healthier, happy lives.* New York, NY: Perigee Trade.

Kabat-Zinn, M., & Kabat-Zinn, J. (1998). *Everyday blessings: The inner work of mindful parenting.* New York, NY: Hyperion.

Miller, K. M. (2007). *Momma Zen: Walking the crooked path of motherhood.* Boston, MA: Trumpeter Books.

Race, K. (2014). *Mindful parenting: Simple and powerful solutions for raising creative, engaged, happy kids in today's hectic world.* New York, NY: St. Martin's Griffin.

Roy, D. (2007). *Momfulness: Mothering with mindfulness, compassion, and grace.* San Francisco, CA: Jossey-Bass.

Ruethling, A., & Pitcher, P. (2003). *Under the Chinaberry tree: Books and inspirations for mindful parenting.* New York, NY: Broadway Books.

Shapiro, S., & White, C. (2014). *Mindful discipline: A loving approach to setting limits and raising an emotionally intelligent child.* Oakland, CA: New Harbinger.

Siegel, D. J., & Bryson, T. P. (2012). *The whole-brain child: 12 revolutionary strategies to nurture your child's developing mind.* New York, NY: Bantam Books.

Siegel, D. J., & Hartzell, M. (2004). *Parenting from the inside out.* New York, NY: Tarcher.

Vieten, C., & Boorstein, S. (2009). *Mindful motherhood: Practical tools for staying sane during pregnancy and your child's first year.* Oakland, CA: New Harbinger.

Emotion

Dalai Lama & Ekman, P. (2009). *Emotional awareness.* New York, NY: Holt Paperbacks.

Ekman, P. (2003). *Emotions revealed: Recognizing faces and feelings to improve communication and emotional life.* (2nd ed.) New York, NY: Henry Holt.

Fredrickson, B. (2009). *Positivity: Top-notch research reveals the 3 to 1 ratio that will change your life.* New York, NY: Three Rivers Press.

Fredrickson, B. (2013). *Love 2.0: Finding happiness and health in moments of connection.* New York, NY: Hudson Street Press.

Goleman, D. (2000). *Working with emotional intelligence.* New York, NY: Bantam Books.

Goleman, D. (2004). *Destructive emotions: How can we overcome them? A scientific dialogue with the Dalai Lama.* New York, NY: Bantam Books.

Goleman, D. (2006). *Emotional intelligence: Why it can matter more than IQ* (10th anniversary ed.). New York, NY: Bantam Books.

Goleman, D. (2007). *Social intelligence: The new science of human relationships.* New York, NY: Bantam Books.

Lyubomirsky, S. (2008). *The how of happiness: A new approach to getting the life you want.* New York, NY: Penguin.

Lyubomirsky, S. (2014). *The myths of happiness: What should make you happy, but doesn't; what shouldn't make you happy, but does.* New York, NY: Penguin.

Segal, J. S. (1997). *Raising your emotional intelligence: A practical guide.* New York, NY: Holt Paperbacks.

Seligman, M. E. P. (2002). *Authentic happiness: Using the new positive psychology to realize your potential for lasting fulfillment.* New York, NY: Free Press.

Seligman, M. E. P. (2012). *Flourish: A visionary new understanding of happiness and well-being.* New York, NY: Free Press.

Children's Books

Alderfer, L. (2011). *Mindful monkey, happy panda.* Somerville, MA: Wisdom.

Biegel, G. M. (2010). *The stress reduction workbook for teens: Mindfulness skills to help you deal with stress.* Oakland, CA: Instant Help Books.

Clarke, C. (2012). *Imaginations: Fun relaxation stories and meditations for kids.* North Charleston, SC: CreateSpace.

Davies, A. (2010). *My first yoga: Animal poses.* Cambridge, MA: My First Yoga.

DiOrio, R. (2010). *What does it mean to be present?* Belvedere, CA: Little Pickle Press.

Eddy, L. (2010). *Every body does yoga.* Houston, TX: Strategic Book Publishing.

Hanh, T. N. (2002). *Under the rose apple tree.* Berkeley, CA: Plum Blossom Books.

Hanh, T. N. (2008). *Mindful movements: Ten exercises for well-being.* Berkeley, CA: Parallax Press.

Hanh, T. N. (2010). *A pebble for your pocket.* Berkeley, CA: Plum Blossom Books.

Hanh, T. N. (2012). *A handful of quiet: Happiness in four pebbles.* Berkeley, CA: Plum Blossom Books.

Lite, L. (2008). *Angry octopus: A relaxation story.* Marietta, GA: Stress Free Kids.

MacLean, K. L. (2004). *Peaceful piggy meditation.* Park Ridge, IL: Albert Whitman.

MacLean, K. L. (2009). *Moody cow meditates.* Somerville, MA: Wisdom.

MacLean, K. L. (2014). *Peaceful piggy yoga.* Park Ridge, IL: Albert Whitman.

McGinnis, M. W. (2013). *An orange for you: A child's book of awareness.* North Charleston, SC: CreateSpace.

Muth, J. J. (2005). *Zen shorts.* New York, NY: Scholastic Press.

Muth, J. J. (2008). *Zen ties.* New York, NY: Scholastic Press.

Silver, G. (2009). *Anh's anger.* Berkeley, CA: Plum Blossom Books.

Snel, E. (2013). *Sitting still like a frog: Mindfulness exercises for kids (and their parents).* Boston, MA: Shambhala.

Thomson, B., & Hoffsteader, N. (2013). *Meditation, my friend: Meditation for kids and beginners of all ages.* New York, NY: Betsy Thomson.

Verdick, E. (2010). *Calm-down time.* Minneapolis, MN: Free Spirit.

Yoo, T. E. (2012). *You are a lion! And other fun yoga poses.* New York, NY: Nancy Paulsen Books.

Mindfulness-Based Programs

This resource section contains links to school-based mindfulness-based programs for teachers and students. The most comprehensive resource on programs for teachers or students that involve a contemplative approach can be found on the Garrison Institute website. The link below will take you to a searchable database of these programs: http://www.garrisoninstitute.org/contemplation-and-education/contemplative-education-program-database

Programs for Children and Youth

Calm Classroom
Chicago, IL
http://calmclassroom.com

Calmer Choice
Cotuit, MA
http://calmerchoice.org

Education for Excellence
New York, NY, and other locations worldwide
http://educationforexcellence.com

Every Kid's Yoga
New York, NY
http://www.everykidsyoga.com

Flourish Foundation
Ketchum, ID
http://flourishfoundation.org

Friends Council on Education
Philadelphia, PA, and other US locations
http://www.friendscouncil.org
Growing Minds
Milwaukee, WI
http://www.growingmindstoday.com

Holistic Life Foundation
Baltimore, MD, and other US locations
http://hlfinc.org

Inner Explorer
Franklin, MA
http://innerexplorer.org

Inner Kids
Los Angeles, CA, and other US locations
http://www.susankaisergreenland.com/inner-kids.html

Inner Resilience Program
New York, NY, and other US locations
http://www.innerresilience-tidescenter.org

Inward Bound Mindfulness Education
North Andover, MA, and other US locations
http://ibme.info

Kripalu
Stockbridge, MA, and other US locations
http://www.kripalu.org/be_a_part_of_kripalu/812/

Learning to BREATHE
Philadelphia, PA, and other US locations
http://learning2breathe.org

Little Flower Yoga
Croton on Hudson, NY, and other US locations
http://littlefloweryoga.com

Mind Body Awareness Project
Oakland, CA
http://www.mbaproject.org

Mindfulness in Schools (.b)
Oxford, UK, and other locations worldwide
http://mindfulnessinschools.org

Mindfulness without Borders
Tiburon, CA, and other locations worldwide
http://mindfulnesswithoutborders.org

Mindful Schools
Oakland, CA, and other US locations
http://www.mindfulschools.org/

MindUp
Santa Monica, CA, and other locations worldwide
http://thehawnfoundation.org/mindup/

Move this World
East Coast, US and other locations worldwide
http://movethisworld.org

Relax to Learn
Baton Rouge, LA
http://relaxtolearn.com

Resilient Kids
Providence, RI
http://www.resilientkids.org

Shanti Generation
Southern California
http://shantigeneration.com/programs/
mindful-life-skills-for-classrooms/

Still Quiet Place
Menlo Park, CA, and other US locations
http://www.stillquietplace.com

Transformative Life Skills
Oakland, CA, and other locations worldwide
http://www.niroga.org/

Wake Up Schools
Escondido, CA
http://wakeupschools.org

Wellness and Resilience Program
South Burlington School District
South Burlington, VT
http://sbsd.schoolfusion.us/modules/cms/pages.phtml?pageid=195
404&sessionid=c93577

Wellness Works in Schools
Lancaster, PA
http://www.wellnessworksinschools.com

Yoga in Schools
Pittsburgh, PA, and other US locations
http://yogainschools.org

Programs for Teachers

Antioch University New England
Certificate Program in Mindfulness for Educators
Keene, NH, and other US locations
http://www.mindfulinquiry.org/certificate/

Center for Courage and Renewal
Courage to Teach
Seattle, WA, and other locations worldwide
http://www.couragerenewal.org/courage-to-teach

Cultivating Awareness and Resilience in Education (CARE for Teachers)
Garrison Institute
Garrison, NY, and other locations worldwide
http://www.care4teachers.org

Inner Resilience Program
New York, NY, and other locations worldwide
http://www.innerresilience-tidescenter.org

Mindfulness-Based Emotional Balance
San Francisco Bay Area and other US locations
http://www.margaretcullen.com/programs/

Naropa University
Contemplative Education Program
Boulder, CO
http://www.naropa.edu/academics/snss/grad/
contemplative-education-low-residency-ma/

SMART in Education (Two organizations deliver this program)
1. Passageworks
Boulder, CO, and other US locations
http://passageworks.org
http://passageworks.org/courses/smart-in-education/

2. University of British Columbia, Okanagan Campus
Kelowna, BC, Canada, and other locations in Canada
http://ok-edu.sites.olt.ubc.ca

Wellness and Resilience Program
South Burlington School District
South Burlington, VT
http://sbsd.schoolfusion.us/modules/cms/pages.phtml?pageid=195
404&sessionid=c93577

Programs for the General Public

Cultivating Emotional Balance Program
http://www.cultivatingemotionalbalance.org

Mindsight Institute
https://www.mindsightinstitute.com

Mindfulness-Based Stress Reduction (MBSR)
University of Massachusetts School of Medicine
Center for Mindfulness
http://www.umassmed.edu/Content.aspx?id=41254

Other Resources

Free Audio Recordings

Center for Mindfulness at the University of California San Diego
(UCSD)
http://health.ucsd.edu/specialties/mindfulness/mbsr/Pages/audio.
aspx

Mindful Awareness Research Center at the University of California Los Angeles (UCLA)
http://marc.ucla.edu/body.cfm?id=22

Mindful Self-Compassion audio by Christopher Germer
http://www.mindfulselfcompassion.org/meditations_downloads.php

Mindfulness Apps

Buddhify
http://buddhify.com

Calm
https://itunes.apple.com/us/app/calm-meditate-sleep-relax/id571800810?mt=8

ConZentrate
https://itunes.apple.com/us/app/conzentrate/id493897333?mt=8

Get Some Headspace
http://www.getsomeheadspace.com/shop/headspace-meditation-app.aspx

Insight Timer
https://insighttimer.com

Mind
https://itunes.apple.com/us/app/id419702358

The Mindfulness App
http://www.mindapps.se/?lang=en

Mindfulness Daily
http://mindfulnessdailyapp.com

Mindfulness Meditation App
http://www.mentalworkout.com/store/programs/mindfulness-meditation/

Simply Being: Guided Meditation for Relaxation and Presence
https://itunes.apple.com/us/app/simply-being-guided-meditation/id347418999?mt=8

Organizations and Conferences

Association for Mindfulness in Education (AME)
http://www.mindfuleducation.org

Bridging Hearts and Minds
UC San Diego School of Medicine, Continuing Medical Education
(Holds an annual conference in February)
https://cme.ucsd.edu/bridging/

Garrison Institute Initiative on Contemplative Teaching and Learning
(Holds an annual conference in the fall)
http://www.garrisoninstitute.org

Mindfulness in Education Network (MIEN)
(Holds an annual conference in the spring)
http://www.mindfuled.org

Omega Institute
Reinbeck, NY
(Mindfulness and Education Conference, July)
http://www.eomega.org

References

Abbott, R. D., O'Donnell, J., Hawkins, J. D., Hill, K. G., Kosterman, R., & Catalano, R. F. (1998). Changing teaching practices to promote achievement and bonding to school. *Journal of Orthopsychiatry, 68,* 542–552.

Allington, R. L. (1980). Poor readers don't get to read much in reading groups. *Language Arts, 57,* 872–876.

Angell, A. V. (1991). Democratic climates in elementary classrooms: A review of theory and research. *Theory and Research in Social Education, 19,* 241–266.

Atomic education urged by Einstein. (1946, May 25). *New York Times,* p. 11.

Auguste, B., Kihn, P., & Miller, M. (2010*). Closing the talent gap: Attracting and retaining top third graduates to a career in teaching.* New York, NY: McKinsey & Company.

Battistich, V., Solomon, D., Watson, M., & Schaps, E. (1997). Caring school communities. *Educational Psychologist, 32,* 137–151.

Baumann, P., & Taft, M. W. (2011). *Ego: The fall of the twin towers and the rise of an enlightened humanity.* San Francisco, CA: NE Press.

Benn, R., Akiva, T., Arel, S., & Roeser, R. W. (2012). Mindfulness training effects for parents and educators of children with special needs. *Developmental Psychology, 48,* 1476–1487.

Benson, H., & Klipper, M. Z. (2009). *The relaxation response* (Kindle edition). New York, NY: HarperCollins.

Benson, H., Kornhaber, A., Kornhaber, C., LeChanu, M. N., Zuttermeister, P. C., Myers, P., & Friedman, R. (1994). Increases in positive psychological characteristics with a new relaxation-response curriculum in high school students. *Journal of Research and Development in Education, 27,* 226–231.

Benson, H., Wilcher, M., Greenberg, B., Huggins, E., Ennis, M., Zuttermeister, P.C., . . . Friedman, R. (2000). Academic performance among middle school students after exposure to a relaxation response curriculum. *Journal of Research and Development in Education, 33,* 156–165.

Bernier, A., Carlson, S. M., & Whipple, N. (2010). From external regulation to self-regulation: Early parenting precursors of young children's executive functioning. *Child Development, 81,* 326–339.

Birch, S., & Ladd, G. W. (1998). Children's interpersonal behaviors and the teacher–child relationship. *Developmental Psychology, 34,* 934–946.

Blase, J. J. (1986). A qualitative analysis of sources of teacher stress: Consequences for performance. *American Educational Research Journal, 23,* 13–40.

Bredekamp, S., & Copple, C. (Eds.). (1997). *Developmentally appropriate practice in early childhood programs* (Rev. ed.). Washington, D.C.: National Association for the Education of Young Children.

Broderick, P. C. (2013). *Learning to BREATHE: A mindfulness curriculum for adolescents to cultivate emotion regulation, attention, and performance.* Oakland, CA: New Harbinger.

Broderick, P. C., & Metz, S. (2009). Learning to BREATHE: A pilot trial of a mindfulness curriculum for adolescents. *Advances in School Mental Health Promotion, 2,* 35–46.

Brophy, J. (2006). History of research on classroom management. In C. M. Evertson & C. S. Weinstein (Eds.), *Handbook of classroom management: Research, practice, and contemporary issues* (pp. 17–43). Mahwah, NJ: Erlbaum.

Brown, K. W., & Ryan, R. M. (2003). The benefits of being present: Mindfulness and its role in psychological well-being. *Journal of Personality and Social Psychology, 84,* 822–848.

Brown, K. W., Ryan, R. M., & Creswell, J. D. (2007). Mindfulness: Theoretical foundations and evidence for its salutary effects. *Psychological Inquiry, 18,* 211–237.

Bruner, J. (1995). The cognitive revolution in children's understanding of mind: Commentary. *Human Development, 38,* 203–213.

Bryan, T., & Bryan, J. (1991). Positive mood and math performance. *Journal of Learning Disabilities, 24,* 490–494.

Bryan, T., Mathur, S., & Sullivan, K. (1996). The impact of positive mood on learning. *Learning Disability Quarterly, 19,* 153–162.

Carson, R. L., & Templin, T. J. (2007, April). *Emotion regulation and teacher burnout: Who says that the management of emotional expression doesn't matter?* Paper presented at the American Education Research Association Annual Convention, Chicago, IL.

Casteel, J. D., & Stahl, R. J. (1973). *The Social Science Observation Record (SSOR): Theoretical construct and pilot studies.* Gainesville, FL: P.K. Yonge Laboratory School.

Chan, D. (2010). Gratitude, gratitude intervention and subjective well-being among Chinese school teachers in Hong Kong. *Educational Psychology, 30,* 139–153.

Chang, M. (2013). Toward a theoretical model to understand teacher emotions and teacher burnout in the context of student misbehavior: Appraisal, regulation and coping. *Motivation and Emotion, 37,* 799–817.

Chiesa, A., Calati, R., & Serretti, A. (2011). Does mindfulness training improve cognitive abilities? A systematic review of neuropsychological findings. *Clinical Psychology Review, 31,* 449–464.

Chiesa, A., & Serretti, A. (2009). Mindfulness-based stress reduction for stress management in healthy people: A review and meta-analysis. *Journal of Alternative and Complementary Medicine, 15,* 593–600.

Colzato, L. S., Ozturk, A., & Hommel, B. (2012). Meditate to create: The impact of focused-attention and open-monitoring training on convergent and divergent thinking. *Frontiers in Psychology, 3*(116), 1–5.

Conduct Problems Prevention Research Group. (1992). A developmental and clinical model for the prevention of conduct disorder: The FAST Track Program. *Development and Psychopathology, 4,* 509–527.

Costa, A. L., & Kallick, B. (n.d.). *Describing 16 habits of mind.* Retrieved from http://www.habitsofmindinstitute.org/about-us/hear-art/

Darling-Hammond, L., Ancess, J., & Ort, S. W. (2002). Reinventing high school: Outcomes of the coalition campus schools project. *American Educational Research Journal, 39,* 639–673.

Darwin, C. (1998). *The expression of the emotions in man and animals* (3rd ed.). New York, NY: Oxford University Press. (Original work published 1872)

Davidson, R. J., Kabat-Zinn, J., Schumacher, J., Rosenkranz, M., Muller, D., Santorelli, S. F., . . . Sheridan, J. F. (2003). Alterations in brain and immune function produced by mindfulness meditation. *Psychosomatic Medicine, 65,* 564–570.

Davis, J. I., Senghas, A., Brandt, F., & Ochsner, K. N. (2010). The effects of BOTOX injections on emotional experience. *Emotion, 10,* 433–440.

Desbordes, G., Negi, L. T., Pace, T. W. W., Wallace, B. A., Raison, C. L., & Schwartz, E. L. (2012). Effects of mindful-attention and compassion meditation training on amygdala response to emotional stimuli in an ordinary, non-meditative state. *Frontiers in Neuroscience, 6*(292), 1–15.

DeVries, R., & Zan, B. (1994). *Moral classrooms, moral children: Creating a constructivist atmosphere in early education.* New York, NY: Teachers College Press.

Dodge, K. A., & Coie., J. D. (1987). Social-information-processing factors in reactive and proactive aggression in children's peer groups. *Journal of Personality and Social Psychology, 53,* 1146–1158.

Dottin, E. S. (2009). Professional judgment and dispositions in teacher education. *Teaching and Teacher Education, 25,* 83–88.

Dreikurs, R. (1968). *Psychology in the classroom: A manual for teachers.* New York, NY: HarperCollins.

Dreikurs, R., Grunwald, B. B., & Pepper, F. C. (1998). *Maintaining sanity in the classroom: Classroom management techniques.* Philadelphia, PA: Taylor & Francis.

Dreikurs, R., & Soltz, V. (1964). *Children: The challenge.* New York, NY: Hawthorn/Dutton.

Droit-Volet, S., Meck, W. H., & Penney, T. B. (2007). Sensory modality and time perception in children and adults. *Behavioural Processes, 74,* 113–220.

Duncan, L., Coatsworth, D., & Greenberg, M. (2009). A model of mindful parenting: Implications for parent–child relationships and prevention research. *Clinical Child and Family Psychology Review, 12,* 255–270.

Durlak, J. A., Weissberg, R. P., Dymnicki, A. B., Taylor, R. D., & Schellinger, K. B. (2011). The impact of enhancing students' social and emotional learning: A meta-analysis of school-based universal interventions. *Child Development, 82,* 405–432.

Dweck, C. (2007). *Mindset: The new psychology of success.* New York, NY: Ballantine Books.

Dwyer, K., Osher, D., & Warger, C. (1998). *Early warning, timely response: A guide to safe schools.* Washington, D.C.: U.S. Department of Education.

Easterbrook, J. A. (1959). The effect of emotion on cue utilization and the organization of behavior. *Psychological Review, 66,* 183–201.

Ekman, P. (1994). All emotions are basic. In P. Ekman & R. J. Davidson (Eds.), *The nature of emotion: Fundamental questions* (pp. 15–19). New York, NY: Oxford University Press.

Ekman, P. (2007a). *Emotions revealed: Recognizing faces and feelings to improve communication and emotional life* (2nd ed.). New York, NY: Henry Holt.

Ekman, P. (2007b). The directed facial action task: Emotional responses without appraisal. In J. A. Coan & J. J. B. Allen (Eds.), *Handbook of emotion elicitation and assessment* (pp. 47–53). New York, NY: Oxford University Press.

Ekman, P., Davidson, R. J., & Friesen, W. V. (1990). The Duchenne smile: Emotional expression and brain physiology II. *Journal of Personality and Social Psychology, 58,* 342–353.

Ekman, P., & Friesen, W. V. (1971). Constants across cultures in the face and emotion. *Journal of Personality and Social Psychology, 17,* 124–129.

Ekman, P. E., Sorenson, R., & Friesen, W. V. (1969). Pan-cultural elements in facial displays of emotion. *Science, 164,* 86–88.

Elias, M. J., Zins, J. E., Weissberg, R. P., Frey, K. S., Greenberg, M. T., Haynes, N. M. . . . Shriver, T. P. (1997). *Promoting social and emotional learning: Guidelines for educators.* Alexandria, VA: Association for Supervision and Curriculum Development.

Emmons, R. A., & McCullough, M. E. (2003). Counting blessings versus burdens: Experimental studies of gratitude and subjective well-being in daily life. *Journal of Personality and Social Psychology, 84,* 377–389.

Farb, N. A. S., Segal, Z. V., Mayberg, H., Bean, J., McKeon, D., Fatima, Z., & Anderson, A. K. (2007). Attending to the present: Mindfulness meditation reveals distinct neural modes of self-reference. *Social Cognitive and Affective Neuroscience, 2,* 313–322.

Farber, B. A., & Miller, J. (1981). Teacher burnout: A psycho-educational perspective. *Teachers College Record, 83,* 235-243.

Feldman, G., Greeson, J., & Senville, J. (2010). Differential effects of mindful breathing, progressive muscle relaxation, and loving-kindness meditation on decentering and negative reactions to repetitive thoughts. *Behaviour Research and Therapy, 48,* 1002–1011.

Flook, L., Goldberg, S. B., Pinger, L., Bonus, K., & Davidson, R. J. (2013). Mindfulness for teachers: A pilot study to assess effects on stress, burnout, and teaching efficacy. *Mind, Brain, and Education, 7,* 182–195.

Flook, L., Smalley, S. L., Kitil, M. J., Galla, B. M., Kaiser Greenland, S., Locke, J., . . . Kasari, C. (2010). Effects of mindful awareness practices on executive functions in elementary school children. *Journal of Applied School Psychology, 26,* 70–95.

Fonagy, P., & Target, M. (1997). Attachment and reflective function: Their role in self-organization. *Development and Psychopathology, 9,* 679–700.

Fox, L., & Lentini, R. H. (2006). "You got it!" Teaching social and emotional skills. *Beyond the Journal: Young Children on the Web.* Retrieved from http://www.naeyc.org/files/yc/file/200611/BTJFox-Lentini.pdf

Frank, J. L., Bose, B., & Schrobenhauser-Clonan, A. (2014). Effectiveness of a school-based yoga program on adolescent mental health, stress coping strategies, and attitudes toward violence: Findings from a high-risk sample. *Journal of Applied School Psychology 30,* 29–49.

Frankl, V. E. (1988). *Man's search for meaning.* New York, NY: Pocket Books.

Fredrickson, B. L. (2001). The role of positive emotions in positive psychology: The broaden-and-build theory of positive emotions. *American Psychologist, 56,* 218–226.

Fredrickson, B. L. (2009). *Positivity.* New York, NY: Three Rivers Press.

Fredrickson, B. L. (2013). Positive emotions broaden and build. In P. Devine & A. Plant (Eds.), *Advances in experimental social psychology* (Vol. 47, pp. 1–53). New York, NY: Elsevier.

Fredrickson, B. L, & Branigan, C. (2005). Positive emotions broaden the scope of attention and thought-action repertoires. *Cognition and Emotion, 19,* 313–332.

Fredrickson, B. L., & Cohn, M. A. (2008). Positive emotions. In M. Lewis, J. M. Haviland-Jones, & L. F. Barrett (Eds.), *Handbook of emotions* (3rd ed., pp. 777–796). New York, NY: Guilford Press.

Fredrickson, B. L., & Levenson, R. W. (1998). Positive emotions speed recovery from the cardiovascular sequelae of negative emotions. *Cognition and Emotion, 12,* 191–220.

Fried, R. L. (1995). *The passionate teacher.* Boston, MA: Beacon Press.

Froh, J. J., & Bono, G. (2011). Gratitude in youth: A review of gratitude interventions and some ideas for applications. *Communiqué, 39*(5), 1–28.

Froh, J. J., Bono, G., & Emmons, R. (2010). Being grateful is beyond good manners: Gratitude and motivation to contribute to society among early adolescents. *Motivation and Emotion, 34,* 144–157.

Froh, J. J., Kashdan, T. B., Ozimkowski, K. M., & Miller, N. (2009). Who benefits the most from a gratitude intervention in children and adolescents? Examining positive affect as a moderator. *Journal of Positive Psychology, 4,* 408–422.

Gambone, M. A., Klem, A. M., & Connell, J. P. (2002). *Finding out what matters for youth: Testing key links in a community action framework for youth development.* Philadelphia, PA: Youth Development Strategies/Institute for Research and Reform in Education.

Garrison Institute. (2005). *Contemplation and education: Current status of programs using contemplative techniques in K–12 educational settings: A mapping report.* Retrieved from http://www.garrisoninstitute.org/component/docman/doc_view/56-contemplative-techniques-in-k-12-education-a-mapping-report?Itemid=66

Gettinger, M., & Kohler, K. M. (2006). Process-outcome approaches to classroom management and effective teaching. In C. M. Evertson & C. S. Weinstein (Eds.), *Handbook of classroom management: Research, practice, and contemporary issues* (pp. 73–95). Mahwah, NJ: Erlbaum.

Gilliam, W. S. (2005). *Prekindergarteners left behind: Expulsion rates in state prekindergarten programs.* Unpublished manuscript, Yale University Child Study Center, New Haven, CT.

Ginott, H. G. (1993). *Teacher and child: A book for parents and teachers.* New York, NY: Collier.

Gladwell, M. (2000). *The tipping point: How little things can make a big difference.* New York, NY: Little, Brown and Company.

Glasser, W. (1988). *Choice theory in the classroom.* New York, NY: HarperCollins.

Glasser, W. (1998). *The quality school: Managing students without coercion.* New York, NY: HarperCollins.

Goleman, D. (2003). *Destructive emotions.* New York, NY: Bantam Books.

Goleman, D. (2005). *Emotional intelligence: Why it can matter more than IQ* (10th anniversary ed.). New York, NY: Bantam Books.

Gordon, T. (2003). *Teacher effectiveness training: The program proven to help teachers bring out the best in students of all ages.* New York, NY: Three Rivers Press.

Gross, J. J. (2002). Emotion regulation: Affective, cognitive, and social consequences. *Psychophysiology, 39,* 281–291.

Halifax, J. (2014). G.R.A.C.E. for nurses: Cultivating compassion in nurse/patient interactions. *Journal of Nursing Education and Practice, 4,* 121–128.

Hamre, B. K., & Pianta, R. C. (2001). Early teacher–child relationships and the trajectory of children's school outcomes through eighth grade. *Child Development, 72,* 625–638.

Hamre, B. K., & Pianta, R. C. (2006). Student–teacher relationships. In G. G. Bear & K. M. Minke (Eds.), *Children's needs: III. Development, prevention, and intervention* (pp. 59–71). Washington, D.C.: National Association of School Psychologists.

Hargreaves, A. (1998). The emotional practice of teaching. *Teaching and Teacher Education, 14,* 835–854.

Hargreaves, A. (2000). Mixed emotions: Teachers' perceptions of their interactions with students. *Teaching and Teacher Education, 16,* 811–826.

Hawn Foundation. (2011). *The MindUP Curriculum: Grades PreK–2: Brain-focused strategies for learning—and living.* New York, NY: Scholastic.

Hiebert, E. (1983). An examination of ability grouping for reading instruction. *Reading Research Quarterly, 18,* 231–255.

Hofmann, S. G., Grossman, P., & Hinton, D. E. (2011). Loving-kindness and compassion meditation: Potential for psychological interventions. *Clinical Psychology Review, 31,* 1126–1132.

Hölzel, B. K., Carmody, J., Vangel, M., Congleton, C., Yerramsetti, S. M., Gard, T., & Lazar, S. W. (2011). Mindfulness practice leads to increases in regional brain gray matter density. *Psychiatry Research: Neuroimaging, 191,* 36–42.

Honea, J. M., Jr. (1982). Wait-time as an instructional variable: An influence on teacher and student. *Clearing House, 56,* 167–170.

Humans change the world. (n.d.). Retrieved from http://humanorigins.si.edu/human-characteristics/change

Isen, A. M. (1987). Positive affect, cognitive processes, and social behavior. In L. Berkowitz (Ed.), *Advances in experimental social psychology* (Vol. 20, pp. 203–253). San Diego, CA: Academic Press.

Isen, A. M., Johnson, M. M., Mertz, E., & Robinson, G. F. (1985). The influence of positive affect on the unusualness of word associations. *Journal of Personality and Social Psychology, 48,* 1413–1426.

Ivanovski, B., & Malhi, G. S. (2007). The psychological and neurophysiological concomitants of mindfulness forms of meditation. *Acta Neuropsychiatrica, 19,* 76–91.

Jackson, A. W., & Davis, G. A. (2000). *Turning points 2000: Educating adolescents in the 21st century.* New York, NY: Teachers College Press.

James, W. (1950). *The principles of psychology.* New York, NY: Dover.

Jennings, P. A. (2008). Contemplative education and youth development. *New Directions for Youth Development, 118,* 101–105.

Jennings, P. A., Frank, J. L., Snowberg, K. E., Coccia, M. A., & Greenberg, M. T. (2013). Improving classroom learning environments by Cultivating Awareness and Resilience in Education (CARE): Results of a randomized controlled trial. *School Psychology Quarterly, 28,* 374–390.

Jennings, P. A., & Greenberg, M. (2009). The prosocial classroom: Teacher social and emotional competence in relation to child and classroom outcomes. *Review of Educational Research, 79,* 491–525.

Jennings, P. A., Lantieri, L., & Roeser, R. W. (2012). Supporting educational goals through cultivating mindfulness: Approaches for teachers and students. In P. M. Brown, M. W. Corrigan, & A. Higgins-D'Alessandro (Eds.), *Handbook of prosocial education* (pp. 371–397). Lanham, MD: Rowman & Littlefield.

Jennings, P. A., Snowberg, K. E., Coccia, M. A., & Greenberg, M. T. (2011). Improving classroom learning environments by Cultivating Awareness and Resilience in Education (CARE): Results of two pilot studies. *Journal of Classroom Interaction, 46,* 37–48.

Jimenez, S. S., Niles, B. L., & Park, C. L. (2010). A mindfulness model of affect regulation and depressive symptoms: Positive emotions, mood regulation expectancies, and self-acceptance as regulatory mechanisms. *Personality and Individual Differences, 49,* 645–650.

Johnson, D. W., & Johnson, R. (1991). *Teaching students to be peacemakers.* Edina, MN: Interaction Book Company.

Jones, W., Cash, M., & Osher, D. (2013). *Ohio Skills for Life evaluation: Final report.* Washington, D.C.: American Institutes for Research.

Jussim, L., & Harber, K. D. (2005). Teacher expectations and self-fulfilling prophecies: Knowns and unknowns, resolved and unresolved controversies. *Personality and Social Psychology Review, 9,* 131–155.

Kabat-Zinn, J. (1994). *Wherever you go, there you are: Mindfulness meditation in everyday life.* New York, NY: Hyperion.

Kabat-Zinn, J. (2009). *Full catastrophe living: Using the wisdom of your body and mind to face stress, pain, and illness.* New York, NY: Delta Trade.

Kaiser Greenland, S. (2010). *The mindful child: How to help your kid manage stress and become happier, kinder, and more compassionate.* New York, NY: Free Press.

Kashdan, T. B., & Rottenberg, J. (2010). Psychological flexibility as a fundamental aspect of health. *Clinical Psychology Review, 30,* 865–878.

Keller, T. E., Spieker, S. J., & Gilchrist, L. (2005). Patterns of risk and trajectories of preschool problem behaviors: A person-oriented analysis of attachment in context. *Development and Psychopathology, 17,* 349–384.

Kemeny, M. E., Foltz, C., Cavanagh, J. F., Cullen, M., Giese-Davis, J., Jennings, P. A., . . . Ekman, P. (2012). Contemplative/emotion training reduces negative emotional behavior and promotes prosocial responses. *Emotion, 12,* 338–350.

Keng, S., Smoski, M. J., & Robins, C. J. (2011). Effects of mindfulness on psychological health: A review of empirical studies. *Clinical Psychology Review, 31,* 1041–1056.

Kohn, A. (1996). *Beyond discipline: From compliance to community.* Alexandria, VA: Association for Supervision and Curriculum Development.

Kounin, J. S. (1970). *Discipline and group management in classrooms.* New York, NY: Holt, Rinehart & Winston.

Kraft, T. L., & Pressman, S. D. (2012). Grin and bear it: The influence of manipulated facial expression on the stress response. *Psychological Science, 23,* 1372–1378.

Kuyken, W., Weare, K., Ukoumunne, O. C., Vicary, R., Motton, N., Burnett, R., . . . Huppert, F. (2013). Effectiveness of the Mindfulness in Schools Programme: Non-randomised controlled feasibility study. *British Journal of Psychiatry, 203,* 126–131.

Lantieri, L. (2008). *Building emotional intelligence: Techniques to cultivate inner strength in children.* Boulder, CO: Sounds True.

Lantieri, L., Nambiar, M., & Chavez-Reilly, M. (2006). Building inner preparedness. In Teachers College Press & M. Grolnick (Eds.), *Forever after: New York City teachers on 9/11* (pp. 107–122). New York, NY: Teachers College Press.

Lawler-Row, K. A., Younger, J. W., Piferi, R. L., & Jones, W. H. (2006). The role of adult attachment style in forgiveness following an interpersonal offense. *Journal of Counseling and Development, 84,* 493–502.

Lazarus, R. S. (1991). *Emotion and adaptation.* New York, NY: Oxford University Press.

Learning First Alliance. (2001). *Every child learning: Safe and supportive schools.* Washington, D.C.: Author.

Levin, J., & Nolan, J. (2014). *Principles of classroom management: A professional decision-making model* (7th ed.). Boston, MA: Pearson.

Levine, A. R. (2005). The social face of shame and humiliation. *Journal of the American Psychoanalytic Association, 53,* 525–534.

Lowry, L. (1989). *Number the stars.* New York, NY: Houghton Mifflin Harcourt.

Lowry, L. (1993). *The giver.* New York, NY: Random House.

Lutz, A., Brefczynski-Lewis, J., Johnstone, T., & Davidson, R. J. (2008). Regulation of the neural circuitry of emotion by compassion meditation: Effects of meditative expertise. *PLoS One, 3*(3), e1897.

Ma, S. H., & Teasdale, J. D. (2004). Mindfulness-based cognitive therapy for depression: Replication and exploration of differential relapse prevention effects. *Journal of Consulting and Clinical Psychology, 72,* 31–40.

Maines, B., & Robinson, G. (1995). Assertive discipline: No wheels on your wagon: A reply to Swinson and Melling. *Association of Educational Psychologists Journal, 11*(3), 9–11.

Martens, B. K., & Meller, P. J. (1990). The application of behavioral principles to educational settings. In T. B. Gutkin & C. R. Reynolds (Eds.), *The handbook of school psychology* (2nd ed., pp. 612–634). Oxford, UK: Wiley.

Marzano, R. J., Marzano, J. S., & Pickering, D. J. (2003). *Classroom management that works: Research-based strategies for every teacher.* Alexandria, VA: Association for Supervision and Curriculum Development.

Marzano, R. J., Pickering, D. J., & Pollock, J. E. (2001). *Classroom instruction that works: Research-based strategies for increasing student achievement.* Alexandria, VA: ASCD.

Maslach, C., Jackson, S. E., & Leiter, M. P. (1997). Maslach Burnout Inventory. In C. P. Zalaquett & R. J. Wood (Eds.), *Evaluating stress: A book of resources* (pp. 191-218). Lanham, MD: Scarecrow Education.

Masters, J. C., Barden, R. C., & Ford, M. E. (1979). Affective states, expressive behavior, and learning in children. *Journal of Personality and Social Psychology, 37,* 380–390.

McCullough, M. E., Emmons, R. A., & Tsang, J. (2002). The grateful disposition: A conceptual and empirical topography. *Journal of Personality and Social Psychology, 82,* 112–127.

McEwen, B. S. (1998). Protective and damaging effects of stress mediators. *New England Journal of Medicine, 338,* 171–179.

McGill, V. J., & Welch, L. (1946). A behaviorist analysis of emotions. *Philosophy of Science, 13,* 100–122.

McNeely, C. A., Nonnemaker, J. M., & Blum, R. W. (2002). Promoting school connectedness: Evidence from the National Longitudinal Study of Adolescent Health. *Journal of School Health, 72,* 138–146.

Mendelson, T., Greenberg, M. T., Dariotis, J. K., Feagans Gould, L., Rhoades, B. L., & Leaf, P. J. (2010). Feasibility and preliminary outcomes of a school-based mindfulness intervention for urban youth. *Journal of Abnormal Child Psychology, 38,* 985–994.

MetLife. (2012). *The MetLife Survey of the American Teacher: Executive Summary.* Retrieved from https://www.metlife.com/assets/cao/foundation/MetLife-Teacher-Survey-Exec-Summary.pdf

Metz, S. M., Frank, J. L., Reibel, D., Cantrell, T., Sanders, R., & Broderick, P. C. (2013). The effectiveness of the Learning to BREATHE program on adolescent emotion regulation. *Research in Human Development, 10,* 252–272.

Mitchell-Copeland, J., Denham, S. A., & DeMulder, E. K. (1997). Q-sort assessment of child–teacher attachment relationships and social competence in the preschool. *Early Education and Development, 8,* 27–39.

Montessori, M. (1973). *The Montessori elementary material.* New York, NY: Schocken Books. (Original work published 1917)

Murray, C., & Greenberg, M. T. (2000). Children's relationship with teachers and bonds with school. An investigation of patterns and correlates in middle childhood. *Journal of School Psychology, 38,* 423–445.

National Commission on Teaching and America's Future. (2007). *Policy brief: The high cost of teacher turnover.* Retrieved from http://

nctaf.org/wp-content/uploads/2012/01/NCTAF-Cost-of-Teacher-Turnover-2007-policy-brief.pdf

National Council for Accreditation of Teacher Education. (2008). *Professional standards for the accreditation of teacher preparation institutions.* Washington, D.C.: Author.

Nelsen, J. (2011). *Positive discipline* (Rev. ed.). New York, NY: Ballantine Books.

New England Network for Child, Youth & Family Services. (2009). *Evaluation of the S. Burlington Inner Resilience Pilot Program.* Retrieved from http://www.innerresilience-tidescenter.org/documents/S.Burlington_Inner_Resilience_Pilot_Eval_final.pdf

Noddings, N. (2003). *Caring: A feminine approach to ethics and moral education* (2nd ed.). Berkeley, CA: University of California Press.

Noddings, N. (2005a). Identifying and responding to needs in education. *Cambridge Journal of Education, 35,* 147–159.

Noddings, N. (2005b). *The challenge to care in schools: An alternative approach to education.* New York, NY: Teachers College Press.

Noddings, N. (2010). *The maternal factor: Two paths to morality.* Berkeley, CA: University of California Press.

Noggle, J. J., Steiner, N. J., Minami, T., & Khalsa, S. B. S. (2012). Benefits of yoga for psychosocial well-being in a US high school curriculum: A preliminary randomized controlled trial. *Journal of Developmental Behavioral Pediatrics, 33,* 193–201.

Osher, D., Dwyer, K., & Jackson, S. (2002). *Safe, supportive, and successful schools: Step by step.* Rockville, MD: U.S. Department of Health and Human Services, Substance Abuse and Mental Health Services Administration, Center for Mental Health Services.

Osher, D., Sprague, J., Weissberg, R. P., Axelrod, J., Keenan, S., Kendziora, K., & Zins, J. E. (2007). A comprehensive approach to promoting social, emotional, and academic growth in contemporary schools. In A. Thomas & J. Grimes (Eds.), *Best practices in school psychology* (Vol. 4, 5th ed., pp. 1263-1278). Bethesda, MD: National Association of School Psychologists.

Ostafin, B. D., & Marlatt, G. A. (2008). Surfing the urge: Experiential acceptance moderates the relation between automatic alcohol motivation and hazardous drinking. *Journal of Social and Clinical Psychology, 27,* 404–418.

Pace, T. W. W., Negi, L. T., Adame, D. D., Cole, S. P., Sivilli, T. I., Brown, T. D., . . . Raison, C. L. (2009). Effect of compassion meditation on neuroendocrine, innate immune and behavioral responses to psychosocial stress. *Psychoneuroendocrinology, 34,* 87–98.

Park, N., Peterson, C., & Seligman, M. E. P. (2004). Strengths of character and well-being. *Journal of Social and Clinical Psychology, 23,* 603–619.

Pedersen, E., Faucher, T. A., & Eaton, W. W. (1978). A new perspective on the effects of first-grade teachers on children's subsequent adult status. *Harvard Educational Review, 48,* 1–31.

Pianta, R. C. (2006). Classroom management and relationships between children and teachers: Implications for research and practice. In C. M. Evertson & C. S. Weinstein (Eds.), *Handbook of classroom management: Research, practice and contemporary issues* (pp. 685–709). Mahwah, NJ: Erlbaum.

Pianta, R. C., Hamre, B., & Stuhlman, M. (2003). Relationships between teachers and children. In W. M. Reynolds & G. E. Miller (Eds.), *Comprehensive handbook of psychology* (Vol. 7, pp. 199–234). New York, NY: Wiley.

Pianta, R. C., La Paro, K. M., & Hamre, B. (2003). *Classroom assessment scoring system.* Baltimore, MD: Brooks.

Pickert, K. (2014, February 3). The art of being mindful. *Time,* pp. 40–48.

Potts, R., Morse, M., Felleman, E., & Masters, J. C. (1986). Children's emotions and memory for affective narrative content. *Motivation and Emotion, 10,* 39–57.

Rilke, R. M. (2002). *Letters to a young poet* (R. Snell, Trans.). Mineola, NY: Dover.

Roeser, R. W., Schonert-Reichl, K. A., Jha, A., Cullen, M., Wallace, L., Wilensky, R., . . . Harrison, J. (2013). Mindfulness training and reductions in teacher stress and burnout: Results from two randomized, waitlist-control field trials. *Journal of Educational Psychology, 105,* 787–804.

Roeser, R. W., Skinner, E., Beers, J., & Jennings, P. A. (2012). Mindfulness training and teachers' professional development: An emerging area of research and practice. *Child Development Perspectives, 6,* 167–173.

Roeser, R. W., & Zelazo, P. D. (2012). Contemplative science, education and child development: Introduction to the special section. *Child Development Perspectives, 6,* 143–145.

Rowe, M. B. (1972, April). *Wait-time and rewards as instructional variables: Their influence on language, logic and fate control.* Paper presented at the annual meeting of the National Association for Research on Science Teaching, Chicago, IL.

Rowe, M. B. (1987). Wait time: Slowing down may be a way of speeding up. *American Educator, 11,* 38–43, 47.

Ryan, T. (2013). *A mindful nation: How a simple practice can help us reduce stress, improve performance, and recapture the American spirit.* Carlsbad, CA: Hay House.

Safran, J. D., & Segal, Z. V. (1990). *Interpersonal process in cognitive therapy.* New York, NY: Basic Books.

Salzberg, S. (1995). *Lovingkindness: The revolutionary art of happiness.* Boston, MA: Shambhala Publications.

Sapolsky, R. M. (2004). *Why zebras don't get ulcers* (3rd ed.). New York, NY: Henry Holt.

Scharmer, C. O. (2009). *Theory U: Leading from the future as it emerges.* San Francisco, CA: Berrett-Koehler.

Scharmer, C. O. (2014). *Addressing the blind spot of our time.* Retrieved from https://www.presencing.com/sites/default/files/page-files/Theory_U_Exec_Summary.pdf

Schell, L. M., & Rouch, R. L. (1988). The low reading group: An instructional and social dilemma. *Journal of Reading Education, 14,* 18–23.

Schön, D. A. (1983). *The reflective practitioner: How professionals think in action.* New York, NY: Basic Books.

Schonert-Reichl, K. A., & Lawlor, M. S. (2010). The effects of a mindfulness-based education program on pre- and early adolescents' well-being and social and emotional competence. *Mindfulness, 1,* 137–151.

Selman, R. L. (1980). *The growth of interpersonal understanding: Developmental and clinical analysis.* San Diego, CA: Academic Press.

Selman, R. L. (2003). *The promotion of social awareness: Powerful lessons from the partnership of developmental theory and classroom practice.* New York, NY: Russell Sage.

Shapiro, S. L., Brown, K. W., & Biegel, G. M. (2007). Teaching self-care to caregivers: Effects of mindfulness-based stress reduction on the mental health of therapists in training. *Training and Education in Professional Psychology, 1,* 105–115.

Shapiro, S. L., Carlson, L. E., Astin, J. A., & Freedman, B. (2006). Mechanisms of mindfulness. *Journal of Clinical Psychology, 62,* 373–386.

Shonk, S. M., & Cicchetti, D. (2001). Maltreatment, competency deficits, and risk for academic and behavioral maladjustment. *Developmental Psychology, 37,* 3–17.

Siegel, D. J. (2007). *The mindful brain: Reflection and attunement in the cultivation of well-being.* New York, NY: W. W. Norton.

Siegel, D. J. (2010). *Mindsight: The new science of personal transformation.* New York, NY: Bantam Books.

Siegel, D. J. (2012). *The developing mind: How relationships and the brain interact to shape who we are* (2nd ed.). New York, NY: Guilford.

Simon, A., Harnett, S., Nagler, E., & Thomas, L. (2009). *Research on the effect of the Inner Resilience Program on teacher and student wellness and classroom climate: Final report.* New York, NY: Metis Associates.

Soussignan, R. (2002). Duchenne smile, emotional experience, and autonomic reactivity: A test of the facial feedback hypothesis. *Emotion, 2,* 52–74.

Stahl, R. J. (1990). *Using "think-time" behaviors to promote students' information processing, learning and on-task participation: An instructional module.* Tempe, AZ: Arizona State University.

Sutton, R. E. (2004). Emotional regulation goals and strategies of teachers. *Social Psychology of Education, 7,* 379–398.

Sutton, R. E., & Wheatley, K. E. (2003). Teachers' emotions and teaching: A review of the literature and directions for future research. *Educational Psychology Review, 15,* 327–358.

Swift, J. N., & Gooding, C. T. (1983). Interaction of wait time feedback and questioning instruction on middle school science teaching. *Journal of Research in Science Teaching, 20,* 721–730.

Thomas, D., & Brown, J. S. (2011). *A new culture of learning: Cultivating the imagination for a world of constant change.* Seattle, WA: CreateSpace.

Tobin, K. (1987). The role of wait time in higher cognitive level learning. *Review of Educational Research, 57,* 69–95.

Tobin, K. G., & Capie, W. (1982). *Wait-time and learning in science.* Burlington, NC: Carolina Biological Supply Company.

Tomlinson, C. A. (1999). *The differentiated classroom: Responding to the needs of all learners.* Alexandria, VA: Association for Supervision and Curriculum Development.

Tomlinson, C. A. (2001). *How to differentiate instruction in mixed-ability classrooms* (2nd ed.). Alexandria, VA: Association for Supervision and Curriculum Development.

Trevarthen, C., & Aitken, K. J. (2001). Infant intersubjectivity: Research, theory, and clinical applications. *Journal of Child Psychology and Psychiatry, 42,* 3–48.

Tronick, E. Z. (1989). Emotions and emotional communication in infants. *American Psychologist, 44,* 112–119.

U.S. Department of Health and Human Services. (1999). *Mental health: A report of the Surgeon General.* Rockville, MD: U.S. Department of Health and Human Services, Substance Abuse and Mental Health Services Administration, Center for Mental Health Services, National Institutes of Health, National Institute of Mental Health.

Wadlinger, H. A., & Isaacowitz, D. M. (2006). Positive mood broadens visual attention to positive stimuli. *Motivation and Emotion, 30,* 89–101.

Watkins, P. C. (2004). Gratitude and subjective well-being. In R. A. Emmons & M. E. McCullough (Eds.), *The psychology of gratitude* (pp. 167–192). New York, NY: Oxford University Press.

Watson, M. (2003). *Learning to trust.* San Francisco, CA: Jossey-Bass.

Watson, M., & Battistich, V. (2006). Building and sustaining caring communities. In C. S. Weinstein & C. M. Evertson (Eds.), *Handbook of classroom management: Research, practice, and contemporary issues* (pp. 253-279). Mahwah, NJ: Erlbaum.

Webster-Stratton, C., Reid, M. J., & Hammond, M. (2004). Treating children with early-onset conduct problems: Intervention outcomes for parent, child, and teacher training. *Journal of Clinical Child and Adolescent Psychology, 33,* 105–124.

Weinstein, C. S. (1999). Reflections on best practices and promising programs. In H. J. Freiberg (Ed.), *Beyond behaviorism: Changing the classroom management paradigm* (pp. 145–163). Boston, MA: Allyn & Bacon.

Wentzel, K. R. (1998). Social relationships and motivation in middle school: The role of parents, teachers, and peers. *Journal of Educational Psychology, 90,* 202–209.

Woolfolk Hoy, A., & Weinstein, C. S. (2006). Student and teacher perspectives on classroom management. In C. M. Evertson & C. S. Weinstein (Eds.), *Handbook of classroom management: Research, practice, and contemporary issues* (pp. 181–219). Mahwah, NJ: Erlbaum.

Yoon, J. S. (2002). Teacher characteristics as predictors of teacher–student relationships: Stress, negative affect, and self-efficacy. *Social Behavior and Personality, 30,* 485–493.

Zelazo, P. D., & Cunningham, W. (2007). Executive function: Mechanisms underlying emotion regulation. In J. Gross (Ed.), *Handbook of emotion regulation* (pp. 135–158). New York, NY: Guilford.

Zhang, Q., & Sapp, D. A. (2008). A burning issue in teaching: The impact of perceived teacher burnout and nonverbal immediacy on student motivation and affective learning. *Journal of Communication Studies, 1,* 152–192.

Zins, J. E., Weissberg, R. P., Wang, M. C., & Walberg, H. J. (Eds.). (2004). *Building academic success on social and emotional learning.* New York, NY: Teachers College Press.

Index